SHORTLIST

Venice

WHAT'S NEW | WHAT'S ON | WHAT'S BEST

www.timeout.com/venice

Contents

Venice by Area

Essentials

Published by Time Out Guides Ltd
Universal House
251 Tottenham Court Road
London W1T 7AB
Tel: + 44 (0)20 7813 3000
Fax: + 44 (0)20 7813 6001
Email: guides@timeout.com
www.timeout.com

Editorial/Managing Director Peter Fiennes
Editorial Director Ruth Jarvis
Deputy Series Editor Dominic Earle
Business Manager Gareth Garner
Guides Co-ordinator Holly Pick
Accountant Kemi Olufuwa

Time Out Guides is a wholly owned subsidiary of Time Out Group Ltd.

© Time Out Group Ltd
Chairman Tony Elliott
Financial Director Richard Waterlow
Time Out Magazine Ltd MD David Pepper
Group General Manager/Director Nichola Coulthard
Time Out Communications Ltd MD David Pepper
Production Director Mark Lamond
Group Marketing Director John Luck
Group Art Director John Oakey
Group IT Director Simon Chappell

Time Out and the Time Out logo are trademarks of Time Out Group Ltd.

This edition first published in Great Britain in 2007 by Ebury Publishing
A Random House Group Company
Company information can be found on www.randomhouse.co.uk
10 9 8 7 6 5 4 3 2 1

For details of distribution in the Americas, see www.timeout.com

ISBN 10: 978184670 0415
ISBN 13: 1-84670-041-8

A CIP catalogue record for this book is available from the British Library

Colour reprographics by Wyndeham Icon, 3 & 4 Maverton Road, London E3 2JE

Printed and bound in Germany by Appl

Papers used by Ebury Publishing are natural, recyclable products made from wood grown
in sustainable forests

Venice Shortlist

The **Time Out Venice Shortlist** is one of a new series of guides that draws on Time Out's background as a magazine publisher to keep you current with everything that's going on in town. As well as Venice's classic sights and the best of its eating, drinking and entertainment options, the guide picks out the most exciting venues to have recently opened, and gives a full calendar of annual events. It also includes features on the important news, trends and openings, all compiled by locally based editors and writers. Whether you're visiting for the first time in your life, or you're a frequent repeat visitor, you'll find the *Time Out Venice Shortlist* guide contains everything you need to know, in a portable and easy-to-use format.

The guide divides central Venice into seven areas, each of which contains listings for Sights & Museums, Eating & Drinking, Shopping, Nightlife and Arts & Leisure, along with maps pinpointing all their locations. At the front of the book are chapters rounding up each of these scenes city-wide, and giving a shortlist of our overall picks in a variety of categories. We also include itineraries for days out, as well as essentials such as transport information and hotels.

Our listings use phone numbers as dialled from within Italy. From abroad, use your country's exit code followed by 39 (the country code for Italy) and the number given, including the initial '0'. We have noted price categories by using one to four euro signs (€-€€€€),

representing budget, moderate, expensive and luxury. Major credit cards are accepted unless otherwise stated. We also indicate when a venue is NEW and give **Event highlights**.

All our listings are double-checked, but businesses do sometimes close or change their hours or prices, so it's a good idea to call a venue before visiting. While every effort has been made to ensure accuracy, the publishers cannot accept responsibility for any errors that this guide may contain.

Venues are marked on the maps using symbols numbered according to their order within the chapter and colour-coded according to the type of venue they represent:

❶ Sights & Museums
❶ Eating & Drinking
❶ Shopping
❶ Nightlife
❶ Arts & Leisure

SHORTLIST
Online

The *Time Out Venice Shortlist* is as up to date as it is possible for a printed guidebook to be. And to keep it completely current, it has a regularly updated online companion, at **www.timeout. com/venice**. Here you'll find news of the latest openings and exhibitions, as well as picks from visitors and residents – ideal for planning a trip. Time Out is the city specialist, so you'll also find travel information for more than 100 cities worldwide on our site, at www.timeout.com/travel.

Time Out Venice Shortlist

EDITORIAL
Editor Anne Hanley
Copy Editor Jan Fuscoe
Proofreader Sylvia Tombesi-Walton

STUDIO
Art Director Scott Moore
Art Editor Pinelope Kourmouzoglou
Senior Designer Josephine Spencer
Graphic Designer Henry Elphick
Junior Graphic Designer Kei Ishimaru
Digital Imaging Simon Foster
Ad Make-up Jenni Prichard
Picture Editor Jael Marschner
Deputy Picture Editor Tracey Kerrigan
Picture Researcher Helen McFarland

ADVERTISING
Sales Director/Sponsorship
   Mark Phillips
International Sales Manager
   Ross Canadé
International Sales Executive
   Simon Davies
Advertising Sales Fabio Giannini
Advertising Assistant Kate Staddon

MARKETING
Marketing Manager Yvonne Poon
Sales & Marketing Director, North America Lisa Levinson
Marketing Designer Anthony Huggins

PRODUCTION
Production Manager Brendan McKeown
Production Co-ordinator Caroline Bradford

CONTRIBUTORS
This guide was researched and written by Anne Hanley, with the exception of Tintoretto's Last Suppers (Gregory Dowling); Glass Beads (JoAnn Titmarsh); Alive and pretty well (JoAnn Titmarsh); Celluloid Rivalry (Lee Marshall); Hotels (Nicky Swallow).

PHOTOGRAPHY
All photography by Olivia Rutherford; except: pages 25, 43, 45, 46, 56, 58, 61, 104, 106 Alys Tomlinson; page 31 © Fototeca Enit/Vito Arcomano.

The following pictures were provided by the featured establishments/artists: pages 119, 157.
Cover photograph: Pictures Colour Library

MAPS
LS International Cartography, via Decemviri 8, 20138 Milan, Italy (www.geomaker.com)

Thanks to Fulvio Marsigliani at LS International, JoAnn Titmarsh, Jill Weinrich and Kate Davies, and all contributors to past editions of *Time Out Venice*.

About Time Out

Founded in 1968, Time Out has expanded from humble London beginnings into the leading resource for those wanting to know what's happening in the world's greatest cities. As well as our influential what's-on weeklies in London, New York and Chicago, we publish more than a dozen other listings magazines in cities as varied as Beijing, Beirut and Mumbai. The magazines established Time Out's trademark style: sharp writing, informed reviewing and bang up-to-date inside knowledge of every scene.

Time Out made the natural leap into travel guides in the 1980s with the City Guide series, which now extends to over 50 destinations around the world. Written and researched by expert local writers and generously illustrated with original photography, the full-size guides cover a larger area than our Shortlist guides and include many more venue reviews, along with additional background features and a full set of maps.

Throughout this rapid growth, the company has remained proudly independent, still owned by Tony Elliott nearly four decades after he started Time Out London as a single fold-out sheet of A5 paper. This independence extends to the editorial content of all our publications, this Shortlist included. No establishment has been featured because it has advertised, and no payment has influenced any of our reviews. And, for our critics, there's definitely no such thing as a free lunch: all restaurants and bars are visited and reviewed anonymously, and Time Out always picks up the bill.
For more about the company, see www.timeout.com.

Don't Miss

San Marco p50

Sights & Museums

With very few exceptions, there's nothing cutting-edge – or even remotely modern – about the way Venice presents its immense cultural wealth.

Were they to return today, the visitors who have flocked to this watery city since the 15th century – for commerce, edification or just plain fun – would have no difficulty recognizing the city they saw then: certainly, the Gallerie dell'Accademia wasn't created until the early 19th century, but many of the works in it had hung in Venice's churches previously; and constant construction, at least until the fall of the Venetian Republic in 1797, meant that the city's skyscape and architectural make-up have been in constant flux.

But the overall impression of art and beauty being an intrinsic part of the city's fabric has never changed – to the point, at times, where little effort has been made to exalt those very features that make the city so unique.

So don't expect state-of-the-art museums with all mod cons; be prepared to make do with beauty beyond your wildest expectations: in artworks hung on the walls of dark, incense-perfumed churches; in gem-studded galleries; in rippling reflections of Titianesque colours in quiet canals and in an architectural mish-mash of stunning and endlessly absorbing originality.

Nobody comes to Venice without some idea of what to expect; the big surprise is that it's true. The streets *are* full of water, and there's an otherworldly, fairy-tale quality to the place.

There are, of course, highlights: St Mark's basilica, the Gallerie dell' Accademia and the **Rialto** bridge to name but a few. But in these tourist hotspots you'll never get an impression of Venice's full diversity; for that, you'll have to take your courage (and your map) in your hands and leave the main routes.

Venice is divided into six *sestieri* (districts). They're worth getting to grips with, firstly because all addresses include the *sestiere* name, and secondly because each has a different flavour. Cradled by the great lower bend of the Grand Canal is the *sestiere* of San Marco, the heart of the city; east of here is Castello; stretching to the west and north is Cannaregio. To the west of the Rialto bridge is San Polo; north of that is Santa Croce; while further to the south is Dorsoduro, with its wide Zattere promenade looking across to the long residential island of the Giudecca – the honorary seventh *sestiere*.

Churches

Venice began life as a host of separate island communities, each clustered around its own parish church. There are still well over 100 religious buildings. They contain inestimable artistic treasures.

Most of the major churches have reliable opening times; hours in minor churches depend on the whim of the priest or sacristan. It's well worth exploring these too, since there is not a single one that does not contain some item of interest.

No Sunday opening times are given in listings for churches that open only for Mass. Remember that churches are places of worship: shorts and bare shoulders are frowned upon, as are visits while services are going on.

SHORTLIST

Unmissable
- Gallerie dell'Accademia (p139)
- Grand Canal (p38)
- Rialto bridge (p112)
- St Mark's basilica (p51)
- St Mark's square (p50)

Great views
- Campanile (San Giorgio Maggiore, p148)
- Campanile (St Mark's, p57)
- Campanile (Torcello, p155)
- Scala Contarini del Bòvolo (p69)

Peaceful picnic spots
- Giardini Pubblici (p84)
- Parco Savorgnan (p144)
- Sant'Elena gardens (p84)
- Zattere (p130)

Top Titians
- *Annunciation* in San Salvador (p65)
- *Assumption* in I Frari (p109)
- *Pietà* in Accademia (p139)
- *St John* in San Zaccaria (p79)
- *St Lawrence* in I Gesuiti (p102)

Gothic glory
- Ca' d'Oro (p102)
- Doge's Palace (p59)
- I Frari (p109)
- Santi Giovanni e Paolo (p79)

Renaissance splendour
- San Michele (p152)
- Santa Maria dei Miracoli (p102)
- Torre dell'Orologio (p63)
- Façade of Scuola Grande di San Marco (p74)

Contemporary
- Bevilacqua La Masa Foundation (p65)
- La Biennale (p33)
- Palazzo Grassi (p68)
- Peggy Guggenheim Collection (p140)

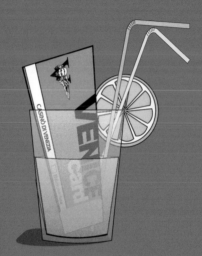

Museums, galleries and *scuole*

On the whole, Venice's museums and galleries are rather old-fashioned containers for beautiful and/or instructive things, rather than innovative exhibition-experience spaces. Slowly, the city is catching up with new exhibiting techniques (see box p136). It still has a way to go.

In the meantime, the city's beautiful things are peerlessly beautiful, and traditional Venetian instruction can be fun. The Museo Storico Navale provides a colourful introduction to Venice's maritime past, while a grasp of the elaborate mechanisms of Venetian government will turn the slog around the Palazzo Ducale (Doge's Palace) into a voyage of discovery.

Then there are the curiosities – Ca' d'Oro, where a patchy gallery with the occasional gem is housed inside one of the city's most extraordinary architectural frames; Ca' Rezzonico, where 18th-century Venice is recreated in all its finery and foppery; and the smaller but eclectic Museo della Fondazione Scientifica Querini Stampalia, a private foundation with a fascinating collection of scenes of 18th-century Venetian life and a glorious Bellini (the painter, not the cocktail).

As well as museums in the strict sense of the word, Venice also boasts **scuole**, establishments that were a blend of art-treasure house and social institution. Essentially, they were devotional lay brotherhoods, subject to the state rather than the Church. The earliest were founded in the 13th century; by the 15th century there were six *scuole grandi* and as many as 400 minor ones, or *scuole*. The *scuole grandi* had annually elected officers drawn from the 'citizen' class (those sandwiched between the governing patriciate and the unenfranchised *popolani*). While the *scuole grandi* (such as Scuola di San Rocco and Scuola di San Giovanni Evangelista) drew their members mainly from the wealthier professional classes, the humbler *scuole piccole* were either exclusively devotional groups, trade guilds or confraternities of foreign communities (such as Scuola di San Giorgio degli Schiavoni).

The wealthier confraternities devoted a great deal of time and expense to beautifying their meeting houses (the *scuole* themselves), sometimes hiring one major painter to decorate the whole building; this was the case of Tintoretto in the Scuola di San Rocco and Carpaccio in the Scuola di San Giorgio degli Schiavoni, so that these buildings are essential viewing for anyone interested in their art.

Admission and tickets

In high season, expect to queue to enter St Mark's, the Accademia and the Palazzo Ducale. Other sights rarely present any overcrowding problems except during special exhibitions. April and May are traditional months for Italian school trips: this can mean sharing your Titians and Tintorettos with gangs of bored teenagers.

Entry to all state-owned museums is, theoretically, free (or at least reduced) for citizens under 18 and over 65. Charges and concessions at city-run and privately owned museums vary; it pays to carry whatever ID cards you can muster (student card, press card, motoring association card and so on).

For one week each spring – designated the *Settimana dei Beni Culturali* (Cultural Heritage Week) – most state-owned (but not city-owned) galleries and museums are free. See www.beniculturali.it for details.

Multi-entrance tickets

Many of Venice's landmarks offer multi-entrance tickets, cutting costs if you are planning to visit all the sights covered by a given ticket (see box p55). Schemes include:

Musei Civici Veneziani

Venice's city-owned museums offer two multi-entrance options, both of which can be bought at participating establishments. The major museums (Musei di Piazza San Marco, Ca' Rezzonico and Ca' Pesaro) accept credit cards (MC, V). Note that the Musei di Piazza San Marco can **only** be entered on a cumulative ticket.

For the others (Ca' Rezzonico, Carlo Goldoni's House, Museo di Palazzo Mocenigo, Ca' Pesaro, Museo Fortuny, the Glass Museum and Lace Museum), individual tickets are also available. See also www.museicivicivenezaini.it.
• **Musei di Piazza San Marco** (Palazzo Ducale, Biblioteca Marciana, Museo Correr, Museo Archeologico, Torre dell'Orologio) €12; €6.50 concessions.
• **Museum Pass** (all the Musei Civici) €18; €12 concessions.

State Museums

The state-owned Gallerie dell'Accademia, Ca' d'Oro and Museo Orientale can be visited on a multi-entrance ticket costing €11 (€5.50 concessions) from participating sights. No credit cards except for online advance bookings. Information on www.artive.arti.beniculturali.it.

Chorus

A number of Venice's churches belong to the Chorus scheme (041 275 0462, www.chorusvenezia.org), which funds upkeep by charging for entry. There's a fee of €2.50 for each church, or you can get a multi-entrance ticket (€8; €5 over-65s and students under 30). Single- and multi-entrance tickets can be bought in participating churches. No credit cards.

Gallerie dell'Accademia p139

Alla Palanca p145

WHAT'S BEST
Eating & Drinking

More than any other Italian city, Venice has its own particular customs when it comes to dining, and drinking, out.

Of course there are *ristoranti* (many of them, in this tourist-orientated place, of execrable quality along with exorbitant prices); but there are also *bacari* – a cross between a drinking den and a traditional fast-food outlet. It is this latter establishment that sets Venice apart… and that has spearheaded a recent renaissance in Venetian cuisine.

Venetians differ from other Italians, too, in that they are drinkers. Not to excess, mind you: but a shot of fiery grappa in your breakfast coffee takes the damp

from the canals out of your marrow, and a stopover – or four, or five – on the way home from work for a quick *spritz* or an *ombra* (see box p99) with friends is an essential part of socialising *alla veneziana*.

What's on the plate

The lagoon city has a long culinary tradition based on fresh seafood, game and vegetables, backed up by northern Italy's three main carbohydrate fixes: pasta, risotto rice and polenta. Outside of a handful of top-notch restaurants, you will invariably eat better if you go with the flow of *la cucina veneta*.

This requires a certain spirit of experimentation. If you've never

eaten *garusoli* (sea snails) or *canoce* (mantis shrimps), Venice is the place to try these marine curios.

The once-strong local tradition of creative ways with meat is kept alive in a handful of restaurants (Ai Gondolieri and Vini da Arturo) and one marvellous trattoria, Dalla Marisa; it can also be found in *bacaro*-counter *cicheti* like *nervetti* (veal cartilage) and *cotechino* (spicy pig's intestine parcels filled with pork).

Vegetarians may be horrified to learn that here's not a single vegetarian restaurant in the city, but Venetian cuisine relies heavily on seasonal veggies, so eating a meat-free meal is not difficult. La Zucca is always a safe bet, and Algiubagio offers a range of vegetarian dishes.

There is something of the Spanish tapas mentality about the Venetian approach to eating: *antipasti* (hors d'oeuvres) often engulf the whole meal. If you nodded vigorously when the waiter suggested bringing 'one or two' seafood *antipasti*, you may start to regret it when the fifth plate arrives – but it is perfectly okay just to eat some pasta afterwards, or to skip to the *secondo*, or dessert.

What's in the glass

Except in the more upmarket restaurants and one or two born-again *bacari*, wines will mostly be local. Luckily, the wine-growing area that stretches from the Veneto north-east to Friuli is one of Italy's strongest, with good white wines like tocai and soave backed up by solid red wines such as valpolicella and cabernet franc. This means that even in humbler establishments the house wine is usually drinkable and often surprisingly refined.

For what to drink in bars, see box p99.

DON'T MISS

Al Garanghelo p114

Eating

Restaurants

Steer well clear of those restaurants – mainly around St Mark's and the Rialto – that employ sharply dressed waiters to stand outside and persuade passing tourists to come in for a meal: an immediate recipe for rip-off prices and mediocre fare. Following our recommendations will spare you unpleasant surprises.

Bacari

With their blackened beams and rickety wooden tables, *bacari* (accent on the first syllable) are often hidden down backstreets or in quiet *campielli*. Most look age-old; many, however, are recent arrivals or makeovers... which doesn't detract from the bounty of what's on offer.

Locals crowd the bar, swiftly downing a glass or two of wine (*un'ombra*), and taking the edge off their appetites with one of the *cicheti* (snacks) that line the counter (see box p112). If you sit down at a table and order from the menu – which will include more abundant portions of those *cicheti*, plus a few hot dishes – you can expect prices to be a bit higher.

Pizzerie

Venice has its fair share of pizza joints, though the standard here is not particularly high. Still, prices in *pizzerie* are low-ish, which makes them a good standby for a carbohydrate-and-protein injection between more expensive meals. Note that beer, rather than wine, is the traditional accompaniment for pizza.

Drinking

Cafés & bars

Italian bars and cafés (the terms are pretty much interchangeable) are multi-purpose establishments. To the usual Italian breakfast, light snacks, pastries and alcoholic beverages routine, Venice adds its own specialities: the *ombra* and the *spritz*.

Many of Venice's bars also double up as cake and ice-cream emporia. Locals consume freshly prepared goodies throughout the day, and with early-evening *aperitivi*.

Rules of engagement

There are two timescales for eating in Venice. Smart restaurants serve lunch from around 1pm to 3pm and dinner from 7.30pm until at least 10pm. *Bacari* and neighbourhood *trattorie* follow Venetian workers' rhythms, with lunch running from noon to 2pm and dinner from 6.30pm to 9pm.

Menus are often recited out loud; waiters are used to doing off-the-cuff English translations. If you want to know how much dishes cost, ask. Note that the price of fish is often quoted by weight – generally by the *etto* (100 grammes).

A double pricing policy applies in many eateries, with one tariff for locals and another (the one given on the menu, if it exists) for tourists. There is not much you can do about this unofficial congestion charge.

Always ask for a written *conto* (bill) at the end of the meal, as it is, in theory, illegal to leave the restaurant without one.

The usual practice in Italian bars is to decide what you want, pay at the till, then order at the counter. Remember that anything ordered at the counter must be consumed there. If you want to sit at a café table, you should sit down and order (or at the very least indicate that you are planning to sit down); the privilege of occupying a table will push your bill up – a little in smaller, more hidden-away places, but jaw-droppingly in, say, St Mark's square, especially in the evening, when a surcharge is added for the palm orchestras.

Note that many bars that remain open until late and/or offer live music in the evenings have been listed under Nightlife headings in the Venice by Area section pp50-160.

For advice on tipping, see p187.

Reading the listings

In this guide, we have used the € symbol to indicate price ranges. € means a cheap meal at €20 or less; €€ is anything up to €40; €€€ is up to €60; €€€€ is over €60. These figures cover a three-course meal for one, with house wine. Prices may seem high, but remember that it is perfectly okay just to order a pasta course, a salad and a coffee – which may halve the price.

Where we have given 'meals served' times in the Venice by Area listings, this refers to the kitchen's opening hours, when full meals can be ordered; establishments may function well before and/or after these times as wine- and snack-serving *bacari*.

DON'T MISS

Maison de Laurent p81

Rialto market p108

Shopping

For centuries, merchants from all over Europe met with those from the Levant in this extraordinary entrepôt between East and West. An endless array of goods, from exotic spices and raw silks to humble salt, was imported for resale by Venetian traders. In the Renaissance, the two-week *La Sensa* trade fair drew people from all over the Mediterranean basin and further north in Europe; it was particularly popular for purchasing wedding trousseaux.

Traders of different nations each had their *fondaco* (alternatively spelled *fontaco* or *fondego*), a warehouse-cum-lodging. So successful – and so desirous of making an impression – were the German traders in Venice that their Fondego dei Tedeschi (now the main post office) was adorned with frescoes by Titian and Giorgione.

The sumptuous brocades and damasks, Burano lace and Murano glassware still produced and found in the city are all legacies of *La Serenissima*'s thriving commerce. Though the prices of such authentic Venetian-made goods can be prohibitive, a recent resurgence of local artisans – cobblers, jewellers, carpenters, mask-makers and blacksmiths – has led to slightly more competitive rates, and has helped to keep traditional techniques alive.

Where & what to buy

The Mercerie – the maze of crowded, narrow alleyways leading

from piazza San Marco to the Rialto – and the streets known collectively as the Frezzeria, immediately to the west of St Mark's square, have been the main retail areas in this city for the past 600 years or so. The densest concentration of big-name fashion outlets can be found around calle larga XXII Marzo where top names such as Prada, Fendi, Versace and Gucci have all staked their boutiques.

Devotees of kitsch should not miss the stalls and shops near the train station, where plastic gondolas, illuminated gondolas, flashing gondolas, musical gondolas and even gondola cigarette lighters reign supreme. Stalls around both ends of the Rialto bridge are also a good source of tack, though nylon football strips and fake Nikes dominate here.

For more tasteful souvenirs, Venice's glass, lace, fabrics and handmade paper are legendary – as are the made-in-Taiwan substitutes

Tragicomica p120

that are passed off as the genuine article by unscrupulous traders. Sticking to the outlets listed in our Venice by Area section will help you to avoid unpleasant surprises.

The steady demographic drop has led to the demise of 'everyday' shops: bread, fruit and veg, milk and meat are increasingly difficult to get hold of. Some supermarkets have opened, but the flip side of this is the threat now posed to the livelihood of the few remaining greengrocers, bakers and butchers. For fresh fruit, vegetables, fish and a magnificent taste of exuberant Venetian life, head for the open-air market at the north-west foot of the Rialto bridge (Mon-Sat mornings). Fruit and vegetables can also be purchased from the market-boats that are moored at the eastern end of via Garbaldi in the *sestiere* of Castello, and on the rio San Barnaba in Dorsoduro.

Opening hours

Most food shops are closed on Wednesday afternoons, while some non-food shops stay shut on Monday mornings. During high season many shops abandon their lunchtime closing and stay open all day, even opening on Sundays.

It pays to be sceptical about the hours posted on the doors of smaller shops. If you want to be sure of not finding the shutters drawn, call before you set out.

Tax rebates

If you are not an EU citizen, remember to keep your official receipt (*scontrino*) as you are entitled to a rebate on *IVA* (sales tax) paid on purchases of personal goods costing more than €154, as long as they leave the country unused and are bought from a shop that provides this service. In shops displaying the tax-free sign in the window, ask for the form, which you'll need to show at customs upon departure. See the Italian government website (www.agenziadogane.gov.it) for more information about customs in English.

Fondamenta della Misericordia

WHAT'S BEST
Nightlife

The city described by Byron as 'revel of the Earth' can no longer lay any claim to the status of Europe's party capital. But despite a shrinking, ageing population, Venice still conceals a surprising amount of life after dark.

A typical Venetian night out starts with a post-work, pre-prandial *spritz* (see box p99) in one of the bars around the Rialto market area; this might develop into a *giro de ombre*, a bar-crawl Venetian-style. For those still standing when the traditional *bacari* (wine bars) close, there's a network of late-opening bars hidden away all over town – by the Rialto, along the northern fondamenta della Misericordia or in ever-lively campo Santa Margherita.

Stringent noise-pollution regulations combined with a lack of adequate venues have effectively pulled the plug on large music events, except during Carnevale (during the months of January and February) and summer festivals (pp30-36). There's better news for serious jazz heads: regular high-quality jazz and experimental music events are put on by local cultural organisations like Caligola (www.caligola.it) or Vortice (www.provincia.venezia.it/vortice).

Thanks to the tenacity of the few bar owners still willing to wrestle with red tape and persist in the face of party-pooping petitioning neighbours, it's still possible, however, to hear live music in a handful of *locali* around

SHORTLIST

Dancefloors
- Piccolo Mondo (p142)
- Round Midnight (p137)

Live sounds
- Centrale Restaurant
  Lounge – varies (p68)
- Centro Zitelle Culturale
  Multimediale – varies (p147)
- Do Fradei – Wed & Fri (p97)
- Iguana – Tue or Thur (P101)
- Paradiso Perduto – Fri & Sun
  (P101)
- Santo Bevitore – Mon (p97)
- Torino@Notte – Wed (p71)

Foreign (student) hangouts
- Bacaro Jazz (p67)
- Café Blue (p135)
- Da Baffo (p120)
- Do Fradei (p97)

Great wines
- Il Caffè (p137)
- La Mascareta (p80)
- Naranzaria (p117)

Gay events
- Aurora (p63)
- Centrale Restaurant
  Lounge (p68)

Cool places to be seen
- Da Baffo (p120)
- Muro Vino e Cucina (p116)
- Naranzaria (p117)
- Orange (p137)

town. Venetian vibes tend to be laid-back, and these small, free gigs are almost always reggae, jazz or blues, with the occasional rock, Latino or world session.

Note that many of the bars listed under Nightlife in the Venice by Area section operate through the day as regular cafés and even lunch spots. Likewise, most of the venues listed under Eating & Drinking remain open into the evening.

Clubs

If it's clubs you're after, you've come to the wrong city. Round Midnight has a tiny dancefloor; Piccolo Mondo has another. For serious club culture, make for the mainland (see box p103).

Information and tickets

Listings are carried by the two local dailies, *Il Gazzettino* and *La Nuova Venezia*. For a more complete overview of concerts and festivals, with English translations, the monthly listings magazine *Venezia News* is indispensable. Also keep your eyes peeled around town for posters advertising upcoming gigs and events.

Tickets are usually available at venues, but in some cases they can be bought in advance at the CD shop Parole e Musica (Castello

Art reviews, festivals, fairs & sales, exhibitions, tours, walks. Time In plugged in, TV listings, film of the day, terrestrial choice, digital choice, radio, podcast of the week. Nightlife night pass, house, electro & techno, social club, after-dark diary, compilation corner. Food & Drink reviews, food & drink 50, what to drink this weekend. Around Town previews, events, museums. Music gigs, listings, critics' choice, jazz, folk, latin, rock, pop, dance, on the up, classical, it happened here, booking ahead, booking of the week, opera. Theatre musicals, west end, fringe, plays, show of the week, openings. Books reviews, how I write, book of the week. Comedy listings, venues, critics' choice. Dance shows, bookings, critics' choice. Film reviews, close-up, film of the week, critics' choice, the directors, film listings, festivals & seasons, other cinema, DVD of the week, box office top ten. Gay & Lesbian listings, critics' choice. Kids events, weekend choice, outings, shows. Sport things to watch, sportsboard, things to do, touchlines. Consume london lives, check out, streets of London, travel solutions. Health & Fitness clubs & classes.

For the Londoner and the visitor

The best of London every week

Online
timeout.com/london

To your door
timeout.com/subscribe
0800 068 0050

In Store
at shops across London

Piccolo Mondo p142

5673, salizada San Lio, 041 521 2215) or via the national ticket agency www.boxoffice.it.

Gay & lesbian

Venice might seem to provide the perfect backdrop for most fantasies. But gays and lesbians looking for something fast-paced may be disappointed.

In Venice proper, the laid-back gay scene is tucked neatly away in the private sphere, where dinner parties or quiet drinks at the local *bacaro* or wine bar define the way the city's (by no means small) gay community goes about its business. Il Muro (at the lagoon end of the piazzetta San Marco, turn right towards the Giardinetti Reale and keep walking), one of the city's oldest cruising institutions, is no longer as popular as it once was, but it still attracts a fair number of post-midnight visitors in the summer months.

Across on the mainland, however, Mestre and Marghera have newer, flashier clubs and bars pulling in a younger crowd from around the province.

The twain meet in the summer in large numbers at Alberoni on the Lido, its rather secluded beach area and surrounding dunes allowing people to indulge in nude sunbathing and cruising.

The national gay rights group ArciGay (www.arcigay.it) sponsors activities, festivals and counselling. ArciGay membership is needed for entry to several of the venues listed below. A one-month ArciGay *tessera* (membership card) for non-Italian nationals costs €7 (annual membership costs €14) and can be purchased at the door of venues requiring it, or at the nearest ArciGay chapter (corso Garibaldi 41, Padua, 049 876 2458, open 9-11.30pm Tue, 6-8pm Wed, 6.30-8pm Thur).

Tango in campo San Giacomo dell'Orio

Arts & Leisure

Night after night in the 17th and 18th centuries, Venetians flocked to their city's theatres. With audiences demanding constant novelty, competing houses renewed their repertoires frequently. As a result, play production was prolific, as was operatic output, with as many as 1,274 operas being produced in Venice in just over a generation.

Today's theatregoers are less demanding than their 18th-century counterparts. The growth and revamping in recent years of small theatres have finally given a little more space for experiments in the avant-garde. But on the whole, the performing-arts scene remains a victim of Venice's musical tradition, with Vivaldi pouring out of its churches and *scuole*, more often than not performed by bewigged and costumed players of varying standards.

Exceptions are the Venice Baroque Orchestra, a global success story (see box p56), and the orchestra of La Fenice, one of the best in the country. As well as its opera and ballet seasons, La Fenice has at least two concert seasons a year. The Teatro Malibran shares the Fenice's programmes and also has its own chamber-music season.

Lovers of sacred music should catch two regular Sunday events: the sung Mass at St Mark's (10.30am) and the Gregorian chant on the island of San Giorgio (11am).

SHORTLIST

Classic venues
- La Fenice – opera, concerts and classical dance (p72)
- Teatro Malibran – chamber music, opera and dance (p107)

Sporting fixtures
- Stadio PL Penzo – Venice's football stadium (p29). See box p89.

Experimental theatre
- Teatrino Groggia (p97)
- Teatro Junghans (p147)

Film
- Arena di Campo San Polo (p120)
- See box p157.

Vivaldi-in-silk
- See box p85.

Visiting foreign choirs often give free one-off performances in Venice's fabulous churches. Look out for posters around town. The city also has two resident gospel choirs, The Venice Gospel Ensemble (www.venicegospel.com) and the Joy Singers of Venice (www.joysingers.it); both perform frequently at venues around town, and particularly during the Venice Gospel Festival (www.venezia gospelfestival.it).

What's on when

Venice's theatre and dance season stretches from November to June – though La Fenice keeps on going most of the year, closing only for August. Tourist-oriented classical music concerts are held all year.

The summer brings a plethora of contemporary theatre, dance and music performances, as part of the Biennale di Venezia Danza-Musica-Teatro (www.labiennale.it).

Summer also brings a chance to watch or even join in tango performances in campo San Giacomo dell'Orio, on the steps of the station, or in front of the Salute basilica (www.tangoaction.com).

Information & tickets

Tickets can usually be purchased at theatre box offices immediately prior to shows, at the tourist information office near piazza San Marco and at HelloVenezia offices (p181).

For high-profile or first-night productions at prestigious venues such as La Fenice or Teatro Malibran, seats sell out days or even weeks in advance: reserve at the theatres themselves or online.

Local newspapers *Il Gazzettino* and *La Nuova Venezia* carry listings of theatrical events, as does the bilingual monthly *Venezia News*.

The silver screen

Once Venice had a host of cinemas; these days, most of them have been converted into supermarkets. But it's a pretty accurate reflection of local demand, with a diminishing population signifying decreasing numbers of movie-goers.

Injecting a little life into the film scene are the annual Film Festival (see box p157) in September, when the Lido's bikini-clad hordes rub shoulders with photographers, journalists and a constellation of international stars; and the Circuito Cinema (www.comune.venezia.it/cinema), a city council-backed hive of film-related research and activity that also runs and programmes a group of local arthouse cinemas, the newest of which is the plush Sala Perla, housed in the former Casinò on the Lido (lungomare Marconi, 041 524 1320).

The dearth of original-language films infuriates expats and cinema buffs alike. Outside the festival, screenings in *versione originale* are few and far between.

The sporting life

No other Italian city puts its inhabitants through their paces like Venice. In return for tramping miles on foot each day and being forced into compulsory step aerobics every ten paces, Venetians are rewarded with longevity and general good health into ripe old age.

Watery pursuits are what web-footed Venetians like best. Over 120 regattas are held throughout the year (see box p35).

This doesn't mean, however, that more familiar exercise routines can't be stuck to. Many of the city's rowing clubs have well-equipped gyms. If you like to take your morning run in company, head for the lagoon-side pavement near the Giardini Pubblici or in the park by the Sant'Elena vaporetto stop. Cycling is best done on the Lido or as a means of exploring the island of Sant'Erasmo. If spectating is more appealing than participating, then catch a football match at the PL Penzo stadium, on a island off Castello – a truly unique experience.

Fondazione Bevilacqua La Masa p65

WHAT'S ON
Calendar

Carnevale

Many of Venice's best-known festivals – Carnevale, for example, and the Regata Storica – are late 20th-century reinventions of popular revelries stamped out by the French when they took control of the city in the early 1800s. By that time Venice's celebrations had become frantic and excessive, the tawdry death-throes of a city in terminal decline. In the Republic's heyday, however, Venice's rulers used pageantry both to assert the hierarchical nature of society and to give the lower orders the chance to let off steam. Official celebrations were declared in honour of anything from the end of a plague epidemic to victory in a naval battle. For the working classes, there were the corse al toro (bullfights) in campo Santo Stefano, or bloody battles between rival factions of the populace.

Nowadays you could be forgiven for thinking that *feste* such as **Carnevale** are merely media and tourism events. Yet Venetians continue to take festivals seriously, especially if they take place on the water. There are more than 120 regattas on the lagoon each year (see box p35).

The following are the pick of the annual events that take place in Venice. Further information and exact dates can be found nearer the time in the city's two dailies, *Il Gazzettino* and *La Nuova Venezia*, and in the monthly *Venezia News*. Posters around the city advertise concerts and other happenings. Dates highlighted in **bold** are public holidays. *See also* http://english.comune.venezia.it.

January

1 Jan New Year's Day

Hardy swimmers take a bracing dip in the waters off the Lido.

6 Jan **La Befana (Epiphany)**

A rowing race along the Grand Canal in which the competitors, all aged over 50, are dressed up as an ugly witch, La Befana.

26 Jan-5 Feb 2008 **Carnevale**

Venice's 'traditional' pre-Lent Carnevale festivities were resuscitated in the late 1970s, and now draw masked revellers from all over the world.

February

Ongoing Carnevale

March

2 Mar 2008 **Su e Zo per i Ponti**

www.tgseurogroup.it/suezo
Literally 'Up and Down Bridges'. Participants in this non-competitive race on the fourth Sunday of Lent are given a map and a list of checkpoints (many of them bars) in the city of Venice to tick off.

23 Mar 2008 **Pasqua (Easter Sunday)**

Basilica di San Marco

At dusk, the lights are turned off inside St Mark's basilica, and a fire is lit in the narthex (entrance porch) for the *benedizione del fuoco* (blessing of fire).

24 Mar 2008 **Pasquetta (Easter Monday)**

April

8 Apr 2007 **Pasqua (Easter Sunday)**

Basilica di San Marco

At dusk, the lights are turned off inside St Mark's basilica, and a fire is lit in the narthex (entrance porch) for the *benedizione del fuoco* (blessing of fire).

9 Apr 2007 **Pasquetta (Easter Monday)**

25 Apr **Feast of San Marco**

Mass in the basilica, followed by a gondola regatta between the island of Sant'Elena and the Punta della Dogana. Red rosebuds are given to wives and lovers.

May

1 May **Festa del Lavoro (Labour Day)**

17 May 2007/1 May 2008 **Festa & Regata della Sensa**

Venice's film festival p33

Under the Republic, the doge boarded a glorious state barge and threw a gold ring overboard near the outlet to the Adriatic, to symbolise *lo sposalizio del mare* – marriage with the sea. Today the mayor throws a wreath at San Nicolò on the Lido; a regatta follows.

27 May 2007 **Vogalonga**
www.vogalonga.com
Venetians, and many out-of-towners, cover a 33km/20.5 mile route in non-motorised boats of all descriptions. Starts in front of the lagoon façade of the Doge's Palace at 8.30am.

June

10 June-21 Nov 2007 **Biennale d'Arte Contemporanea**
Giardini della Biennale and various other venues
www.labiennale.org
This *Jeux sans Frontières* of the contemporary art world has been going strong since 1895.

Week around 29 June **Feast of San Pietro**
San Pietro in Castello
The most villagey of Venice's local festivals, this one has a week of concerts, food stands and bouncy castles.

July

Ongoing 2007 Biennale d'Arte Contemporanea

3rd weekend in July **Feast of the Redentore**
A pontoon bridge is built from San Marco to the Giudecca. On Saturday evening, illuminated boats full of picnickers gather off the Punta della Dogana to watch a firework display.

Week around 25 July **Feast of San Giacomo dell'Orio**
Concerts, barbecues and a charity raffle in the eponymous *campo*.

Late July-mid Aug **Teatro in Campo**
Campo Pisani
www.pantakin.it
Good drama and opera performances in a square behind the Accademia.

Late July-Sept **Cinema all'Aperto**
Campo San Polo
www.comune.venezia.it/cinema
A huge screen is set up to show current films, mostly dubbed into Italian, and some offerings from the Film Festival.

August

Ongoing 2007 Biennale d'Arte Contemporanea

15 Aug **Ferragosto (Feast of the Assumption)**
Venice closes down. There's usually a free concert on the island of Torcello.

29 Aug-9 Sept 2007 **Mostra Internazionale d'Arte Cinematografica (Film Festival)**
Various venues on the Lido
www.labiennale.org
The brightest stars of the film firmament descend on Venice for this fest.

September

Ongoing 2007 Biennale d'Arte Contemporanea

Ongoing Mostra Internazionale d'Arte Cinematografica (Film Festival)

Carnevale p31

EW

EXPRESSWAY
Car Rental

RESERVATIONS
+39 041.5223000
FAX:
+39 041.5200000
www.expressway.it

Messing about in boats

It doesn't take much to get a Venetian into a boat: give them a blue-skied Sunday or even a dry evening after a frustrating day at work, and they'll take to the water for a leisurely saunter to a deserted sandbank for a picnic, or a punishing, head-clearing row across a lonely backwater.

Two traditional activities dominate on the mosquito-infested lagoon: Venetian rowing (*voga alla veneta*) and three-sail sailing (*vela al terzo*).

In *voga alla veneta* the rower stands up, facing the direction of travel. There are various types of *voga alla veneta*: team rowing is one; the solo, cross-handed, two-oar method called *voga alla valesana* is another; and the most famous is *voga ad un solo remo* (one-oar rowing) as practised by Venetian gondoliers. The gondolier only ever puts his oar in the water on the right side of the boat, where it rests in a *forcola* (rowlock). Pushing on the oar makes the craft turn to the left. The trick consists in using the downstroke to correct the direction. In theory, a gondolier uses little energy rowing a gondola, though that

doesn't quite explain how they get those bodybuilder biceps.

Depending upon their length, *vela al terzo* boats can hoist one or two square sails, plus the classic triangular jib. They can also be rowed in the traditional standing-up position.

All of these boating methods are employed by participants in the 120-plus regattas that take place on the lagoon each year.

The most famous is the Regata Storica, held on the first Sunday of September: the pageantry may make it look like a tourist-board creation, but locals take the racing part of it very seriously indeed.

For sheer numbers of craft in the water, the Vogalonga – held one Sunday in May – takes the prize. Anything without a motor can, and does, take part, from all the regular variations on the gondola, to dragon boats and things that look suspiciously like bathtubs. In the 2005 event, 1,462 craft carried 1,121 Venetian rowers and 2,531 rowers from outside Italy.

The city's website provides a list (in Italian) of the major rowing events at www2.comune.venezia. it/turismo/feste/stagioneremiera/

Campo San Polo's film screening p33

2 Sept 2007/7 Sept 2008
Regata Storica
Grand Canal
After an historical procession, races take place along the Grand Canal.

16 Sept 2007 **Sagra del Pesce Burano**
Fried fish and lots of white wine are consumed between Burano's brightly painted houses on the third weekend of September.

Mid Sept-mid Nov 2008 **Biennale d'Architettura**
Giardini della Biennale and various other venues
www.labiennale.org
This extensive look at the latest in world architecture spreads into spectacular areas inside the Arsenale.

October

Ongoing 2007 Biennale d'Arte Contemporanea
Ongoing 2008 Biennale d'Architettura

6-7 Oct 2007 **Sagra del Mosto**
Sant'Erasmo
This festival on the first weekend in October is a great excuse for Venetians to get light-headed on the first pressing of wine.

21 Oct 2007 **Venice Marathon**
www.venicemarathon.it
The marathon starts in the town of Stra, near Padua, and ends on the riva Sette Martiri.

November

Ongoing 2007 Biennale d'Arte Contemporanea
Ongoing 2008 Biennale d'Architettura

1 Nov **Ognissanti (All Saints' Day)**

11 Nov **Feast of San Martino**
Kids armed with mamma's pots and spoons raise a ruckus around the city centre. Horse-and-rider-shaped San Martino cakes proliferate in cake shops.

21 Nov **Feast of the Madonna della Salute**
The patriarch (archbishop) leads a procession across the Grand Canal on a pontoon bridge from campo Santa Maria del Giglio to the Salute church.

December

8 Dec **L'Immacolata (Feast of the Immaculate Conception)**

25 Dec **Natale (Christmas Day)**

26 Dec **Santo Stefano (St Stephen's Day/Boxing Day)**

Itineraries

The Grand Canal

Nothing else in Venice will give you the same grasp of what this extraordinary city is all about like a trip down its high street: the Grand Canal. In quintessentially Venetian fashion, the magnificent *palazzi* that line this three-and-a-half kilometre (2.2-mile) stretch were both statement of clout and taste, and solid commercial enterprise: their design is as practical as it is eye-catching.

Most of the buildings date from between the 12th and 18th centuries. When a palazzo was rebuilt, the basic structure was retained, for the good reason that the same foundations could be used.

A *palazzo* typically had a water entrance opening on to a large hall with storage space on either side; a *mezzanino* with offices; a *piano nobile* with spacious reception halls and residential rooms; and a land entrance at the back.

Setting out from the railway station, the façades of the Scalzi (L) and San Simeone (R) churches greet the visitor before the vaporetto passes beneath the **Scalzi bridge**, built in 1934.

Beyond, the church of San Geremia (L) stands just before the wide Cannaregio canal forks off. Placed with its main façade on the Cannaregio canal is the 18th-century **Palazzo Labia**; now the regional HQ of the RAI (the Italian state broadcaster), it contains sumptuous frescoes by Tiepolo.

Beyond the Riva di Biasio stop, just before the rio del Megio, is the **Fontego dei Turchi** (R), a 19th-century reconstruction a Veneto-Byzantine building leased to Turkish traders in the 17th century as a residence and warehouse; it now houses the **Museo di Storia Naturale**. Across the *rio*, the **Depositi del**

Megio (state granaries) have a battlemented plain-brick façade.

After the San Marcuola stop is **Palazzo Vendramin Calergi** (L), designed by Mauro Codussi in the early 16th century, with porphyry insets in the façade. Wagner died here in 1883; it now plays host to the **Casinò**.

After the baroque church of **San Stae** (R), with its exuberant sculpture, comes **Ca' Pesaro**, a splendid example of Venetian baroque by Baldassare Longhena. After two smaller *palazzi* stands **Palazzo Corner della Regina**, with a rusticated ground floor featuring grotesque masks; the palazzo dates from the 1720s.

On the left bank, a fairly uneventful stretch ends at the **Ca' d'Oro**, the most gorgeously ornate Gothic building on the Grand Canal. It has an open loggia on the *piano nobile*.

Just beyond, on the right bank, a covered **Pescaria** (fish market) has occupied a site here since the 14th century. The current neo-Gothic construction was built in 1907. Beyond it is the longest façade on the Grand Canal, with an endless parade of arches. This belongs to Sansovino's **Fabbriche Nuove**, built in 1554-6 for Venice's financial judiciary; it now houses the Court of Assizes.

Just before the rio dei Santi Apostoli (L) is **Palazzo Mangilli Valmarana**, built in 1751 for Joseph Smith, the British consul, who amassed the Canaletto paintings that now belong to Queen Elizabeth II. Beyond the *rio* is the **Ca' da Mosto**, once the site of the Leon Bianco (white lion) Hotel, and currently being returned to its original vocation as a luxury hotel. This is one of the earliest Veneto-Byzantine *palazzi* on the canal. It still has three of the original five arches of its water entrance and

a long array of Byzantine arches on the first floor. As the vaporetto swings round the bend here, the Rialto bridge comes into view.

On the right bank, the **Fabbriche Vecchie** was designed by Scarpagnino in the early 16th century. If you're doing this trip in the morning, you'll see the crowds stocking up at the fruit and vegetable part of the Rialto markets beside the *fabbriche*.

At the foot of the Rialto bridge is the **Fondego dei Tedeschi** (L), a huge residence-cum-warehouse leased to the German community from the 13th century onwards. The present building – now the main post office – was designed by Spavento and Scarpagnino in 1505-8. The façade once had frescoes by Titian and Giorgione.

Opposite, the **Palazzo dei Camerlenghi** (1523-5; R) is built around the curve of the canal; the walls lean noticeably. It was the headquarters of the Venetian Exchequer, with a debtors' prison on the ground floor.

Under the bridge, but before the Rialto vaporetto stop, the **Palazzo Manin Dolfin** (L) has a portico straddling the *fondamenta* (canal path). The façade is by Sansovino (late 1530s); the rest was rebuilt by Ludovico Manin, the last doge of Venice. It now belongs to the Bank of Italy.

On the left after the Rialto vaporetto stop, **Palazzetto Dandolo** is a Gothic building that appears to have been squeezed in. Enrico Dandolo, the blind doge who led the ferocious assault on Constantinople in 1204, was born in an earlier palazzo here.

Palazzo Farsetti and **Palazzo Loredan** (L) are Veneto-Byzantine buildings that now house the city hall. Though heavily restored, these two adjoining *palazzi* are among the few surviving examples of the

ITINERARIES

Time Out
Travel Guides

Italy

Available at all good bookshops
and at timeout.com/shop

Scalzi bridge p38

typical 12th-century Venetian house, with its first-floor polyforate window.

The austerely classical **Palazzo Grimani** is one of the largest *palazzi* on the Grand Canal. Its creator, Michele Sanmicheli, was famous for his military architecture, and this building is characteristically assertive.

Seven *palazzi* further on, before the rio Michiel, stands the pink **Palazzo Benzon** (L), home of Countess Marina Querini-Benzon, a society figure in the late 18th century. Byron was charmed by her when she was already in her 60s.

Facing off across the canal at the Sant'Angelo vaporetto stop are the small **Palazzo Corner** (L), built in the last decade of the 15th century by Mauro Codussi, with a rusticated ground floor, elegant balconies and double-arched windows; and the 16th-century **Palazzo Cappello Layard** (R), once the home of Sir Henry Austen Layard, archaeologist and British ambassador to Constantinople.

Almost opposite the San Tomà stop stand the four **Palazzi Mocenigo** (L), with blue-and-white poles in the water. The central double palazzo (16th century) was where Byron lived in 1818-9.

On the right bank, **Palazzo Pisani Moretta**, a large Gothic 15th-century palazzo, is just before the San Tomà stop; it's often hired out for Hollywood-style parties. After the stop, **Palazzo Balbi** (1582-90) – with obelisks, indicating that an admiral lived here – is the seat of the Veneto Regional Council.

Next door, across the rio Ca' Foscari, come three magnificent mid-15th-century Gothic *palazzi*. The first and largest is **Ca' Foscari**, now the HQ of Venice University. The next two are the **Palazzi Giustinian**; Wagner stayed in one of them in the winter of 1858-9, composing part of *Tristan und Isolde*. The horn prelude to the third act was inspired by the mournful cries of the gondoliers.

Just before the San Samuele vaporetto stop is the heavy, grey-white **Palazzo Grassi** (L), designed by Giorgio Massari. This was the last of the great patrician *palazzi*, built in 1748-72 when the city was already in terminal decline. It now belongs to French magnate François Pinault, who began his reign in 2006 with a show of works from his own post-war art collection. **Ca' Rezzonico** (R) is a baroque masterpiece by Longhena, begun in

1667. Robert Browning died here, while staying with his talentless son Pen. It's now the museum of 18th-century Venice.

A little further round the bend, **Ca' del Duca** (L) incorporates a part of the aggressively rusticated base and columns of a palace that Bartolomeo Bon was going to build for the Cornaro family; the massive project was never completed.

At the right foot of the Accademia bridge stand the **Gallerie dell' Accademia**; once the church and monastery of Santa Maria della Carità, they now boast an unrivalled collection of Venetian paintings.

Beyond the bridge, at its left foot, is **Palazzo Franchetti**, built in the 15th century but much restored and altered in the 19th; it's now used for conferences and exhibitions.

Immediately beyond this are two **Palazzi Barbaro** (L): part of the first – 15th-century Gothic, with a fine Renaissance water entrance – still belongs to the Curtis family, who hosted Henry James in 1870-5.

After the bridge on the right bank are four fine Renaissance *palazzi*, then campo San Vio, one of few *campi* on the Grand Canal. In the corner is the Anglican church of **St George**. To one side of the campo is the 16th-century **Palazzo Barbarigo**, with eye-catching but tacky 19th-century mosaics. Next is the pretty Gothic **Palazzo da' Mula**.

Just before one of the few Grand Canal gardens comes the bashful **Casetta delle Rose** (L), set behind its own small trellised garden. Canova had a studio here. Nearby, the massive rusticated ground floor of the **Palazzo Corner della Ca' Grande** (now the Prefecture) influenced Longhena's baroque *palazzi*. The imposing pile was commissioned in 1537 from Sansovino and built after 1545.

Work on the single-storey **Palazzo Venier dei Leoni** (R) ground to a halt in 1749. It was acquired in 1949 by the flamboyant Peggy Guggenheim, and now contains the **Peggy Guggenheim Collection**.

Next but one comes the pure, lopsided charm of the Renaissance **Ca' Dario**, built in the 1470s, with decorative use of coloured marbles. Venetians say it's cursed, as many of its owner have met sticky ends. Gaudy 19th-century mosaics on **Palazzo Salviati** advertise the products of that family's glass works. Further on, the large neo-Gothic **Palazzo Genovese**, built in 1892 on the site of the abbey of **San Gregorio**, was being converted into yet another luxury hotel as this guide went to press.

The new hostelry faces a Venetian classic across the way: the ultra-luxurious **Palazzo Gritti** (L), with its 15th-century Gothic façade. Three *palazzi* further on is the narrow Gothic **Palazzo Contarini Fasan**, traditionally known as Desdemona's house. The beautiful balconies have wheel tracery.

Lording it over the end of the right bank is the wonderfully curvy church of **Santa Maria della Salute**, an audacious baroque creation by Baldassare Longhena (1671). At the very tip is the **Dogana di Mare** (Customs House, 1677), with its tower, gilded ball and weathervane figure of Fortune; the warehouses at the Punta are in the process of becoming exhibition spaces (see box p133).

The last notable building on the left bank is **Ca' Giustinian**, built in the late Gothic style of the 1470s, and once a hotel where Verdi, Gautier, Ruskin and Proust stayed. At the corner of calle Vallaresso is **Harry's Bar**, the near-legendary Venetian watering hole founded in the 1930s. Just beyond the Vallaresso stop lie the pretty **Giardinetti Reali** and **piazza San Marco**.

Tintoretto's Last Suppers

No one ever accused Tintoretto (1518-94) of being a slacker. His paintings, nearly all on a huge scale, are to be found in almost every major church in Venice. And while other big producers – such as the depressingly ubiquitous Palma il Giovane – tended to repeat themselves unashamedly, Tintoretto always astonishes by the fertility of his imagination.

This is even more apparent if you study his variations on one theme. One subject in particular seemed to hold an unending fascination for the mystically minded Tintoretto: the Last Supper. There are seven paintings of this subject by the artist in Venice: they give a good idea of the development of his techniques and style, and also offer an insight into the deepest workings of his imagination.

The following itinerary covers much of the central, western and northern part of the city. Given how compact Venice is, you could cover the ground in a determined morning or afternoon. It would be far better, however, to stretch it out over a whole Tintoretto-packed day, perhaps pausing for a reviving lunch before or after visiting the Scuola di San Rocco (below).

Tintoretto's earliest *Last Supper* is in the church of San Marcuola (p95), by the vaporetto stop of that name. In this early work Tintoretto still organises the mainly horizontal composition in terms of symmetry and narrative clarity, adopting the same classical structure found in

ITINERARIES

Leonardo's more famous version of the subject. The main innovation with respect to Leonardo is the greater dynamism: the apostles are all caught in mid movement; the action spills over to either side of the table, with busy serving women and children participating in the scene. This background movement would increase in later paintings, until it almost came to dominate the scenes.

From San Marcuola, head towards the railway station and cross the Scalzi bridge; take the *calle* directly at the foot of the bridge, turn left at the end and cross a canal. Here, in the church of San Simeone Profeta (p123; aka San Simeone Grande), hangs a comparatively small *Last Supper*, tentatively dated 1560. The most striking elements of this painting, probably done with the help of assistants, are the spectral figure of the man who commissioned the work (probably the parish priest) in the background on the left, and the fine candelabra hanging over the table.

Some deft map-reading will be needed to get to campo San Polo. The *Last Supper* (1568) in the church of the same name (p113) has the same floor of red and white squares as in the San Marcuola painting, but the composition is no longer classically symmetrical. The first thing we notice is the apostle at the centre of the painting turning away from the table to offer a crust of bread to a beggar lying on the floor in the foreground. This shadowy figure, startlingly foreshortened, serves to pull us into the painting, making us feel part of the scene. The table now slants diagonally upwards to the right, and the apostles are all in swirling movement around the central figure of Christ.

It's a short hop west from here past the great bulk of the Frari to the Scuola di San Rocco (p113), where the *Last Supper* (1578-81) has an elevated stage setting used in an earlier painting in the church of Santo Stefano (below); the same dog seems to stand quivering on the steps in the foreground, although here he is strangely spectral, with the lines of the stairs visible through his body. The setting appears to be a fairly grandiose 16th-century palazzo. The table is set low, with the apostles squatting or kneeling around it; Christ himself is kneeling, with his bare soles protruding from beneath his red robes. All around the table and in the background, everyday life goes on, with servants in the kitchen baking bread and clearing away dishes. This only adds to the visionary quality of what is happening in the centre of the painting.

Follow the flow southwards to San Trovaso (p131), which contains a *Last Supper* dated 1556. Though this is an early version, it's original in concept, with a greater emphasis on realism. The setting seems to be a tavern, and the apostles are sitting on all four sides of a square table. Each of them seems to be caught in mid move, one reaching for a flagon of wine at the very bottom of the painting, another twisting round to take the lid off a pot that a cat seems eager to inspect, another leaning forward in apparent surprise towards Christ. A chair lies overturned in the foreground, with its cane bottom and legs towards the viewer. In contrast to all this earthy realism, above Christ's head is a mysterious view beyond the tavern to a classical landscape, with diaphanous figures poised against sunlit arches and pillars.

Make your way across the nearby Accademia bridge into campo Santo Stefano. Hanging in the sacristy of the eponymous church (p69) is Tintoretto's first truly large-scale version of the Last Supper theme

San Giorgio Maggiore p148

(1576). Although it contains a good deal of studio work, the design is clearly by the maestro and paves the way for the great painting in the Scuola di San Rocco. The setting is strikingly different from the earlier versions, with the table on an elevated platform; the steps leading up to it provide the foreground of the painting, with a child sprawled across them and a dog poised expectantly, looking up at the laden table with an eager, quivering nose. The area in front of the stairs contains two figures that seem to mediate between the viewer and the miraculous scene: on the right is a half-naked beggar, lying and looking wistfully up at the table; on the left is a striking female figure, who may be a servant but whose open-armed gesture seems curiously beneficent, even benedictory. For the first time Christ is viewed from behind, with the apostles leaning across the table towards him and the viewer.

For Tintoretto's final version, make your way through St Mark's square to the riva degli Schiavoni, and take a vaporetto to the island of San Giorgio Maggiore. The vast painting (1591) hanging to the right of the high altar is a magnificent work intended to dazzle the viewer, with its bewildering mixture of lights and shadows, movement and stillness: the long table occupies the left half of the painting, and angels appear mysteriously in the swirling smoke from the oil lamps above. The right-hand side of the painting is dominated by two striking figures of servants at work; a girl kneels beside a basket (which is being investigated by another curious cat) and offers a dish to a servant in blue clothes and orange apron; he is caught in an elegant balletic pose, his head turned left to the girl while his body and right arm reach towards a table on the right. These figures provide an interesting solid counterpoint to the evanescent swirl of angelic figures floating mysteriously above and around them. The combination of earthy realism and visionary mysticism is here taken to startling new levels.

ITINERARIES

Marina & Susanna Sent p142

Glass beads

Though Venice has more glassware shops than grocery stores, many of them serve up endless variations on the same mass-produced tat. Nowhere is this truer than with glass beads, a Venetian-produced luxury good that was coveted for centuries throughout the civilised world. Nowadays, high-quality glass jewellery is as hard to find as hen's teeth, but if you are prepared to put in some legwork, there are a few havens of quality and design.

A dedicated bead-hunter could whip through this itinerary in a morning – depending, of course, on how long you dally in each store. However, if you are planning on fitting in some culture on the way, this route combines satisfying jewellery experiences with more than a weekend's worth of some of the best sightseeing to be had in the city.

Hop off the vaporetto at the Salute stop and pop into the towering wedding-cake church before taking the bridge closest to the Grand Canal and heading to campo San Gregorio, where you'll find one of Venice's leading names in glass manufacture. **Giorgio Nason** (Dorsoduro 167, campo San Gregorio, 041 523 9426) comes from a glass-blowing dynasty (his brother has a glass shop just down the road). He and his American wife Trina Tygrett produce exquisitely coloured glass beads from which they design their modern jewellery, often incorporating silver elements (designed by Trina) into the pieces. Though their classic chunky glass rings look similar to many you will see throughout Venice, each one is hallmarked; if you ever happen to crack or chip the item, the designers will repair it for you. They will adapt pieces to suit particular requirements, such as shortening necklaces, and will also help you to conjure up a design of your own. Prices start at around €48, but a long glass and silver necklace will set you back about €300.

Head down calle San Gregorio, cross the bridge, and in a few moments you'll find yourself at the entrance of the Peggy Guggenheim Collection. (Note that Tuesday is Peggy's day off, thus many of the galleries and shops in the neighbourhood are also shut.)

Take in the Peggy Guggenheim collection, take a break in the gallery's lovely café, then start out afresh on your bead quest. Exiting from the Guggenheim, take a right and follow the *fondamenta* (canal path) until you reach campo San Vio, home to the English Protestant church. Tucked away in the corner of the square to your left is **Sent**, Marina and Susanna Sent's glass emporium (p142). Like Nason, the Sent sisters come from a long line of glass-makers and create what look like Liquorice Allsort necklaces and soap-bubble bracelets out of glass, offering a unique vision of glass jewellery-making. It is no

surprise that their designs have been snapped up MoMA's online store.

From Sent, head over the bridge on the left and carry on straight until you reach rio terà Antonio Foscarini. Turn right, and you'll see the Grand Canal at the point where the Accademia bridge crosses it. Nestling on the right at the foot of the bridge is **Totem-Il Canal** (Dorsoduro 878B, campo Carità, 041 522 3641, www.totemilcanale. com), a contemporary art gallery specialising in African art, but also a purveyor of gorgeous antique Venetian glass beads, often rethreaded with silver beads to create ethnic-looking jewellery. Totem is right next door to the Gallerie dell'Accademia, currently undergoing major restoration work that will see the exhibition space expand, so that even more of the extraordinary collection of Old Masters can be put on display.

After a dutiful traipse around the Accademia's masterpieces, a sugar fix may be in order. Exiting from the gallery, turn left, take calle Corfu Gambara, then cross over the first bridge you come to. Turn left

Attombri p118

at the end, and you'll find yourself at **Faggiotto** (p135), chocaholics' heaven. After the caffeine hit of an espresso of hot chocolate, you'll be ready to carry on your bead mission.

Leaving the shop, turn left and left again. In calle Toletta is **Antichità** (p134). Among the lace finery and antiques is a selection of hand-painted antique glass beads that can be purchased individually for you to thread your own creations – though lazy beadistas can purchase ready-made pieces. Check out the dainty glass birds on glass leaves incorporated into necklaces in various hues.

After revelling in the old, the next glass pit stop is a paean to the new. Situated in campo San Barnaba, **Madera** (p135) appears to be a groovy kitchenware store, but actually contains some of the best contemporary glass jewellery around. Great chunky rings that look like they're made from marble or granite are the work of Antares, while the beautiful pendants are by Alberto Nason (yes, that dynasty again).

From Madera, turn right into calle del Traghetto, at the end of which is the museum of 18th-century Venice at Ca' Rezzonico. Alternatively, cross the square and take the bridge to the left of the greengrocer's barge into one of the liveliest squares in town: campo Santa Margherita; stop for a breather on one of the many benches, and enjoy viewing Venice going about its daily business.

Leaving the square down calle della Chiesa, cross the bridge and take the alleyway to the right of the church of San Pantalon. Tucked away behind the church is **Officina Veneziana** (Dorsoduro 3752A, calle San Pantalon, 041 720 313). Like Madera, glass does not take precedence in Sonia Dorizza's shop. However, the pretty rings and bracelets made of tiny glass beads

threaded on to invisible strands are delicate and dazzling, sturdy and yet surprisingly spongy to touch.

If you're now teetering, perk yourself up with a cake from one of the best-loved *pasticcerie* in the city: at the end of calle San Pantalon, Tonolo awaits with its calorific delights.

Literally round the corner from Tonolo, more culture is in store at the church and *scuola* of San Rocco, and the basilica of the Frari… after which you can appease the gods of consumerism and continue towards the next bead venue. Leaving the Frari, cross the only bridge you can see and head east towards campo San Polo. At the bottom of the bridge, leading into the square, is one of the three **Perle e Dintorni** stores (San Polo 2102A, campo San Polo, 041 710 031; p70). This Aladdin's cave of beads offers a vast array of baubles for DIY jewellery-making, as well as a whole host of ready-made necklaces. Many of the beads are modern takes on antique designs.

Stop off at the church of San Polo for a few more masterpieces, before continuing east towards the Rialto bridge, where the Pearly Kings of Venice await under the arches. Stefano and Daniele **Attombri** (p118) make exquisite pieces from delicate antique beads. Recent creations include necklaces with antique beads hunted down on the glass-making island of Murano, combined with modern glass mini-sculptures as centrepieces. Winners of the New Talents prize at the 2006 Milan Design Fair, the Attombri brothers offer a perfect fusion of Venetian contemporary design and centuries-old craftsmanship.

After making your glassy purchases, risk becoming glassy-eyed yourself by heading to nearby Bancogiro or Muro for a hard-earned celebratory *aperitivo* and/or meal.

Venice by Area

Piazza San Marco

San Marco

VENICE BY AREA

This *sestiere* is the heart of the city, and at the heart's core is the great square with the splendid church that gives the area its name. However, a stroll off the beaten track will soon reveal that a host of other major sights are concealed here.

Main routes lead from St Mark's square to the Rialto bridge, from the Rialto to the Accademia bridge, and from the Accademia back to St Mark's. For a respite from the jostling crowds, simply wander off these routes: you're never far from a haven of uniquely Venetian calm.

Piazza San Marco

Napoleon referred to St Mark's square as the 'drawing room of Europe', a description that catches the quality of the place: it may not be homey, but it is a supremely

civilised meeting place. Byzantine rubs shoulders with Gothic, late Renaissance and neo-classical.

The north side of the square dates from the early 16th century. Here resided the procurators of St Mark's, who were in charge of maintaining the basilica – hence the name of this wing, the Procuratie Vecchie. At its eastern end is the **Torre dell'Orologio**.

Construction of the Procuratie Nuove on the south side took most of the first half of the 17th century. In the early 19th century, Napoleon joined the two wings at the far end to create that essential imperial mod con: a ballroom. The Ala Napoleonica now houses the **Museo Correr**.

The **campanile** (bell tower) and **basilica di San Marco** (St Mark's basilica) close off the square to the east.

DI PIAZZA SAN MARCO

Museo Correr Museo
Archeologico
Nazionale Sale Monumentali
della Biblioteca
Nazionale Marciana

Sights & muse

Basilica di San
(St Mark's basil

San Marco, piazza San
522 5205). Vaporetto S
or Vallaresso.

Basilica, Chancel & P
Treasury Open *May-Sep* 9.45am-
5.30pm Mon-Sat; 2-4pm Sun. *Oct-Apr*
9.45am-4.30pm Mon-Sat; 2-4pm Sun.
Admission *Basilica* free. *Chancel &*
Pala d'Oro €1.50; €1 concessions.
Treasury €2; €1 concessions.
Loggia & Museo Marciano Open
Apr-Oct 9.45am-5pm daily. *Nov-Mar*
9.45am-4pm daily. **Admission** €3;
€1.50 concessions. No credit cards.
Map p53 F3 ❶

The basilica is open for mass and private prayer 7-9.45am, with entrance from the piazzetta dei Leoncini door.

In the Middle Ages any self-respecting city state had to have a truly important holy relic. So when two Venetian merchants swiped the body of St Mark from Alexandria in 828, they were going for the very best: an evangelist, and an entire body at that. Fortunately, there was a legend (or one was invented) that the saint had once been caught in a storm in the lagoon, and so it was fitting that this should be his final resting place.

The Venetians were traders, but they never looked askance at a bit of straightforward looting. The basilica – like the city as a whole – is encrusted with trophies brought back from Venice's greatest spoliatory exploit, the Sack of Constantinople in 1204, during the free-for-all that went under the name of the Fourth Crusade.

The present basilica is the third on the site. It was built mainly between 1063 and 1094, although the work of decoration continued until the 16th century. The church became Venice's cathedral only in 1807, ten years after the fall of the Republic; until then the bishop exerted his authority from San Pietro in Castello. Venetians who worshipped here were very aware that they were guests of the doge, not the pope.

Between the basilica and the lagoon, the *piazzetta* is the real entrance to Venice: for centuries, foreign visitors disembarked here, to be awestruck by all that pomp and magnificence. At the end are two granite columns, erected in the 12th century. What appears to be a winged lion on top of the easternmost column is in fact a chimera from Persia, Syria or maybe China; the wings and book are Venetian additions. On top of the other one is St Theodore, Venice's first patron saint.

West of here are the Giardinetti Reali (royal gardens). The dainty neo-classical coffee house designed by Gustavo Selva is now a tourist information office (p187).

Head the opposite way from the *piazzetta* for the ponte della Paglia (Bridge of Straw). If you can manage to elbow your way to the side of the bridge, there is a wonderful photo opportunity view of the Bridge of Sighs.

VENICE BY AREA

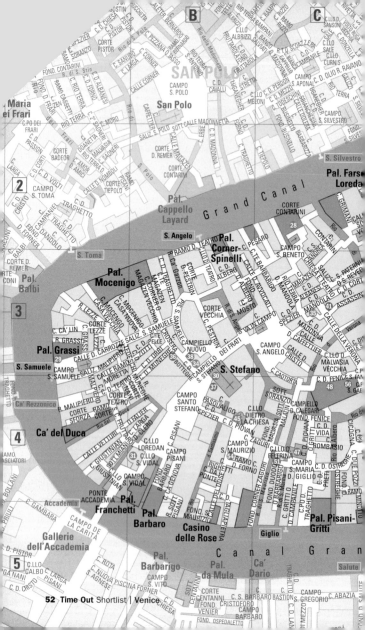

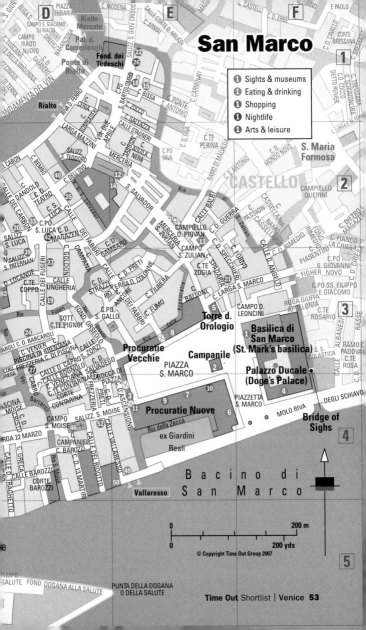

San Marco

1 Sights & museums
1 Eating & drinking
1 Shopping
1 Nightlife
1 Arts & leisure

CASTELLO

S. Maria Formosa

1 Basilica di San Marco (St. Mark's basilica)

Palazzo Ducale (Doge's Palace)

Torre d. Orologio

Procuratie Vecchie

Campanile

PIAZZA S. MARCO

Procuratie Nuove

PIAZZETTA S. MARCO

MOLO RIVA

Bridge of Sighs

ex Giardini Reali

B a c i n o   d i
S a n   M a r c o

Vallaresso

0   200 m
0   200 yds

© Copyright Time Out Group 2007

Piazza San Marco p50

Exterior

The façade consists of two orders of five arches, with clusters of columns in the lower order; the upper arches are topped by fantastic Gothic tracery.

The only original mosaic is the one over the north door, *The Translation of the Body of St Mark to the Basilica*, which contains the earliest-known representation of the church, from around 1260. Of curiosity value is the 17th-century mosaic over the south door, which shows the body of St Mark being filched from Alexandria, with Muslims reeling back in disgust, because it was wrapped in pork.

The real treasures, though, are the sculptures, particularly the group of three carved arches around the central portal, a Romanesque masterpiece. The inner curve of the outer arch is the liveliest, with its detailed portrayals of Venetian trades, crafts and pastimes.

The south façade was the first side seen by visitors from the sea and is richly encrusted with trophies proclaiming Venice's might. At the corner stand the Tetrarchs, a fourth-century porphyry group of conspiratorial-looking kings. These come from Constantinople, and are thought to represent Diocletian and his imperial colleagues.

The two free-standing pillars in front of the baptistry door, with Syrian carvings from the fifth century, come from Acre, as does the stumpy porphyry column on the corner, known as the Pietra del Bando, where official decrees were read.

The north façade, facing piazzetta dei Leoncini, is also studded with loot. The carving of 12 sheep on either side of a throne bearing a cross is a seventh-century Byzantine work. Note the beautiful 13th-century Moorish arches of the Porta dei Fiori, which enclose a Nativity scene.

The narthex (entrance porch) has an opus sectile marble floor. A series of fine 13th-century mosaics shows scenes from the Old Testament.

Interior

The basilica is Greek cross in form, surmounted by five great 11th-century domes. There are more than four square kilometres (1.5 square miles) of mosaics, the result of 600 years of labour. The finest pieces, dating from the 12th and 13th centuries, are the work of Venetian craftsmen influenced by Byzantine art. The chapels and baptistry were decorated in the 14th and 15th centuries; a century later, replacements of earlier mosaics were made using cartoons by such artists as Titian and Tintoretto.

In the apse, Christ Pantocrator is a faithful 16th-century reproduction of a Byzantine original. Beneath, in what may be the oldest mosaics inside the church, are four saint-protectors of Venice: St Nicholas, St Peter, St Mark and St Hermagoras. The central dome of the Ascension, with its splendidly poised angels and apostles, dates from the early 13th century. The Passion scenes (12th century) on the west vault are a striking blend of Romanesque and Byzantine styles. The Pentecost dome (towards the entrance) was probably the first to be decorated; it shows the descent of the Holy Spirit. Four magnificent angels hover in the pendentives.

The scene of the *Miraculous Rediscovery of the Body of St Mark* in the right transept refers to an episode that occurred after the second basilica was destroyed by fire. When no one could remember where the saint's body was, the evangelist obligingly opened up the pillar where his sarcophagus had been hidden (it's just opposite and marked by an inlaid marble panel).

Baptistry & Zen Chapel

The baptistry (for private prayer only) contains the Gothic tomb of Doge Andrea Dandolo and some interesting mosaics. The adjoining Zen Chapel, with its bronze 16th-century tomb of Cardinal Zen (a common Venetian surname), was closed for restoration as this guide went to press.

Chancel & Pala d'Oro

The chancel is separated from the body of the church by the iconostasis, a red marble rood screen by the Gothic sculptors Jacobello and Pier Paolo

Make the cut

From its €5-a-trip vaporetto tickets and €1-a-go toilets to the unofficial 'tax' levied by many restaurateurs on non-local diners, Venice is not a cheap city to visit.

You can take some of the sting out of your stay by investing in a **Venice Card**. This is a one-, three- or seven-day card that gives an array of discounts on museums and services around the city; its primary selling point, however, is that it allows unlimited use of the city's extortionate public transport. It's fiendishly complicated, with colour-coded cards giving different benefits: for details, and to buy it online, see www.venicecard.it.

Visitors aged between 14 and 29 can sign up for the **Rolling Venice** programme (information on the Venice Card site); this €4 card gives discounts at selected hotels, museums (up to 50 per cent), restaurants and shops (10-15 per cent), as well as cut-price (€15) three-day vaporetto passes. You can pick one up at any HelloVenezia (p181) or APT office (p187).

If you're planning to move about a lot without visiting many museums, consider a vaporetto season ticket (24-hour – €12; 36-hour – €20; 72-hour – €25), which can be purchased at most vaporetto stops, at *tabacchi* and at HelloVenezia offices.

Alternatively, if plan to soak up culture, look into multi-entrance cards, which include the **Museum Pass**, themed multi-entrance tickets to Venice's city-owned museums, and the **Chorus** pass for churches. For all, see p12.

Tune!

Once upon a time you could catch regular concerts by conductor, harpsichordist and organist Andrea Marcon and his Venice Baroque Orchestra at the Scuola di San Rocco. These days you're more likely to hear the award-winning musician in Vienna, New York or London.

From its birth in 1997, it was clear that the VBO was no peddlar of baroque faves to tourists: Marcon's dedicated rooting-out of neglected works played on period instruments, made sure of this.

The VBO strove to recapture the spirit of the period, injecting its music with the kind of energy, emotion and extravagance that makes the art and architecture of the baroque so recognisable.

The orchestra has won widespread acclaim for its renditions of previously unrecorded works by Claudio Monteverdi and Antonio Vivaldi, and for reviving long-forgotten operas such as Handel's *Siroe* (2000) and *L'Olimpiade* (2006) by Baldassarre Galuppi.

But even golden oldies take on a new lease of life in VBO hands: listening to virtuoso violinist Giuliano Carmignola perform the *Four Seasons* is like hearing that work for the first time.

You're unlikely to find the VBO in its native city except during October's Venice Music Festival (www.venicemusicfestival.org). But you'll find its performances on Deutsche Grammophon (www.deutschegrammophon.com): stick them on your iPod and experience baroque Venice.

Dalle Masegne, with fine naturalistic statues of the Madonna, the apostles and St George. Access to the chancel is via the San Clemente Chapel to the right, with a mosaic showing merchants Rustico di Torcello and Buono di Malamocco, apparently about to Fed-Ex the body of St Mark to Venice. St Mark's sarcophagus is visible through the grate underneath the altar.

The indigestibly opulent Pala d'Oro (gold altarpiece) is a Byzantine work made in Constantinople in 976 and further enriched later with amethysts, emeralds, pearls, rubies, sapphires and topaz, topped off with a Gothic frame and resetting in 1345.

The left transept contains the chapel of the Madonna Nicopeia (the victory bringer), named after the tenth-century icon on the altar. The St Isidore Chapel beyond, with its 14th-century mosaics of the life of the saint, is reserved for private prayer and confessions, as is the adjacent Mascoli Chapel, where the Gothic altarpiece features Saints Mark and John the Evangelist, with the Virgin between them. The chapel's mosaics, dating from 1430-50, have a definite Renaissance look to them. They are mostly by Michele Giambono, although some of the figures have been attributed to Jacopo Bellini and to the Florentine Andrea del Castagno.

Loggia & Museo Marciano

Up a narrow stairway from the narthex are the bronze horses that vie with the lion of St Mark as the city's symbol; here too, is Paolo Veneziano's exquisite Pala Feriale, a painted panel that was used to cover the Pala d'Oro on weekdays. The loggia also provides a marvellous view over the square.

The original bronze horses are now kept indoors. They were brought to Venice after the 1204 Sack of Constantinople, where they had stood above the hippodrome. They were put in front of the Arsenale, but around 1250 they found their place of honour on the terrace of the basilica. In 1797 Napoleon snaffled the horses and they didn't return to Venice until after his defeat at Waterloo. They remained on the terrace until 1974, when they were removed for restoration. Since 1982 they have been on display inside, with copies replacing them on the terrace.

Treasury
This contains a hoard of exquisite Byzantine gold and silver work – reliquaries, chalices, candelabras – most of it crusader plunder.

Campanile
San Marco, piazza San Marco. Vaporetto San Zaccaria or Vallaresso. **Open** *Apr-June, Sept-Oct* 9.30am-7pm daily. *July, Aug* 9am-9pm daily. *Nov-Mar* 9.30am-4.15pm daily. **Admission** €6; €3 concessions. No credit cards. **Map** p53 E3 ②
Venice's tallest building – almost 99m (325ft) – was originally built between 888 and 912. Its present appearance, with the stone spire and the gilded angel on top, dates from 1514. The campanile served both as a watchtower and a bell tower. People guilty of 'scandalous behaviour' were hung in a cage from the top.

In July 1902 the whole thing fell down. Old age, weak foundations and lightning damage were blamed. The campanile imploded in a neat pyra~~mid~~ of rubble; the only victim was the ~~cus~~todian's cat. It was rebuilt exactly ~~as~~ it was, where it was', as the town council of the day promised. The view from the top (there's a lift) is superb.

Sansovino's little Loggetta at the foot of the tower was also rebuilt, using bits and pieces found in the rubble. In the 18th century the Loggetta was where the state lottery was drawn.

Museo Correr, Biblioteca Marciana & Museo Archeologico
San Marco 52, piazza San Marco/ sottoportego San Geminian (041 240 5211/www.museicivicivenezianii.it). Vaporetto Vallaresso. **Open** *Apr-Oct* 9am-7pm daily. *Nov-Mar* 9am-5pm daily. **Admission** see p12 Musei Civici Veneziani. **Map** p53 E4 ③
These three adjoining museums are all entered on the same ticket and by the same doorway, which is situated at the western end of piazza San Marco.

Museo Correr
Based on the private collection of Venetian nobleman Teodoro Correr (1750-1830), the Museo Correr covers the history of the republic.

Museo Marciano p56

Torre dell'Orologio p63

The first part of the collection is dedicated to the beautiful if icy sculpture of Antonio Canova, whose first Venetian commission – the statue of Daedalus and Icarus, displayed here – brought him instant fame.

The historical collection, which occupies most of the first floor of the Procuratie Nuove, documents Venetian history and social life in the 16th and 17th centuries. Room 6, devoted to the figure of the doge, features Lazzaro Bastiani's famous portrait of Doge Francesco Foscari (c1460). Room 11 has a collection of Venetian coins, plus Tintoretto's fine *St Justine and the Treasurers*. Beyond are rooms dedicated to the Arsenale.

Upstairs is the Quadreria picture gallery. Rooms 24 to 29 focus on Byzantine and Gothic painters: note Paolo Veneziano's fine *St John the Baptist* and the rare allegorical fresco fragments from a 14th-century private house in Room 27. Room 30 fast-forwards abruptly with the macabre *Pietà* (c.1460) of Cosme Turà.

Room 32 contains an aerial view of Venice by Jacopo de' Barbari, dated 1500. This extraordinary woodcut is so finely detailed that the architectural details of every single church, palazzo and well head can be made out. Beyond here, the Renaissance gets into full swing with Antonello da Messina's *Pietà with Three Angels*, haunting despite the fact that the faces have nearly been erased by cack-handed restoration. The Bellinis get Room 36 to themselves: note the rubicund portrait of Doge Giovanni Mocenigo, painted by Gentile Bellini in 1475.

The gallery's most fascinating work is Vittore Carpaccio's *Two Venetian Noblewomen* – which was long known erroneously as *The Courtesans* – in Room 38. These two bored women are not angling for trade: they're waiting for their husbands to return from a hunt. This was confirmed when *A Hunt in the Valley* in the Getty Museum in Los Angeles was shown to be this painting's other half.

Biblioteca Marciana – Libreria Sansoviniana

In the 1530s, Florentine architect Jacopo Sansovino was appointed to create a library for a collection of Greek and Latin manuscripts left to the state in 1468. With this building, Sansovino brought the new ideas of the Roman Renaissance into Venice. He also appealed to the Venetian love of surface decoration with an abundance of statuary.

The main room has a magnificent ceiling and rows of allegorical medallion paintings. Beyond this is the anteroom, with a collection of classical statues. On the ceiling is *Wisdom*, a late work by Titian.

In a room off the staircase landing is Fra Mauro's map of the world (1459), a fascinating testimony to the precision of Venice's geographical knowledge. There are free guided tours at weekends (to be sure of a tour in English, phone 041 240 7241; tours can also be booked on Thursdays).

Museo Archeologico

This collection is discerning 16th-century humanist Cardinal Domenico Grimani's attempt to surround himself with the classical ideal of beauty. Among the highlights are the original fifth-century BC Greek statues of goddesses in Room 4, and the Grimani Altar in Room 6. There are free guided tours in English (11am Sat & 10.30am Sun); it's best to book in advance (041 522 5978).

Palazzo Ducale (Doge's Palace)

San Marco 1, piazzetta San Marco (041 271 5911/bookings 041 520 9070/www.museiciviciveneziani.it). Vaporetto San Zaccaria. **Open** *Apr-Oct* 9am-7pm daily. *Nov-Mar* 9am-5pm daily. **Admission** see p12 Musei Civici Veneziani. No credit cards. **Map** p53 F4 ❹

There are guided tours (€6) from November to March; call 041 520 9038 for information and bookings.

If St Mark's basilica was the Venetian Republic's spiritual nerve centre, the Doge's Palace was its political and judicial hub. The present site was the seat of ducal power from the ninth century onwards, though most of what we see today dates from the mid-15th century. Devastating fires in 1574 and 1577 took their toll, but after much debate it was decided to restore rather than replace – an enlightened policy for the time.

This is Venice's great Gothic building, but it's also curiously eastern in style. The ground floor was open to the public; the work of government went on above. This arrangement resulted in a curious reversal of the natural order. The building gets heavier as it rises.

The *piazzetta* façade was built in the 15th century as a continuation of the 14th-century waterfront façade. On the corner by the ponte della Paglia (Bridge of Straw) is an exquisite marble relief carving, the *Drunkenness of Noah* from the early 15th century, while on the *piazzetta* corner is a statue of Adam and Eve from the late 14th century. The capitals of the pillars below date from the 14th and 15th centuries, although many of them are 19th-century copies (the originals are on display inside).

The Porta della Carta (Paper Gate, where permits were checked), between the palace and the basilica, is a grand piece of florid Gothic architecture and sculpture (1438-42) by Bartolomeo and Giovanni Bon. The statue of Doge Francesco Foscari and the lion is a copy dating from 1885; French troops smashed the original in 1797.

The visitors' entrance is at the Porta del Frumento, on the lagoon side of the palace. The Museo dell'Opera, to the left of the ticket barrier, has the best of the 14th-century capitals from the external loggia; the ones you see outside are mostly copies.

In the main courtyard stands the Arco dei Foscari, another fine late Gothic work, by Antonio Bregno and Antonio Rizzo. Rizzo also sculpted the figures of Adam and Eve (these, too,

are copies; the originals are in the first-floor *liagò*), which led to his appointment as official architect in 1483. Rizzo oversaw the building of the Scala dei Giganti (Giants' Staircase, where doges were crowned) and some of the interior before he was found to have embezzled 12,000 ducats; he fled, and died soon after.

The route now leads up the ornate Scala d'Oro (golden staircase) by Jacopo Sansovino, with stuccoes by Alessandro Vittoria outlined in 24-carat gold leaf.

First floor: Doge's apartments

In the Sala delle Mappe, a series of 16th-century maps shows the known world as it radiated from Venice. Just to the right of the entrance door is a detailed map of the New World with Bofton (Boston) and Isola Longa (Long Island) clearly marked. Further on, Titian's fresco of St Christopher is hidden above a doorway giving on to a staircase; it took the artist a mere three days to complete.

First floor: State rooms

The Sala dei Censori now leads down to a *liagò* (covered, L-shaped loggia), which gives on to the Sala della Quarantia Civil Vecchia (the civil court) and the Sala del Guariento. The latter's faded 14th-century fresco of *The Coronation of the Virgin* by Guariento looks strangely innocent amid all this worldly propaganda. The shorter arm of the *liagò* has the originals of Antonio Rizzo's sculptures of Adam and Eve.

Next comes the Sala del Maggior Consiglio, the largest room in the palace. This was the Republic's lower house. Before a fire in 1577, the hall was decorated with paintings by Bellini, Titian, Carpaccio and Veronese. When these went up in smoke, they were replaced by less exalted works – with a few exceptions: Tintoretto's immense *Paradise* on the far wall, sketched out by the 70-year-old artist but completed after his death in 1594 by his son Domenico; and the ceiling panels by Veronese and Palma il Giovane. The frieze of ducal portraits

Keeping it real

It's an unlikely looking craft, the Venetian gondola: 11 metres (36 feet) long, riding high in the water, bendy and listing. But it manages to be elegant too, as it weaves its way between the motor boats that stir up the water of the canals and the lagoon... unless, of course, it's fitted out with fluorescent yellow cushions, lashings of gleaming brass fittings and tacky fake-fur rugs.

'It used to be that respect for traditions was taken for granted,' moaned Ente Gondola (gondoliers' association) chairman Roberto Luppi recently. 'Now we have to make it clear that this is Venice, not Las Vegas.'

In a modern take on the sumptuary laws with which rulers of the Serene Republic of Venice banned public displays of conspicuous wealth in past centuries, the Ente Gondola has drawn up strict guidelines forcing its 425 members to stick to more sober trappings, or face losing their lucrative licences.

According to the new rules, *gondole* cushions must be black, bordeaux or dark blue. (The hulls themselves have always been black, due to the pitch used to waterproof them.) Backrests should be low and shiny metal fittings kept to a minimum. Gondoliers' attire has come under scrutiny too, with the Ente establishing a maximum width for the characteristic stripes on their shirts.

For a complete return to tradition, the Ente would have to rule on the songs crooned to star-struck visitors as they make their way along the canals on possibly the most expensive boat ride of their lives: *O sole mio* might seem to match the mood, but it's Neapolitan, not Venetian. And *gondole* would have to be fitted with *felze*, the black cabins that, local lore relates, were the setting for any number of illicit amorous adventures (though it's difficult to imagine the craft remaining upright were the action inside too vigorous).

And *gondole* would have to become a necessary possession of the city's rich and famous. Nowadays, locals zip around their watery world in smaller *topi* or *sandali*. And they cross the Grand Canal on *gondoloni* – the larger *gondole* used for the *traghetto* service (p182). The last private gondola to ply Venice's waterways belonged to American heiress Peggy Guggenheim; it can be seen in the Museo Storico Navale.
■ www.gondolavenezia.it

is by Domenico Tintoretto and assistants; a black veil marks where Marin Falier's face would have been had he not conspired against the state in 1356.

A door leads from the back of the hall into the Sala della Quarantia Civil Nuova and the large Sala dello Scrutinio, where the votes of the *maggior consiglio* were counted; the latter is flanked by vast paintings of victorious naval battles.

Second floor: State rooms

This grandiose series of halls provided steady work for all the great 16th-century Venetian artists. Titian, Tintoretto, Veronese, Palma il Vecchio and Jacopo Bassano left their mark, though the sheer acreage didn't always spur them to artistic heights.

The Sala delle Quattro Porte was where the Collegio – the inner cabinet of the Republic – met until 1574. After substantial renovation it became an ambassadorial waiting room, where humble envoys could gaze enviously at Andrea Vicentino's portrayal of the magnificent reception given to the young King Henry III of France in 1574. The Anticollegio, restored in part by Palladio, has a spectacular gilded stucco ceiling, four Tintorettos and Veronese's blowsy *Rape of Europa*. Beyond here is the Sala del Collegio, where the inner cabinet convened.

The propaganda paintings on the ceiling are by Veronese; note how Justice and Peace are handmaidens to Venice herself. Next door in the Sala del Senato, the Senate would meet to discuss questions of foreign policy, war and trade beneath Tintoretto's ceiling centrepiece, the *Triumph of Venice*.

Beyond are the Sala del Consiglio dei Dieci and the Sala della Bussola, where matters of national security were debated. In the former is Veronese's ceiling panel, *Juno Offering Gifts to Venice* (1553). Here the itinerary heads through a bristling armoury.

Criminal courts & prisons

Backtracking through the Sala del Maggior Consiglio, a small door on the left leads past the Scala dei Censori to the Sala della Quarantia Criminale –

AURORA

Aurora p63

the criminal court. The next room retains some original red and gold leather wall coverings. Beyond is a small gallery of Flemish paintings that includes Hieronymus Bosch's *Inferno*.

The route now leads over the Bridge of Sighs to the Prigioni Nuove (new prisons), where petty criminals were kept. (Lifers were sent down to the waterlogged *pozzi* – wells – in the basement.) When this new prison wing was built in 1589, it was acclaimed as a paragon of comfort.

On the lowest level is a small exercise yard, where an unofficial tavern used to operate. Up the stairs beyond is a display of Venetian ceramics found during excavations, and more cells, one with cartoons and left by 19th-century internees.

Back across the Bridge of Sighs, the tour ends in the Avogaria – the offices of the clerks of court.

Torre dell'Orologio (Clock tower)

San Marco 147, piazza San Marco (041 520 9070/www.museicivici veneziani.it). Vaporetto San Zaccaria. **Open** daily for guided tours, which must be booked 2 days in advance. **Admission** see p12 Musei Civici Veneziani. **Map** p53 E3 **❺**

The clock tower, designed by Maurizio Codussi, was built between 1496 and 1506. Above the clock face is the Madonna. During Ascension week and at Epiphany, the Magi come out and bow to her every hour. At other times of year, the Moors on the roof, made of gunmetal and cast in 1497, strike the hour. Another Moore – Roger – sent a villain flying through the clock face in the film *Moonraker*. The whole building, together with the elaborate mechanism of the clock, has just been restored.

La Zecca (The Mint)

San Marco 7, piazzetta San Marco (041 520 8788). Vaporetto Vallaresso. **Open** 8.10am-7pm Mon-Fri; 8.10am-1.30pm Sat. **Admission** free. **Map** p53 E4 **❻**

The Mint, designed by Sansovino, was completed by 1547. It coined Venice's famous gold ducats – later referred to as *zecchini*, whence the English 'sequins'. It is impregnable in appearance, though the façade had to accommodate large windows for relief from heat. It now houses the civic library.

Eating & drinking

Caffè Florian

San Marco 56, piazza San Marco (041 520 5641/www.caffeflorian.com). Vaporetto Vallaresso. **Open** *May-Oct* 10am-midnight daily. *Nov-Apr* 10am-midnight Mon, Tue, Thur-Sun. Closed 2wks Jan, early Dec-Christmas. **Map** p53 E4 **❼**

This mirrored, stuccoed and frescoed jewel of a café was founded in 1720, though its present appearance, with intimate wooden *séparés*, dates from an 1859 remodelling. Rousseau, Goethe and Byron all hung out here.

Having a drink at Florian will dent your holiday budget, especially if you sit at an outside table, where nothing – not even a humble *caffè* – comes in at less than €10.

Gran Caffè Quadri

San Marco 121, piazza San Marco (041 5222105/fax 041 500 8041/ www.quadrivenice.com). Vaporetto San Zaccaria or Vallaresso. **Open** *Apr-Oct* 9am-11pm daily. *Nov-Mar* 9am-11pm Tue-Sun. **Map** p53 E3 **❽**

With its ornate stucco mouldings, 18th-century murals, huge mirrors and polished wooden furniture, Quadri is every inch the *caffè storico*. People have been drinking here since 1638. Stendhal, Wagner and Balzac were habitués. In the evening, a palm orchestra plays out in the square, and romantics pay small fortunes to sip cocktails under the stars. In neo-classical rooms upstairs, the Quadri has a restaurant that is as expensive as it is elegant.

Shopping

Martinuzzi

San Marco 67A, piazza San Marco (041 522 5068). Vaporetto Vallaresso. **Open** *Mar-Oct* 9am-7.30pm Mon-Sat; 9.30am-7pm Sun. *Nov-Feb* 9am-7pm Mon-Sat. **Map** p53 E4 **❾**

The oldest lace shop in Venice, Martinuzzi has exclusive designs for bobbin-lace items such as place mats, tablecloths and linens.

Nightlife

Aurora

San Marco 49, piazza San Marco (041 528 6405). Vaporetto Vallaresso. **Open** 7pm-2am Tue-Sun. **Map** p53 E4 **❿**

The evening management of this classic café, which sits close by the campanile in St Mark's square, organises 'Queer Wednesdays', as well as hosting eclectic art exhibitions, video projections and DJ sets that go down just as well as the surprisingly affordable cocktails.

VENICE BY AREA

Pastry, Cuisine, Banqueting
The best tradition
in Venice since 1879

Renowned Pasticceria Rosa Salva
just a stone's throw from both
Rialto and Piazza San Marco,
creates traditional mouth-watering cakes,
biscuits and luscious desserts
beloved of the sweet-toothed Venetians.

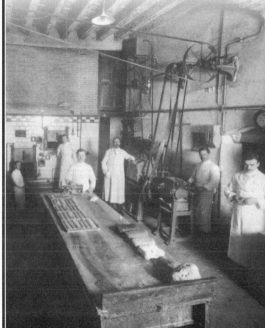

Venezia
San Marco 950
ph. 0415210544

San Marco 5020
ph. 0415227934

Mestre
Via Cappuccina 17
ph. 041988400

www.rosasalva.it
info@rosasalva.it

Arts & leisure

Fondazione Bevilacqua La Masa

Exhibition space *San Marco 71C, piazza San Marco (041 523 7819/ www.bevilacqualamasa.it). Vaporetto Vallaresso.* **Open** *during exhibitions only* noon-6pm Mon, Wed-Sun. **Map** p53 E4 ⓫

Offices & exhibition space *Dorsoduro 2826, fondamenta Gerardini (041 520 7797). Vaporetto Ca' Rezzonico.* **Open** *Office* 9am-1pm Mon, Thur, Fri; 9am-1pm, 2-5pm Tue, Wed. *Exhibition space* varies.

This institution is very active in organising exhibitions and fostering new art. The exhibition space is located on two floors and is dedicated to historical as well as contemporary exhibitions. There are talks, performances and an annual show by Veneto-based artists aged under 30.

Piazza San Marco to the Rialto

Piazza San Marco is linked to the Rialto by the busiest and narrowest of shopping streets: the Mercerie. The name is plural, since the street is divided into five parts: the Merceria dell'Orologio, di **San Zulian** (on which stands the church of the same name), del Capitello, di San Salvador and del 2 Aprile.

Mercerie mean 'haberdashers', but nowadays most of the big-name fashion designers are to be found here, and most of Venice's short-stay tourists too. The ponte dei Baretteri (the Hatmakers' Bridge), in the middle of the Mercerie, is, by the way, a minor record-holder: there are six different roads leading directly off the bridge.

The Mercerie emerge near campo San Bartolomeo, the square at the foot of the Rialto bridge, with the statue of playwright Carlo Goldoni looking down at the milling crowds.

Sights & museums

San Salvador

San Marco, campo San Salvador (041 270 2464). Vaporetto Rialto. **Open** 9am-noon, 4-6.30pm Mon-Sat; 4-6pm Sun. **Map** p53 E2 ⓬

The geometrical sense of space and the use of soft-toned greys and whites in this church – begun by Giorgio Spavento in 1506, continued by Tullio Lombardo and completed by Sansovino in 1534 – exude Tuscan elegance. The church contains two great Titians: the *Annunciation* at the end of the right-hand aisle (with the signature 'Tizianus fecit, fecit'), and the *Transfiguration* on the high altar. There's also some splendid Veneto-Tuscan sculpture, including Sansovino's monument to Doge Francesco Venier, between the second and third altars on the right. At the end of the right transept is the tomb of Cristina Cornaro, the hapless queen of Cyprus (died 1510), who was forced into abdicating the island to Venetian rule. In the left aisle, the third altar has vibrant figures of Saints Roch and Sebastian by Alessandro Vittoria. The sacristy contains delightful 16th-century frescoes of birds and leafage.

San Zulian

San Marco, mercerie San Zulian (041 523 5383). Vaporetto San Zaccaria or Vallaresso. **Open** 8.30am-7pm daily. **Map** p53 E2 ⓭

The classical simplicity of the façade (1553-5) is offset by a grand monument to Tommaso Rangone, a far from self-effacing showman-scholar from Ravenna, who made his fortune with a treatment for syphilis. The interior has paintings by Palma il Giovane of *The Apotheosis of St Julian* on the ceiling and the *Assumption* on the second altar on the right, which also has good statues of St Catherine of Alexandria and Daniel by Alessandro Vittoria. The first altar on the right has a *Pietà* by Paolo Veronese. Mass is celebrated here in English at 11.30am and again at 7pm every Sunday.

Telecom Italia Future Centre

San Marco 4826, campo San Salvador (041 521 3272/www.futurecentre.tele comitalia.it). Vaporetto Rialto. **Open** 10am-6pm Tue-Sun. **Admission** free. **Map** p53 E2 ⑭

The Italian phone company's Future Centre – housed in the 16th-century cloisters of the monastery of San Salvador – offers a tour through the latest innovations in information technology. The first cloister contains computers with playful lessons on Venetian art and history. Don't miss the splendid refectory with a 16th-century frescoed ceiling.

Eating & drinking

Alla Botte

San Marco 5482, calle della Bissa (041 520 9775). Vaporetto Rialto. **Open** 10am-3pm, 5.30-11pm Mon-Wed, Fri-Sat; 10am-3pm Sun. **Map** p53 E1 ⑮

Though it's tucked away in a hidden *calle* close to campo San Bartolomeo, you'll have no trouble finding Alla Botte: just follow the crowds of Venetians of all ages heading there. Don't let the packed bar discourage you from making your way up to the counter, where 25 wines by the glass are available, in addition to some of the city's best bar snacks.

Osteria San Marco

San Marco 1610, Frezzeria (041 528 5242). Vaporetto Vallaresso. **Meals served** 12.30-11pm Mon-Sat. Closed 2wks Jan, 2wks Aug. €€€ **Map** p53 D3 ⑯

This smart, modern *osteria*-wine bar is a breath of fresh air in the tourist-oriented San Marco area. The four young guys behind the operation are serious about food and wine. Among the dishes on offer in the rustic-minimalist dining area are *capesante con porcini su letto di polenta* (scallops with porcini mushrooms on a bed of polenta) and *scampi al forno con timo e zucchine* (baked scampi with thyme and courgettes). Prices are a little on

the high side, but the mark-up on bottles is commendably low.

Shopping

Antichità Marciana

San Marco 1691, Frezzeria (041 523 5666/www.antichitamarciano.it). Vaporetto Vallaresso. **Open** 3.30-7.30pm Mon; 9.30am-1pm, 3.30-7pm Tue-Sat. **Map** p53 D3 ⑰

A tasteful selection of antique baubles can be found in this jewel of a shop; its speciality, however, is the painted velvets created by the owner.

Carteria Tassotti

San Marco 5472, calle de la Bissa (041 528 1881/www.tassotti.it). Vaporetto Rialto. **Open** 10am-1pm, 2-7pm daily. **Map** p53 E1 ⑱

This family business has a charming selection of greeting cards, decorative paper, diaries and notebooks. Wedding invitations and business cards can also be ordered.

Daniela Ghezzo Segalin Venezia

San Marco 4365, calle dei Fuseri (041 522 2115). Vaporetto Rialto or Vallaresso. **Open** 9.30am-12.30pm, 3.30-7.30pm Mon-Fri; 9am-12.30pm Sat. **Map** p53 D3 ⑲

A pair of Daniela Ghezzo's fantastic footware creations will set you back anything between €500 and €1,500.

Fantoni Libri Arte

San Marco 4119, salizada San Luca (041 522 0700). Vaporetto Rialto. **Open** 10am-8pm Mon-Fri; 10am-1.30pm, 4.30-8pm Sat. **Map** p53 D2 ⑳

Beautifully illustrated art, architecture, design, photography and textile books, mostly in Italian. There's also a small selection of cookbooks and works on Venice in English.

Marchini Pasticceria

San Marco 676, calle Spadaria (041 522 9109/www.golosessi.com). Vaporetto Rialto or San Zaccaria. **Open** *Oct-May* 9am-10pm daily. *June-Sept* 9am-8pm Mon, Wed-Sat. **Map** p53 E3 ㉑

Carteria Tassotti p66

Probably Venice's most famous (and most expensive) sweet shop, Marchini sells exquisite chocolate, including *Le Baute Veneziane* – small chocolates in the form of Carnevale masks. Cakes can be ordered.

Nalesso

San Marco 5537, salizada Fontego dei Tedeschi (041 522 1343). Vaporetto Rialto. **Open** 10am-7.30pm Mon-Sat; 11am-7pm Sun. **Map** p53 E1 ㉒
You'll hear the music as you approach this small shop. Specialising in classical Venetian music, Nalesso also sells concert tickets for the Fenice and Malibran theatres, as well as for concerts in various churches.

Pelletterie Silvia

San Marco 4466, calle dei Fuseri (041 523 5749). Vaporetto Rialto or Vallaresso. **Open** 9am-7.30pm Mon-Sat. **Map** p53 D3 ㉓
This stylish shoe store stocks designers such as Lerre and Kalisté, plus an extensive range of bags and a smaller selection of clothing.

Pot-Pourrì

San Marco 1810, ramo dei Fuseri (041 241 0990/www.potpourri.it). Vaporetto Vallaresso. **Open** Nov-Apr, Aug 10am-1pm, 3.30-7.30pm Mon-Sat. Sept-Oct, May-July 10am-1pm, 3.30-7.30pm daily. **Map** p53 D3 ㉔
This shop is like an elegant bedroom: clothes are draped over armchairs or hang from wardrobe doors. This faux-boudoir houses designers such as Cristina Effe and Marzi, as well as homeware.

Rizzo Regali

San Marco 4739, calle dei Fabbri (041 522 5811). Vaporetto Rialto. **Open** 9am-8pm Mon-Sat. **Map** p53 D2 ㉕
Old-fashioned Rizzo sells traditional cakes, sweets and chocolates. If you're unable to find the *torrone* (nougat) you're looking for here, then it probably doesn't exist.

Nightlife

Bacaro Jazz

San Marco 5546, salizada del Fontego dei Tedeschi (041 528 5249/www. bacarojazz.com). Vaporetto Rialto. **Open** 4pm-3am daily. **Map** p53 E1 ㉖
Venice's most central late-night watering hole, Bacaro Jazz is a place to mingle with your fellow tourists or foreign students rather than meet the locals. Happy hour is 4-7pm. Background jazz and killer cocktails invariably keep the party going into the early hours.

Pelletterie Silvia p67

Centrale Restaurant Lounge

San Marco 1659B, piscina Frezzeria (041 296 0664/www.centrale-lounge.com). Vaporetto Vallaresso. **Open** 7pm-2am daily. **Map** p53 D3 ㉗

Despite exposed 16th-century bricks, this cool, contemporary lounge bar is more New York or London than Venice. Owners Franco and Alfredo lay on events like live drum 'n' bass and jazz or a regular international gay night, and serve a full, fresh à la carte menu. Sink into a designer armchair, explore the cocktail menu and chill out to lounge and house sounds.

The Rialto to the Accademia bridge

The route from the Rialto to the Accademia passes through a series of ever-larger squares. From cosily cramped campo San Bartolomeo, the well-marked path leads to campo San Luca, with its bars and cake shops. Beyond that is campo Manin, with its 19th-century statue of Daniele Manin, leader of the 1848 uprising against the Austrian occupiers.

Just before the Accademia bridge, campo Santo Stefano is second only to piazza San Marco in the *sestiere* in size. Until 1802, when part of a stand collapsed, this was where *corse al toro* (bullfights) took place. Nowadays, children ride bikes or kick balls around the statue of 19th-century ideologue Nicolò Tommaseo, known locally as Cagalibri (book-shitter) for reasons that are obvious when the monument is viewed from the rear.

On the Grand Canal to the north-west of campo Santo Stefano is campo San Samuele, home to the massive **Palazzo Grassi**, an exhibition centre recently reopened amid great hype. Nearby, in calle Malipiero (the exact house is not known), 18th-century love machine, Giacomo Casanova, was born.

Sights & museums

Palazzo Fortuny

San Marco 3780, campo San Beneto (041 520 0995). Vaporetto Sant' Angelo. **Open** *during exhibitions only* 10am-6pm Tue-Sun. **Admission** varies. No credit cards. **Map** p52 C3 ㉘

This charming 15th-century palazzo, which belonged to Spanish fashion designer Mariano Fortuny (1871-1949), has been *in restauro* for years. However, the *piano nobile*, where Fortuny had his studio, opens for exhibitions, usually of photography.

Palazzo Grassi

San Marco 3231, campo San Samuele (041 523 1680/www.palazzograssi.it). Vaporetto San Samuele. **Open** *during exhibitions* 10am-7pm daily. **Admission** €10; concessions €6. **Map** p51 A3 ㉙

This superbly – if rather boringly – regular 18th-century palazzo on the Grand Canal was bought in 2005 by French magnate François Pinault, who brought in Japanese architect Tadao Ando for an overhaul that increased exhibition space by 2,000 sq m (6,562 sq ft), but turned it into a rather cold shell. The new-look palazzo was inaugurated in 2006 with a show of post-war works from Pinault's own collection.

Santo Stefano

San Marco, campo Santo Stefano (041 522 5061/www.chorusvenezia. org). Vaporetto Accademia or San Samuele. **Open** 10am-5pm Mon-Sat. **Admission** *Church free. Sacristy* €2.50 (see also p12 Chorus). **Map** p52 B3/4 **30**

Built in the 14th century and altered in the 15th, Santo Stefano has a façade with a magnificent portal in the florid Gothic style. The large interior, with its ship's-keel roof, is a multicoloured treat, with different marbles used for the columns, capitals, altars and intarsia. On the floor is a huge plaque to Doge Morosini (best known for blowing up the Parthenon) and a more modest one to composer Giovanni Gabrielli. In the sacristy are works by Tintoretto: *The Washing of the Feet, The Agony in the Garden* and a *Last Supper*; and three imaginative works by Gaspare Diziani (*Adoration of the Magi, Flight into Egypt, Massacre of the Innocents*).

San Vidal

San Marco, campo San Vidal (041 522 2362). Vaporetto Accademia. **Open** 9.30am-6pm daily. **Map** p52 B4 **31**

This early 18th-century church, with a Palladian-style façade, has been restored and now hosts concerts. Over the high altar is a splendid Carpaccio painting (1514) of St Vitalis riding what appears to be one of the bronze horses of San Marco. The third altar on the right has a painting by Piazzetta (*Archangel Raphael and Saints Anthony and Louis*).

Scala Contarini del Bòvolo

San Marco 4299, corte dei Risi (041 532 2920). Vaporetto Rialto. Closed for restoration, due to reopen 2009. **Map** p53 D3 **32**

This elegant Renaissance spiral staircase was built in c1500 by Giovanni Candi. It was restored in 1986, but further work began recently – a pity, as the view from the top is lovely.

Eating & drinking

Andrea Zanin

San Marco 4589, campo San Luca (041 522 4803). Vaporetto Rialto. **Open** 7.30am-8pm Mon-Sat; 10.30am-7.30pm Sun. No credit cards. **Map** p53 D2 **33**

This long-established cake shop has been refurbished and reinvented by master *pâtisseur* Andrea Zanin, who has stocked it full of his delicious, award-winning goodies. At €2.50 a pop, his miniature-sized cakes are expensive, but for works of art like this, it's worth splashing out.

Bar all'Angolo

San Marco 3464, campo Santo Stefano (041 522 0710). Vaporetto Sant' Angelo. **Open** 6.30am-9pm Mon-Sat. Closed Jan. No credit cards. **Map** p52 B3 **34**

Outside tables are perfect for watching locals saunter through the *campo* as you enjoy a coffee or *spritz*. Inside, stand at the usually crowded bar or relax in one of the comfy seats in the back, where you can enjoy good *tramezzini*, fresh salads and panini served by friendly, if hurried, staff.

Igloo

San Marco 3651, calle della Mandola (041 522 3003). Vaporetto Sant' Angelo. **Open** *May-Sept* 11am-8pm daily. *Oct-mid Nov, Feb-Apr* 11.30am-7.30pm. Closed mid Nov-Carnevale. No credit cards. **Map** p52 C3 **35**

Generous portions of creamy gelato in varieties to please everyone: in summer, fruit flavours such as fig or blackberry are made from the market's freshest produce.

iquus

San Marco 2973 & 3131, calle delle
Botteghe (041 520 6395). Vaporetto
Sant'Angelo. **Open** 10am-12.30pm, 3-
7.30pm Mon-Sat. **Map** p52 B3 **36**

This charming shop has a beautiful
collection of Old Master paintings,
furniture, silver and antique jewellery,
including Moors' heads brooches and
matching earrings.

Ebrû

San Marco 3471, campo Santo Stefano
(041 523 8830/www.albertovalese-
ebru.com). Vaporetto Accademia or
Sant'Angelo. **Open** 10am-1.30pm,
2.30-7pm Mon-Wed; 10am-1pm, 2.30-
7pm Thur-Sat; 11am-6pm Sun. **Map**
p52 B4 **37**

Beautiful marbled handcrafted paper,
scarves and ties. These are Venetian
originals, whose imitators can be found
in other shops around town.

Gaggio

San Marco 3441-3451, calle delle
Botteghe (041 522 8574/www.gaggio.it).
Vaporetto San Samuele or Sant'Angelo.
Open 10.30am-1pm, 4-6.30pm Mon-Fri;
10.30am-1pm Sat. **Map** p52 B3 **38**

Emma Gaggio is a legend among
dressmakers, and her sumptuous
handprinted silk velvets (from €195 a
metre) are used to make cushions and
wall hangings as well as bags, hats,
scarves and jackets.

Godi Fiorenza

San Marco 4261, rio terà San
Paternian (041 241 0866/www.
fiorenzadesign.com). Vaporetto Rialto
or Vallaresso. **Open** 9.30am-12.30pm,
3.30-7.30pm Mon-Sat. **Map** p53
D3 **39**

The London-trained Godi designer
sisters sell exquisite knitwear, stylish
coats and chiffon evening tops, as well
as accessories, including jewellery
and shoes.

Ottico Fabbricatore

San Marco 4773, Calle dell'Ovo (041
522 5263/www.otticofabbricatore.
com). Vaporetto Rialto. **Open**
9am-12.30pm, 3.30-7.30pm Mon-Sat.
Map p53 D2 **40**

This ultra-modern shop specialises in
designer eyewear, with frames in every
material from buffalo horn to titanium.
Designers Francesco Lincetto and
Marianna Leardini also produce
gossamer-like cashmere and sensual
silk apparel, along with a range of luxurious leather bags.

Perle e Dintorni

San Marco 3740, calle della Mandola
(041 520 5068). Vaporetto Sant'
Angelo. **Open** 9.30am-7.30pm Mon-Sat;
noon-7pm Sun. **Map** p52 C3 **41**

Buy bead jewellery or assemble your
own individual pieces by choosing
from a vast assortment of glass beads
– most of which are new versions of
antique designs.

Rizzo Regali p67

Nightlife

Torino@Notte

*San Marco 4591, campo San Luca
(041 522 3914). Vaporetto Rialto.*
Open 8pm-1am Tue-Sat. No credit
cards. **Map** p53 D2 ㊷

This dreary daytime bar switches
management after dark and trans-
forms into a happening hotspot. DJ
sets and live music on Wednesdays
keep the mix of students and older
musos grooving to acid jazz, fusion
and funky tunes.

Vitae

*San Marco 4118, calle Sant'Antonio
(041 520 5205). Vaporetto Rialto.*
Open 8pm-midnight Mon-Fri; 5pm-2am
Sat. No credit cards. **Map** p53 D2 ㊸

Known as *il muro* (the wall), this tiny
bar behind campo San Luca is busy
long into the night with a more mature,
yuppie set who come for mojitos and
background sounds of smooth soul and
acid jazz.

Arts & leisure

Galleria Marina Barovier

*San Marco 3216, salizada San Samuele
(041 523 6748/www.barovier.it).
Vaporetto San Samuele.* **Open** 10am-
12.30pm, 3.30-7.30pm Mon-Sat. No
credit cards. **Map** p51 A3 ㊹

Marina Barovier hosts a collection of
classic masterpieces of Venetian 20th-
century works in glass. The gallery

also represents numerous renowned
artists working in this specialist area.

The Accademia bridge to San Marco

The route from Santo Stefano
back to piazza San Marco zigzags
at first, passing through small
squares, including campo San
Maurizio, with its 19th-century
church now transformed into the
Museo della Musica, and campo
Santa Maria del Giglio (aka
Santa Maria Zobenigo), with the
most boastful church façade in
Venice. It winds past banks and
hotels, along with a few top-dollar
antiques shops, to end in wide via
XXII Marzo, with an intimidating
view of the baroque statuary of
San Moisè. Nearby is the opera
house, **La Fenice**, rebuilt after
a fire in 1996.

Press on, and you are ready for
arguably the greatest view in the
world: piazza San Marco from the
west side.

Sights & museums

Museo della Musica

NEW *San Marco 2601, campo San
Maurizio (041 241 1840). Vaporetto
Giglio.* **Open** 9.30am-7.30pm daily.
Admission free. **Map** p52 B4 ㊺

This small museum, set up in the ex-church of San Maurizio, is run by the Rivoalto recording company. Serving partly as a sales and promotion outlet, the museum also contains an interesting collection of period instruments.

San Moisè

San Marco, campo San Moisè (041 528 5840). Vaporetto Vallaresso. **Open** 9.30am-12.30pm daily. **Map** p53 D4 **46**
The baroque façade of San Moisè is widely considered one of Venice's truly ugly pieces of architecture. Inside, an extravagant baroque sculpture on the high altar represents not only Moses receiving the stone tablets, but Mount Sinai too. Near the entrance is the grave of John Law, author of the disastrous Mississippi Bubble scheme that almost sank the French central bank in 1720.

Santa Maria del Giglio

San Marco, campo Santa Maria Zobenigo (041 275 0462/www.chorus venezia.org). Vaporetto Giglio. **Open** 10am-5pm Mon-Sat. **Admission** €2.50 (see also p12 Chorus). No credit cards. **Map** p52 C4 **47**
This church's façade lacks any Christian symbols (give or take a token angel or two). Built in 1678-83, it's an exercise in defiant self-glorification by Admiral Antonio Barbaro, who was dismissed for incompetence in the War of Candia (Crete). On the plinths of the columns are relief plans of towns where he served; his own statue (in the centre) is flanked by Honour, Virtue, Fame and Wisdom. The interior is more devotional. Little-known Antonio Zanchi (1631-1722) painted *Abraham Teaching the Egyptians Astrology* in the sacristy, and *Ulysses Recognised by his Dog* (an odd subject for a church) in the Cappella Molin. The chapel also contains a *Madonna and Child*, which is proudly but probably erroneously attributed to Rubens. Behind the altar there are two paintings of the evangelists by Tintoretto, formerly organ doors.

Teatro La Fenice

San Marco 1983, campo San Fantin (041 2424/041 786 511/www.teatro lafenice.it). Vaporetto Giglio. **Open** guided tours only 10am-6pm daily. **Admission** €7; concessions €5. No credit cards. **Map** p52 C4 **48**
Tours must be pre-booked on 041 2424. They are suspended during rehearsals and performances. For performance information, p73.

Venice's opera house La Fenice (the phoenix) has a long history of fiery destruction and miraculous rebirth. The latest tragedy came in 1996, when a massive blaze broke out thanks to two electricians engaged in restoration work. The rebuilt theatre – now with state-of-the-art technology behind the scenes – was inaugurated in December 2003.

Eating & drinking

Harry's Bar

San Marco 1323, calle Vallaresso (041 528 5777/www.cipriani.com). Vaporetto Vallaresso. **Open** 10.30am-11pm daily. **€€€€ Map** p53 E4 **49**
This historic watering hole, founded by Giuseppe Cipriani in 1931, has changed little since the days when Ernest Hemingway came here to work on his next hangover... except for the prices and the number of tourists. But a Bellini (fresh peach juice and sparkling wine) at the bar is as much a part of the Venetian experience as a gondola ride (and, at €14, far cheaper). At meal-times, Venetian-themed international comfort food is served upstairs.

Hotel Monaco & Grand Canal Bar

San Marco 1332, calle Vallaresso (041 520 0211/www.hotelmonaco.it). Vaporetto Vallaresso. **Open** 10am-midnight daily. **Map** p53 E4 **50**
The elegant Hotel Monaco & Grand Canal Bar is truly a special place to sit back and savour *La Serenissima*. There's a cosy, compact bar inside and a divine terrace looking across to the the Salute church. Granted, it's an expensive pleasure, but you're paying for sipping in one of the most enchanting spots in the city.

Palazzo Grassi p68

Shopping

Legatoria Piazzesi

San Marco 2511, campiello Feltrina (041 522 1202). Vaporetto Giglio. **Open** 10am-1pm, 3-7pm Mon-Sat. **Map** p52 C4 ⑤①

This Venetian paper-maker uses the traditional wooden-block method of printing to produce colourful hand-painted paper and cards.

Libreria Mondadori

San Marco 1345, salizada San Moisè (041 522 2193/www.libreriamondadori venezia.it). **Open** *Dec-Feb* 10am-8pm Mon-Sat; 11am-7.30pm Sun. *Mar-Nov* upper floors 10am-8pm Mon-Sat; 11am-7.30pm Sun; ground floor 10am-11pm Mon-Sat; 11am-7.30pm Sun. **Map** p53 D4 ⑤②

In Venice's only mega-bookshop the ground floor is reserved for exhibits and book signings; upstairs, there's a wide selection of English books.

Venetia Studium

San Marco 2403, calle larga XXII Marzo (041 522 9281/www.venetia studium.com). Vaporetto Giglio. **Open** 9.30am-7.40pm Mon-Sat; 10.30am-6pm Sun. **Map** p52 C4 ⑤③

Venetia Studium stocks beautiful silks made up into elegant cushions, lamps, scarves, and other acces-sories in a marvellous range of colours. They're not cheap, but they are perfect gifts for those who have it all.

Zancopè

San Marco 2674, campo San Maurizio (041 523 4567/www.jurubeba.it). Vaporetto Giglio. **Open** 10.30am-1pm, 4-7.30pm Mon-Sat. **Map** p52 B4 ⑤④

An eclectic collection of antique, old and contemporary glass at very good prices.

Arts & leisure

Jarach Gallery

NEW *San Marco 1997, campo San Fantin (041 522 1938/www.jarach gallery.com). Vaporetto Giglio.* **Open** 2-8pm Tue-Sun; mornings by appointment only. **Map** p53 D4 ⑤⑤

This large space tucked into a courtyard opposite the Fenice opera house is the latest addition to the Venetian gallery scene. It deals only with photography.

Teatro La Fenice

San Marco 1965, campo San Fantin (041 786 575/041 2424/www.teatro lafenice.it). Vaporetto Giglio. **Open** *Box office* HelloVenezia (p181). *Performances* varies. **Map** p52 C4 ⑤⑥

Newly restored and positively gleam-ing, La Fenice is back in business offer-ing opera, ballet and concert seasons.

VENICE BY AREA

Via Garibaldi p83

Castello

Castello takes its name from a fortress that once stood at the eastern end of the city, protecting it from invasion by sea. It's the largest *sestiere* in the city and probably the most varied in character.

Western Castello

The canal spanned by the Bridge of Sighs, dividing the Doge's Palace from the prison, marks the end of the *sestiere* of San Marco. This means that the **Museo Diocesano di Arte Sacra** and stately **San Zaccaria**, although closely associated with San Marco, actually belong to Castello. But the heart of northern and western Castello lies inland: **campo Santa Maria Formosa**, a bustling, irregular-shaped square on the road to just about everywhere.

North from here is **campo Santi Giovanni e Paolo**, second only to piazza San Marco in monumental magnificence. The Gothic red brick of the Dominican church is set off by the glistening marble façade of the Scuola di San Marco – now a hospital – with its magnificent trompe-l'œil panels by Tullio and Antonio Lombardo, and the freshly restored bronze of the equestrian monument (1488-96) to Bartolomeo Colleoni, a mercenary soldier. (Colleoni's coat of arms on the pedestal includes three fig-like objects, a reference to his name, which in Italian sounds very similar to *coglioni* – testicles, of which this soldier was said to possess three.)

It's a short walk from here through narrow *calli* to the fondamenta Nuove, where the northern lagoon comes into view.

Sights & museums

Museo Diocesano di Arte Sacra

Castello 4312, ponte della Canonica (041 522 9166). Vaporetto San Zaccaria. **Open** depends on exhibition. **Admission** free (donations appreciated). **Map** p76 A3 ❶

In theory, this museum tucked behind the palace of Venice's patriarch (cardinal) displays works of art from local churches brought here for restoration. But in recent months the space has been used for temporary exhibitions, the first of which was a rare glimpse of works by Tintoretto usually kept in the patriarch's palace. As this guide went to press, no one was able to say what the future holds.

Museo della Fondazione Querini Stampalia

Castello 5252, campo Santa Maria Formosa (041 271 1411/www.querini stampalia.it). Vaporetto Rialto. **Open** 10am-6pm Tue-Thur, Sun; 10am-10pm Fri, Sat. **Admission** €8; €6 concessions. **Map** p76 A2 ❷

This Renaissance palazzo and its collection were left to Venice by Giovanni Querini, a 19th-century man of letters and silk-producer, who specified that a reading room should be created to open 'in the evenings for the convenience of scholars'. The Querini Stampalia still exudes something of its founder's spirit: the first-floor library is a great place to study, and the Foundation organises debates and concerts (5pm, 8.30pm Fri, Sat). The ground floor and gardens were redesigned in the 1960s by Carlo Scarpa. On the second floor, the gallery contains important paintings, including a *Presentation in the Temple* by Giovanni Bellini. It also has a fascinating series of minor works, such as Gabriele Bella's 67 paintings of Venetian festivals and customs, and a selection of Pietro Longhi's scenes of 18th-century life. The top-floor gallery was designed by Mario Botta; it hosts contemporary art shows.

Santa Maria dei Derelitti (Ospedaletto)

Barbarie delle Tole 6691 (041 271 9012). Vaporetto Fondamente Nove. **Open** 3.30-6.30pm Thur-Sat. **Admission** (incl guided tour) €2. No credit cards. **Map** p76 B1 ❸

The church was built in 1575 inside the Ospedaletto, a hospice for the poor and aged. Baldassarre Longhena provided the staggering façade (1668-74) with bulging telamons (supports in the shape of male figures). The interior contains 18th-century paintings, including one of Tiepolo's earliest works, *The Sacrifice of Isaac*. The hospice has an elegant music room with frescoes by Jacopo Guarana (1776) depicting girl musicians performing for Apollo.

Santa Maria della Fava

Castello, campo della Fava (041 522 4601). Vaporetto Rialto. **Open** 8.30-11.30am, 4.30-7pm Mon-Sat. **Map** p76 A2 ❹

St Mary of the Fava Bean (the name refers to a popular bean cake produced at a nearby bakery) is an 18th-century church containing paintings by the city's greatest artists of the time: Tiepolo's brightly coloured *Education of the Virgin*, and Giovanni Battista Piazzetta's more sombre *Virgin and Child with St Philip Neri*.

Santa Maria Formosa

Campo Santa Maria Formosa (041 275 0462). Vaporetto Rialto or San Zaccaria. **Open** 10am-5pm Mon-Sat. **Admission** €2.50 (see also p12 Chorus). No credit cards. **Map** p76 A2 ❺

In the seventh century, St Magnus had a vision in which the Virgin appeared as a buxom (*formosa*) matron, and a church was built in this square to commemorate the fact. The present structure was designed by Mauro Codussi in 1492 and has something fittingly bulgy about it. It has two façades, one on the canal (1542), the other on the campo (1604). The first chapel on the right aisle has a triptych by Bartolomeo Vivarini, *Madonna of the*

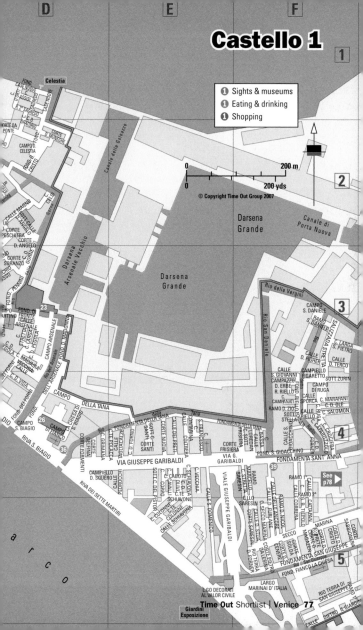

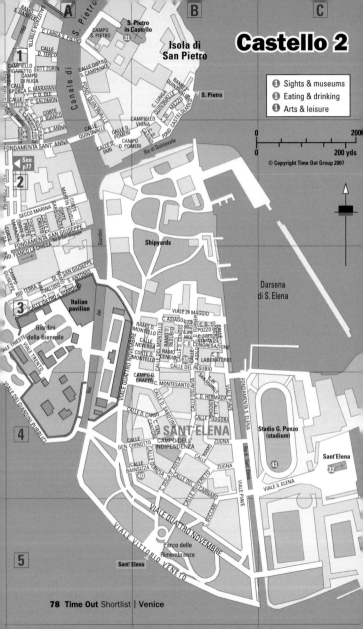

Castello 2

- ① Sights & museums
- ① Eating & drinking
- ① Arts & leisure

0 — 200
0 — 200 yds

© Copyright Time Out Group 2007

Isola di
San Pietro

S. Pietro in Castello

S. Pietro

Shipyards

Darsena
di S. Elena

Italian
pavilion

Giardini
della Biennale

Stadio G. Penzo
(stadium)

Sant'Elena

SANT'ELENA

Parco delle
Rimembranze

Sant' Elena

Misericordia (1473). The altar on the right transept, in the chapel of the Scuola dei Bombardieri, has an altarpiece of St Barbara, patron saint of gunners, by Palma il Vecchio. Half-hidden by the high altar is an 18th-century *Allegory of the Foundation of the Church, with Venice, St Magnus and St Maria Formosa* by Giulia Lama.

Santi Giovanni e Paolo

Campo Santi Giovanni e Paolo (041 523 5913). Vaporetto Fondamente Nove. **Open** 9.30am-6pm Mon-Sat; 1-6pm Sun. **Admission** €2.50. No credit cards. **Map** p76 A/B1 ⑥

Santi Giovanni e Paolo – aka San Zanipolo – was founded by the Dominican order in 1246 but not finished until 1430. Twenty-five doges are buried here. The interior is 101m (331ft) long and packed with monuments. The second altar on the right features an early polyptych by Giovanni Bellini (1465). Further along, the Chapel of St Dominic has a ceiling painting of *St Dominic in Glory* (c1727) by Giovani Battista Piazzetta.

In the right transept is a painting of *St Antonine Distributing Alms* (1542) by Lorenzo Lotto. The Rosary Chapel, off the left transept, was gutted by fire in 1867, just after two works by Titian and Bellini had been placed here for safe keeping. It now contains an *Annunciation*, an *Assumption*, an *Adoration of the Shepherds* and another *Adoration* to the left of the door, all by Veronese.

San Zaccaria

Campo San Zaccaria (041 522 1257). Vaporetto San Zaccaria. **Open** 10am-noon, 4-6pm Mon-Sat; 4-6pm Sun. **Map** p76 B3 ⑦

Founded in the ninth century, San Zaccaria holds the body of St Zacharias, the father of John the Baptist, under the second altar on the right. The current church was begun in 1444 but took decades to complete, making it a curious combination of Gothic and Renaissance. Inside, every inch is covered with paintings.

Giovanni Bellini's magnificent *Madonna and Four Saints* (1505), on the second altar on the left, leaps out of the confusion. On the right aisle is the Chapel of St Athanasius (admission €1), which contains carved 15th-century wooden stalls, *The Birth of St John the Baptist* by Tintoretto and a striking *Flight into Egypt* by Giandomenico Tiepolo. The adjoining Chapel of St Tarasius has three stiff, icon-like altarpieces (1443) by Antonio Vivarini and Giovanni d'Alemagna. The frescoed saints by Florentine artist Andrea del Castagno (1442) in the fan vault have a realistic vitality. In front of the altar there are remains of the mosaic floor originally from the early Romanesque church. There's also a tenth-century crypt, though it's usually flooded.

Eating & drinking

Alle Testiere

Castello 5801, calle del Mondo Novo (041 522 7220). Vaporetto Rialto. **Meals served** noon-2pm, 7-10.30pm Tue-Sat. Closed 3wks Dec-Jan; 4wks July-Aug. €€€€. **Map** p76 A2 ⑧

This tiny (22-cover) restaurant is one of the hottest culinary tickets in Venice, offering creative variations on Venetian seafood, many of them involving herbs and spices; the John Dory fillet sprinkled with aromatic herbs in citrus sauce is a mouth-watering example. There's a small but well-chosen wine list and a marvellous cheeseboard. Desserts are spectacular.

Al Portego

Castello 6015, calle Malvasia (041 522 9038/www.alportego.it). Vaporetto Rialto. **Meals served** noon-2.30pm, 7-9.30pm Mon-Sat. Closed 2wks June. €€. No credit cards. **Map** p76 A1 ⑨

This rustic osteria smacks of the mountain chalet. Alongside a big barrel of wine, the bar is loaded down with a selection of *cicheti*, from meatballs and tuna balls to fried courgette flowers. There are simple pasta dishes, risottos and secondi such as *fegato alla*

veneziana, served up for early lunch (noon-2.30pm). Eat at the bar or queue for a table as no reservations are taken.

Antica Trattoria Bandierette

Castello 6671, Barbaria delle Tole (041 522 0619/www.elmoro.com/bandierette. htm). Vaporetto Ospedale. **Meals served** noon-2pm Mon; noon-2pm, 7-10pm Wed-Sun. Closed 2wks Dec-Jan; 2wks Aug. €€€. **Map** p76 B1 ⑩
Despite bland decor and garish lighting, this trattoria is a favourite with locals who come for good, reasonably priced seafood and friendly service. Among the primi, the tagliatelle with scampi and spinach, and the spaghetti with prawns and asparagus are especially good.

Boutique del Gelato

Castello 5727, salizada San Lio (041 522 3283). Vaporetto Rialto. **Open** June-Sept 10am-11.30pm daily. Oct, Nov, Feb-May 10am-8.30pm daily. Closed Dec, Jan. No credit cards. **Map** p76 A2 ⑪
Most Venetians agree that some of the city's best *gelato* is served in this miniscule shop. Be patient though as there's always a huge queue waiting.

Da Bonifacio

Castello 4237, calle degli Albanesi (041 522 7507). Vaporetto San Zaccaria. **Open** 7am-8.30pm Mon-Wed, Fri-Sun. Closed 3wks Aug, 1wk Christmas. No credit cards. **Map** p76 A3 ⑫
This bar-*pasticceria* is a firm favourite with Venetians, who squeeze inside for coffee, drinks and something from the cake cabinet. Each season brings a new pastry to the line-up.

Da Dante

Castello 2877, corte Nova (041 528 5163). Vaporetto Celestia or San Zaccaria. **Open** 8am-9pm Mon-Sat. Closed Aug. No credit cards. **Map** p76 B3 ⑬
If you want to hang with the locals, head to this out-of-the-way *bacaro*. To accompany the banter of the card-playing Venetians, there's wine out of demi-johns. Dante's wife serves up snack-specialities such as *bovoleti* (snails in garlic) and *folpeti* (baby octopus).

La Mascareta

Castello 5183, calle lunga Santa Maria Formosa (041 523 0744). **Open** 7pm-2am Mon, Tue, Fri-Sun. **Map** p76 B2 ⑭
Genial, bow-tied Mauro Lorenzon serves hundreds of wines, by the

Museo della Fondazione Querini Stampalia p75

bottle or glass, along with plates of cheese, seafood or *crostini*. There are also more filling options – hearty soups, for example – every evening.

Maison de Laurent

NEW *Castello 4509, campo Santi Filippo e Giacomo (041 520 8280). Vaporetto San Zaccaria.* **Meals served** noon-2pm, 7-10pm Mon, Tue, Fri-Sun; 7-10pm Thur. €€€€. **Map** p76 B3 ⓯
High-end restaurant openings are rare in quick-bite Venice, so this elegantly modern gourmet eaterie is one to watch. There are just 12 table settings. The daily changing Gallic-tinged menu is based on a mix of fresh market produce and globally sourced fine foods. The wine list offers a challenging selection of Italian and international crus. Maison de Laurent has lofty ambitions that it doesn't always fulfil – but it's early days yet.

Osteria di Santa Marina

NEW *Castello 5911, campo Santa Marina (041 528 5239/www.osteria disantamarina.it). Vaporetto Rialto.* **Meals served** 7.30-9.30pm Mon; 12.30-2.30pm, 7.30-9.30pm Tue-Sat. Closed 2wks Jan; 2wks Aug. €€€€. **Map** p76 B1 ⓰

This upmarket *osteria* has the kind of professional service and standards that are too often lacking in Venice; the ambience and the high level of the creative, seafood-oriented cuisine justify the weighty price tag. Raw fish features strongly among the *antipasti*; first courses give local traditions a creative twist. The bread is home-made, and between-course tasters turn up unexpectedly. The secret is out, so be sure to book ahead.

Rosa Salva

Castello 6779, campo Santi Giovanni e Paolo (041 522 7949). Vaporetto Fondamente Nove. **Open** 7.30am-8.30pm Mon, Tue, Thur-Sun. No credit cards. **Map** p76 B1 ⓱
Take the time and pay the higher prices to sit down and savour campo Santi Giovanni e Paolo while nursing one of the smoothest *cappuccini* in town and trying one of the delicious cakes. The ice-cream is home-made.

Shopping

Anticlea Antiquariato

Castello 4719A, calle San Provolo (041 528 6946). Vaporetto San Zaccaria. **Open** 10am-1.30pm, 2-7pm Mon-Sat. **Map** p76 B3 ⓲

VENICE BY AREA

Packed with curious antique treasures, as well as an outstanding selection of Venetian glass beads.

Bottiglieria Colonna

Castello 5595, calle della Fava (041 528 5137). Vaporetto Rialto. **Open** 9am-1pm, 4-8pm Mon-Sat. **Map** p76 A1 ⑲
Staff will advise on an extensive selection of regional wines, and even arrange for shipping.

Giovanna Zanella

Castello 5641, calle Carminati (041 523 5500). Vaporetto Rialto. **Open** 9.30am-1pm, 3-7pm Mon-Sat. **Map** p76 A1 ⑳
Venetian designer-cobbler Giovanna Zanella creates a fantastic line of shoes in extraordinary styles and colours: a pair costs €350 to €500. There are bags, hats and gloriously coloured clothes too.

Libreria Marco Polo

Castello 5469, salizada San Lio (041 522 6343/www.libreriamarcopolo.com). Vaporetto Rialto. **Open** 9.30am-8pm Mon-Sat; 11am-7pm Sun. **Map** p76 A2 ㉑
This friendly bookstore specialises in travel. On the ground floor is a good selection of guidebooks and fiction in English. Trade in your used novel for a discount on a new purchase.

Papier Mâché

Castello 5175, calle lunga Santa Maria Formosa (041 522 9995/www.papiermache.it). Vaporetto Rialto. **Open** 9am-7.30pm Mon-Sat; 10am-7pm Sun. **Map** p76 B1 ㉒
This workshop uses traditional techniques to create masks inspired by the works of Klimt, Kandinsky, Tiepolo and Carpaccio. Decoration determines price, with simple designs starting at €40. Ceramics and painted mirrors too.

Eastern Castello

The close-clustered buildings of working-class eastern Castello housed the employees of the **Arsenale** – Venice's dockland –

La Corderia, at Arsenale p84

much of which now lies derelict. Like London's East End or New York's Brooklyn, eastern Castello had its foreign communities, as local churches testify: there's **San Giorgio dei Greci** (Greeks) and **Scuola di San Giorgio degli Schiavoni** (Slavs), with its captivating cycle of paintings by Vittorio Carpaccio. The great promenade along the lagoon – the riva degli Schiavoni – was named after the same community.

Along the *riva* are mementos of Venice's best-known composer, Antonio Vivaldi: he was baptised at the church of **San Giovanni in Bragora** and was choir master at the church of **La Pietà**. Nearby, the **Piccolo Museo della Pietà** is dedicated to the Pietà foundling home and the composer.

Further east, wide via Garibaldi provides proof that Venice is not a dead city: head here in the morning (Mon-Sat) to catch the bustle at the market. Close by, the pleasantly

VENICE BY AREA

leafy Giardini Pubblici give way to the Giardini della Biennale, where international pavilions ranging in style from the seedy to the very pompous come to life for the annual art or architecture fests (p32).

The *riva* ends in the residential district of Sant'Elena, created from 1872, when work began to reclaim the salt marshes between the city and the island of **Sant'Elena**, with its charming Gothic church and gardens.

The church of **San Francesco della Vigna**, with its Palladian façade, is concealed in Castello's northern reaches.

Sights & museums

Arsenale
Campo dell'Arsenale. Vaporetto Arsenale. **Map** p77 D3 ㉓

Museo Storico Navale p86

The word *arsenale* derives from the Arabic *dar sina'a*, meaning 'house of industry': the industry, and efficiency, of Venice's Arsenale was legendary. When the need arose, the *arsenalotti* could assemble a galley in just a few hours. Shipbuilding activities began here in the 12th century and expanded inexorably until the 16th. At the height of the city's power, 16,000 men were employed.

The land gateway by Antonio Gambello (1460) in campo dell' Arsenale is Renaissance, though the capitals of the columns are 11th-century Veneto-Byzantine. The winged lion above holds a book without the traditional words *Pax tibi Marce* (Peace to you, Mark), unsuitable in this military context. Outside the gate, four Greek lions keep guard. Those flanking the terrace were looted from Athens in 1687; the larger one bears runic inscriptions on its side, hacked there in the 11th century by Norse mercenaries. The lion whose head is clearly less ancient than its body came from the Greek island of Delos.

Shipbuilding activity ceased in 1917. For decades the navy has put the property to little apparent use, though shows and concerts are now occasionally put on in the cavernous spaces within the Arsenale's walls. In campo della Tana is the entrance to the Corderia (rope factory), an extraordinary building 316m (1,038 ft) long, used to house the overflow from the Venice Biennale (p119).

La Pietà
Riva degli Schiavoni (041 523 1096). Vaporetto San Zaccaria. **Open** 10am-noon, 4-6pm Mon-Fri; 10am-noon, 4-5.30pm Sat, Sun. **Map** p76 B3 ㉔
By the girls' orphanage of the same name, this church – officially called Santa Maria della Visitazione – employed Antonio Vivaldi as violin teacher and choir master in the 18th century; he wrote some of his finest music for his young charges. The present building by Giorgio Massari was begun in 1745. Music inspired its

Viva Vivaldi!

Vivaldi's La Pietà p84

Venice is the city of Vivaldi, and of classical music in general, though baroque predominates. Churches and institutions ring out to the sounds of classical favourites – but beware: the quality of what's on offer varies. You can be pretty sure, however, that the best renditions are *not* by performers in periwigs and rumpled silk.

Churches that host concerts include the **Frari**, where sacred music performed during spring, autumn and Christmas seasons is of a high standard; see local press for programmes. At **San Giacomo di Rialto**, the Ensemble Antonio Vivaldi (www.ensemble antoniovivaldi.com) performs *il maestro*'s work on Wednesday, Friday and Sunday evenings. **Santa Maria Formosa** stages performances by the Collegium Ducale orchestra (www.collegium ducale.com), as well as hosting concerts by visiting choirs; the latter are often free. Also free are the organ recitals held in **Santa Maria della Salute** at 4pm each Saturday afternoon. **San Vidal**

is the venue for concerts by the highly professional, no-frills Interpreti Veneziani (www.inter pretiveneziani.com).

Concerts can be a way of gaining entrance to some of Venice's *scuole* (p11), though the performances here are not always as splendid as the surroundings. At the 14th-century Scuola Grande di San Giovanni Evangelista (San Polo 2454, campiello della Scuola, 340 546 6965), the masked Musica in Maschera outfit (www.musicainmaschera.it) performs shrink-wrapped opera. There are wigs and silk aplenty at the Scuola Grande di San Teodoro (San Marco 4810, salizada San Teodoro, 041 521 0294) when the Musici Veneziani (www.imusici veneziani.com) dish up Vivaldi or medleys of opera arias.

Other atmospheric venues include the prisons across the Bridge of Sighs from the Doge's Palace (Palazzo delle Prigioni, Castello 4209, ponte della Paglia, 041 984 252) where Collegium Ducale (*see above*) mix Venetian baroque and German romanticism with the occasional jazz concert. Audiences follow strolling players around the 17th-century Palazzo Barbarigo Minotto (San Marco 2504, fondamenta Duodo o Barbarigo, 340 971 7272) while they perform opera arias; for information, see www.musica palazzo.com. Just off St Mark's square, the Virtuosi di Venezia/ San Marco Chamber Orchestra (www.virtuosidivenezia.com) serve up Vivaldi's favourite hits in the Ateneo San Basso (San Marco 315A, piazzetta dei Leoncini, 041 528 2825).

architecture: the interior has the oval shape of a concert hall. The ceiling has a *Coronation of the Virgin* (1755) by Giambattista Tiepolo.

Museo dell'Istituto Ellenico

Castello 3412, ponte dei Greci (041 522 6581). Vaporetto San Zaccaria. **Open** 9am-5pm daily. **Admission** €4; €2 concessions. No credit cards. **Map** p76 B3 ㉕

There have been a Greek church, college and school on this site since the end of the 15th century. The oldest piece in the museum's collection is the 14th-century altar cross behind the ticket desk. The icons on display mainly follow the dictates of the Cretan School, with no descent into naturalism. The best pieces are those that are resolute in their hieratic (traditional-style Greek) flatness, such as *Christ in Glory Among the Apostles* and the Great Deesis from the early 14th century.

Museo Storico Navale

Castello 2148, campo San Biagio (041 520 0276). Vaporetto Arsenale. **Open** 8.45am-1.30pm Mon-Fri; 8.45am-1pm Sat. **Admission** €1.55. No credit cards. **Map** p77 D4 ㉖

This museum dedicated to ships and shipbuilding continues an old tradition. Under the Republic, the models made for shipbuilders were kept in the Arsenale; some of the ones on display are survivors from that collection. The ground floor has warships, cannons and dodgy-looking manned torpedoes, plus models of Venetian fortresses. On the first floor are naval instruments and models of Venetian ships. Here, too, is a replica of the Bucintoro, the doges' state barge. On the third floor is a display of gondolas, including a 19th-century example with a fixed cabin, and the last privately owned covered gondola in Venice, which belonged to Peggy Guggenheim.

Piccolo Museo della Pietà 'Antonio Vivaldi'

NEW *Calle della Pietà 3701 (041 523 9079). Vaporetto Arsenale or San*

Zaccaria. **Open** 11am-4pm Mon, Wed. **Admission** €3. No credit cards. **Map** p76 B3 ㉗

This small museum chronicles the activities of the Ospedale della Pietà, the orphanage where Antonio Vivaldi was violin teacher and choir master. Numerous documents recount such details as the rules for admission of children to the Ospedale and the rations of food allotted them. There is also a selection of period instruments.

San Francesco della Vigna

Campo San Francesco della Vigna (041 520 6102). Vaporetto Celestia. **Open** 8am-12.30pm, 3-7pm Mon-Sat; 3-6.30pm Sun. **Map** p76 C1/2 ㉘

Jacopo Sansovino designed this out-of-the-way church (1534) for the Observant Franciscan order in a simple style to match the monastic rule of its inhabitants. The façade was added by Andrea Palladio in 1568-72.

The interior consists of a single broad nave with side chapels, which are named after the families who paid for them… and who held no truck with Franciscan modesty. The Cappella Giustiniani on the left of the chancel holds a marvellous cycle of early 16th-century bas-reliefs by Pietro Lombardo and school. Along the nave, the fourth chapel on the right has a *Resurrection* (1562) attributed to Veronese. In the right transept is a flowery *Madonna and Child Enthroned* (c1450) by Greek artist Antonio da Negroponte. From the left transept a door leads into the Cappella Santa, which has a *Madonna and Saints* (1507) by Giovanni Bellini. From here you can visit two of the church's Renaissance cloisters. Back in the church, the fifth chapel on the left holds Veronese's first Venetian commission, the stunning *Holy Family with Saints John the Baptist, Anthony the Abbot and Catherine* (c1551). The third chapel has trompe-l'oeil frescoes by Giambattista Tiepolo (1743).

San Giorgio dei Greci

Fondamenta dei Greci (041 523 9569). Vaporetto San Zaccaria.

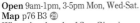
San Francesco della Vigna

Open 9am-1pm, 3-5pm Mon, Wed-Sat.
Map p76 B3 ㉙
When the church of San Giorgio was begun in 1539, the Greek community was well established in Venice. Designed by Sante Lombardo, the church's interior is fully Orthodox in layout, with its women's gallery, and a high altar behind an iconostasis. A heady smell of incense lends the church an eastern mystique, enhanced by dark-bearded priests in flowing robes.

San Giovanni in Bragora

Campo Bandiera e Moro (041 270 2464). Vaporetto Arsenale. **Open** 9-11am, 3.30-5.30pm Mon-Sat.
Map p76 C3 ㉚
San Giovanni in Bragora (the meaning of *bragora* is obscure) is an intimate Gothic structure. Composer Antonio Vivaldi was baptised here: a copy of the entry in the register is on show. Above the high altar is a *Baptism of Christ* (1492-5) by Cima da Conegliano with a charming Veneto landscape. A smaller Cima, on the right of the door to the sacristy, shows *Constantine Holding the Cross and St Helen* (1502). On the same wall, just before the second altar,

is a triptych by Bartolomeo Vivarini, *Madonna and Child and Two Saints*, dated 1478. The church also contains a splendidly heroic *Resurrection* (1498) by his nephew, Alvise Vivarini.

San Pietro in Castello

Campo San Pietro (041 275 0462). Vaporetto San Pietro. **Open** 10am-5pm Mon-Sat. **Admission** €2.50 (see also p12 Chorus). No credit cards.
Map p78 A1 ㉛
Until 1807, remote San Pietro in Castello was the cathedral of Venice. There has probably been a church on this site since the seventh century, but the present building was constructed in 1557 by Andrea Palladio. Above the high altar, the funeral urn of Venice's first patriarch San Lorenzo Giustiniani is a magnificent piece of Baroque theatricality by Baldassarre Longhena (1649). In the right-hand aisle is the so-called 'St Peter's Throne', a delicately carved marble work from Antioch containing a Muslim funerary stele and verses from the Koran. In the left transept, the Vendramin Chapel, also by Longhena, contains a 17th-century *Virgin and Child* by the prolific Neapolitan Luca

San Giovanni in Bragora, p87

Giordano. Outside the entrance to the chapel is a late work by Veronese, *Saints John the Evangelist, Peter and Paul*. San Pietro's canalside 'church green', with its punch-drunk *campanile*, is a charming place for a picnic.

Sant'Elena

Servi di Maria 3, campo Chiesa Sant'Elena (041 520 5144). Vaporetto Sant'Elena. **Open** 5-7pm Mon-Sat. **Map** p78 C4 ㉜

The red-brick church of Sant'Elena contains no great works of art, but its austere Gothic nakedness is a relief after all that Venetian ornament. In a chapel to the right of the entrance lies the body of St Helen, the irascible mother of Emperor Constantine and finder of the True Cross. (Curiously enough, her body is also to be found in the Aracoeli church in Rome.)

Scuola di San Giorgio degli Schiavoni

Castello 3259A, calle dei Furlani (041 522 8828). Vaporetto Arsenale or San Zaccaria. **Open** 9.30am-12.30pm, 3.30-6.30pm Tue-Sat; 9.30am-12.30pm Sun. **Admission** €3; €2 concessions. No credit cards. **Map** p76 B2 ㉝

Venice's Slav (*schiavoni*) inhabitants were so numerous and influential by the end of the 15th century that they built this *scuola* (meeting house). In 1502 Vittore Carpaccio was commissioned to paint a series of canvases illustrating the lives of the Dalmatian saints George, Tryphone and Jerome. The paintings contain a remarkable wealth of incidental detail, such as the decomposing virgins in *St George and the Dragon*, or the little dog in the painting of *St Augustine in his Study*, with its humanist paraphernalia (astrolabe, shells, sheet music, archaeological fragments). The upstairs room provided the setting for a scene in Vikram Seth's 1999 novel *An Equal Music*.

Eating & drinking

Al Covo

Castello 3968, campiello della Pescaria (041 522 3812). Vaporetto Arsenale. **Meals served** 12.45-2.15pm, 7.30-10pm Mon, Tue, Fri-Sun. Closed Dec-mid Jan; 2wks Aug. €€€€. **Map** p76 C3 ㉞

Though it's hidden away in a quiet alley, Al Covo is very much on the international gourmet map. Its reputation is based on a single-minded dedication to serving the best and freshest seafood. The restaurant's charming decor should make it ideal for a romantic dinner, but in fact it's more for foodies than lovers, and service can be prickly. Chef/owner Cesare Benelli's American wife Diane talks non-Italian-speakers through the daily changing menu.

Al Diporto

Sant'Elena, calle Cengio 25 (041 528 5978). Vaporetto Sant'Elena. **Meals served** noon-2pm, 7.30-10pm Tue-Sun. **€€**. Map p78 B3 ㉟

There are few places left in Venice that are quite so authentic: Al Diporto's out-of-the-way location helps to limit the tourist hordes. Grab an outside table or dive into the basic but cheerful interior and order the *spaghetti al Diporto* (with seafood), *schie* (grey shrimps) with polenta, and their pièce de résistance, a magnificent *fritto misto* (mixed seafood fry-up).

Angiò

Castello 2142, ponte della Veneta Marina (041 277 8555). Vaporetto Arsenale. **Open** *June-Sept* 7am-midnight Mon, Wed-Sun. *Feb-May, Oct-Dec* 7am-9pm Mon, Wed-Sun. Closed mid Dec-Jan. **Map** p77 D4 ㊱

This café is the finest stopping point along the riva degli Schiavoni. Tables line the water's edge; friendly staff serve up pints of Guinness, freshly made sandwiches and interesting selections of cheese and wine. Regular music events are held on Saturday afternoons in summer.

Corte Sconta

Castello 3886, calle del Pestrin (041 522 7024). Vaporetto Arsenale. **Meals served** 12.30-2.30pm, 7-10pm Tue-Sat. Closed Jan; mid July-mid Aug. **€€€€**. Map p76 C3 ㊲

This seafood restaurant is such a firm favourite on the well-informed tourist circuit that it's a good idea to book in advance. The main act is an endless procession of seafood *antipasti*. The pasta is home-made, and the warm *zabaione* dessert is a delight. Decor is of the modern Bohemian trattoria variety, and the ambience is loud and friendly. In summer, try and snaffle a table in the vine-covered courtyard.

Dai Tosi

Castello 738, secco Marina (041 523 7102). Vaporetto Giardini. **Meals served** noon-2pm Mon, Tue, Thur; noon-2pm, 7-9.30pm Fri-Sun. Closed 2wks Aug. **€** *Pizzeria*. **€€** **Restaurant**. Map p77 F5 ㊳

In a downmarket residential area, this pizzeria is a big hit with local families. (There are two restaurants of the same name on the street: this place is better.) The cuisine is humble but filling, and the pizzas are tasty. Round the meal off with a killer *sgropin* (lemon sorbet, vodka and *prosecco*).

Pasticceria Melita

Castello 1000-1004, fondamenta Sant' Anna (no phone). Vaporetto Giardini. **Open** 8am-2pm, 3.30-8.30pm Tue-Sun. No credit cards. **Map** p77 F4 ㊴

Your senses will reel at the dizzying assortment of pastries on offer here. Staff are gruff, and it's a stand-up or take-away only kind of place, but it's a local favourite.

Vincent Bar

Sant'Elena, viale IV novembre 36 (041 520 4493). Vaporetto Sant'Elena. **Open** 7am-10pm Tue-Sun. No credit cards. **Map** p78 B4 ㊵

When you've had your fill of museums and churches, venture out to the leafy eastern edge of the city, grab a seat outside this bar and join the locals lazily gazing at passing boats. Ice-cream is made on the premises, and there are computers inside with high-speed internet connections (€4.50 per hour).

Arts & leisure

Stadio PL Penzo

Sant'Elena (041 520 6899/www. veneziacalcio.it). Vaporetto Sant'Elena. **Tickets** €50-€210; €40-€130 concessions; €10 under-10s. No credit cards. **Map** p78 C4 ㊶

Probably the world's only football ground surrounded by water, this stadium in the far east of Castello is the HQ of the luckless Venezia team. Tickets can be bought at HelloVenezia offices (p181) and at the ground before matches.

Campo del Ghetto Nuovo p94

Cannaregio

Cannaregio is the second-largest *sestiere* in the city, extending from the station almost to the Rialto bridge. The name may be a contraction of *Canal Regio* (regal canal), or may derive from the *canne* (reeds) that grew along the banks here.

The South & West

Few other cities offer newly arrived tourists such a feast for the eyes: step out of the railway station, and in front of you there's no snarling tangle of buses but the Grand Canal.

For hundreds of years, visitors to Venice arrived by boat, along the Cannaregio canal. With the construction of the railway bridge in the 19th century, the configuration of the *sestiere* changed. The wide lista di Spagna – a kind of highway from the station to the Rialto, now littered with downmarket bars and hotels, and tacky souvenir shops – was driven through the old city, and much industrial activity was concentrated here.

Nowadays, industrial premises have been turned into dwellings or university digs, and though the *lista* remains a heaving mass of short-stay visitors, the quiet *calli* and *campi* immediately off it conceal some great churches, plus sudden surprises such as the original Jewish Ghetto, and a lively morning fruit and veg market by the Guglie bridge over the Cannaregio canal.

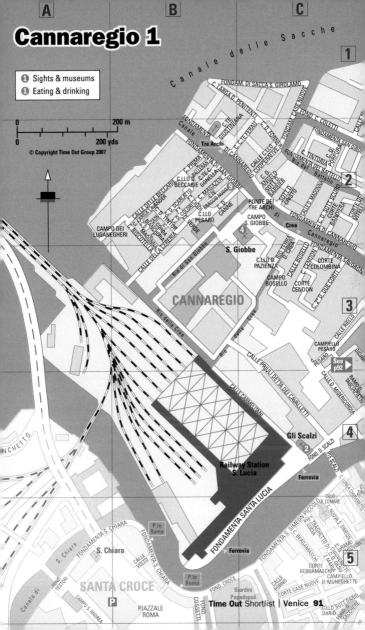

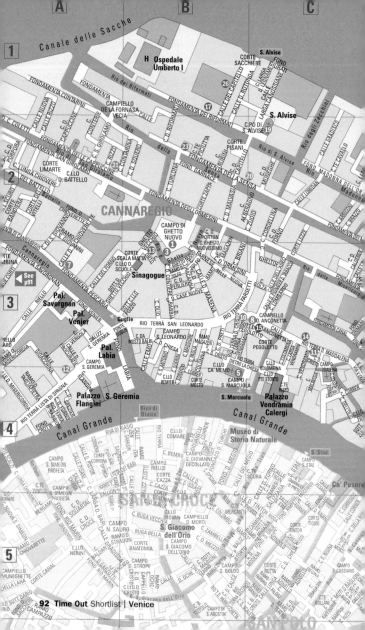

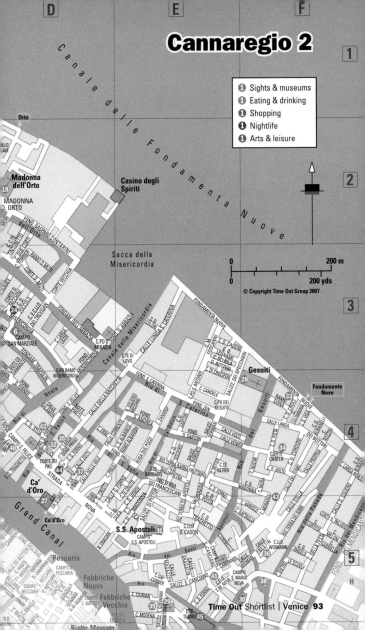

Cannaregio 2

D **E** **F**

1

Canale delle Fondamenta Nuove

Orto

① Sights & museums
① Eating & drinking
① Shopping
① Nightlife
① Arts & leisure

Madonna dell'Orto
18

MADONNA D. ORTO

Casino degli Spiriti

2

Sacca della Misericordia

0   200 m
0   200 yds

© Copyright Time Out Group 2007

3

Canale della Misericordia

FONDAMENTA NUOVE

Gesuiti
28

Fondamente Nove

CAMPO SAN MARZIALE
6

S. Caterina

Rio di

4

34

Ca' d'Oro
27

Ca'd'Oro

CORTE CARITA

43

STRADA NOVA

Grand Canal

S.S. Apostoli
31

CAMPO S.S. APOSTOLI

5

Pescaria

Fabbriche Nuove

CAMPO S. MARIA NOVA

39

30

Fabbriche Vecchie

Market Guglie p90

Sights & museums

Ghetto

Map p92 B3 ❶

The word 'ghetto' is of Venetian origin. It meant an iron foundry, a place where iron was *gettato* (cast). Until 1390, casting was done on a small island in Cannaregio. In 1516 it was decided to confine the city's Jewish population to this island.

Venetian treatment of Jews was not as harsh as in many countries, but neither was it entirely benevolent. It was governed by practical considerations – namely, business. Restrictions were many and tough. Ghetto gates were closed just after sunset; Jews had to wear distinctive badges or headgear. Most trades other than money-lending were barred to them; medicine and music were exceptions.

In the mid-16th century, the Jewish community spread into the confusingly named Ghetto Vecchio (the 'old Ghetto', the site of an earlier foundry) and later into the Ghetto Nuovissimo, but conditions remained cramped; the height of the buildings in the campo del Ghetto Nuovo shows how the inhabitants expanded vertically, creating the first high-rise blocks in Europe. Room was found, however, for five magnificent synagogues, three of which can be visited on the Museo Ebraico tour.

With the arrival of Napoleon in 1797, Jews gained full citizenship rights. During the Nazi occupation in 1943, 202 Venetian Jews were sent to the death camps.

Gli Scalzi

Cannaregio, fondamenta degli Scalzi (041 715 115). Vaporetto Ferrovia. **Open** 7-11.45am, 4-6.45pm Mon-Sat; 4-7pm Sun. **Map** p91 C4 ❷

Santa Maria di Nazareth, which is always known by the name of the *Carmelitani Scalzi* (Barefoot Carmelites) order to which it belongs, was designed by Baldassarre Longhena in 1645. The façade (1672-80) is the work of Giuseppe Sardi. The interior is striking for its coloured marble and massively elaborate baldachin over the high altar. There are many fine baroque statues, including the *St John of the Cross* by Giovanni Marchiori in the first chapel on the right. In 1915, an Austrian shell destroyed the great ceiling fresco by Tiepolo, but spared his *Angels of the Passion*, *Agony in the Garden* and *St Theresa in Glory*.

Museo Ebraico

Cannaregio 2902B, campo del Ghetto Nuovo (041 715 359/www.museo ebraico.it). Vaporetto Guglie or San Marcuola. **Open** *June-Sept* 10am-7pm Mon-Fri, Sun. *Oct-May* 10am-6pm Mon-Fri, Sun. **Admission** *Museum only* €3; €2 concessions. *Museum & synagogues* €8.50; €7 concessions. **Map** p92 B3 ❸
This museum and cultural centre, founded in 1953, has been spruced up recently, with the addition of a book-shop. In the small museum itself, there are ritual objects in silver, sacred vest-ments and hangings, and a series of marriage contracts. It's best to visit the museum as part of a guided tour (hourly) of the Italian, Ashkenazi and Sephardic synagogues.

San Giobbe

Campo San Giobbe (041 524 1889). Vaporetto Crea or Ponte Tre Archi. **Open** 10am-noon, 3-6pm Mon-Sat; 3.30-6pm Sun. **Map** p91 C2 ❹
This church named after Job – an Old Testament figure awarded honorary sainthood – was built to celebrate the visit in 1463 of San Bernardino of Siena, a Franciscan friar and high-profile evan-gelist. Designed by Pietro Lombardo, its interior is unashamedly Renaissance.

There's an atmospheric *Nativity* (1540) by Gerolamo Savoldo, and Antonio Vivarini's *Annunciation with Saints Michael and Anthony* triptych (1445). The Martini Chapel, the second on the left, is a corner of Tuscany in Venice, attributed to Bernardo Rossellino. The 15th-century terracotta medallions of *Christ and the Four Evangelists* are by the Della Robbia studio – the only exam-ples of its work in Venice.

San Marcuola

Cannaregio, campo San Marcuola (041 713 872). Vaporetto San Marcuola. **Open** 10am-noon, 5-6pm Mon-Sat. **Map** p92 B4 ❺
The gleaming interior of this church, designed by 18th-century architect Giorgio Massari, is a surprise after the unfinished brick façade. It contains vig-orous statues by Gianmaria Morleiter and, in the chancel, a *Last Supper* (1547) by Tintoretto. Opposite is a 17th-centu-ry copy of another Tintoretto (*Christ Washing the Feet of His Disciples*).

San Marziale

Cannaregio, campo San Marziale (041 719 933). Vaporetto Ca' d'Oro or San Marcuola . **Open** 4-6.30pm Mon-Sat; 8.30-10am Sun. **Map** p93 D3 ❻

Boscolo

The ceiling of this church has four luminous paintings (1700-5) by the vivacious colourist Sebastiano Ricci. Two depict *God with Angels* and *St Martial in Glory*; the others recount the miraculous tale of the wooden *Madonna and Child* statue that resides on the second altar on the left; apparently, it made its own way here by boat from Rimini. The high altar is a baroque extravaganza.

Eating & drinking

Alla Fontana

Cannaregio 1102, fondamenta Cannaregio (041 715 077). Vaporetto Guglie. **Meals served** *Apr-Oct* 6.30-11pm Mon, Wed-Sat. *Nov-Mar* 7-10pm Mon-Sat. Closed 3wks Jan-Feb. €€€. **Map** p92 A3 ⑦

After its recent shift from wine-and-snack *bacaro* to bona fide restaurant, the Fountain offers a range of filling trattoria dishes with a creative twist: gnocchi with turbot and courgettes, or *spezzatino* (braised strips of veal) with polenta. In summer, tables line the canal outside.

Boscolo

Cannaregio 1818, campiello dell' Anconeta (041 720 731). Vaporetto San Marcuola. **Open** 6.40am-8.40pm Tue-Sun. Closed 2wks Feb; July. No credit cards. **Map** p92 C3 ⑧

Locals flock to this bar-*pasticceria* to enjoy a coffee with one of the excellent selection of sweet things, or an extra-strong *spritz al bitter* with home-made *pizzette*. Chocolates in the form of Kama Sutra positions have made this confectioner's famous.

Dalla Marisa

Cannaregio 652B, fondamenta San Giobbe (041 720 211). Vaporetto Crea or Tre Archi. **Meals served** noon-2.30pm Mon, Wed, Sun; noon-2.30pm, 8-9.15pm Tue, Thur-Sat. Closed Aug. €€. No credit cards. **Map** p91 B2 ⑨

Signora Marisa is a culinary legend; locals call days in advance to ask her to prepare recipes such as *risotto con le secoe* (risotto made with a cut of beef from around the spine). Pasta dishes include the excellent *tagliatelle con sugo di masaro* (in duck sauce), while *secondi* range from tripe to roast stuffed pheasant. In summer, tables spill out on to the *fondamenta*.

Do Colonne

Cannaregio 1814C, rio terà San Leonardo (041 524 0453). Vaporetto San Marcuola. **Open** 10am-8.30pm Mon-Fri, Sun. No credit cards. **Map** p92 B3 ⑩

The large counter in this bar hosts a variety of offerings, from rye bread – *tramezzini* – to *polpette* (meatballs) and a few hot dishes that change daily. Wash everything back with a glass of wine or *prosecco*.

Il Gelatone

Cannaregio 2063, rio terà Maddalena (041 720 631). Vaporetto San Marcuola. **Open** *May-Sept* 11am-10.30pm daily. *Oct-mid Dec, mid Jan-Apr* 11am-8pm daily. Closed mid Dec-mid Jan. No credit cards. **Map** p92 C3 ⑪
The luscious gelato in this ever-popular spot comes in gorgeous flavours and generous portions: the yoghurt variety with sesame seeds and honey is especially good.

Mirai

Cannaregio 227, lista di Spagna (041 220 6517). Vaporetto Ferrovia. **Meals served** 7.30-11.30pm Tue-Sun. Closed 3wks Jan. €€€€. **Map** p92 A3/4 ⑫
This Japanese restaurant, run by a Japanese-Brazilian chef, has built up a steady local following. It does all the classics – sushi, sashimi of salmon, tuna and bream, tempura – and it does them well. They've recently added a garden out back.

Shopping

Laboratorio Blu

Cannaregio 1224, campo del Ghetto Vecchio (041 715 819). Vaporetto Guglie. **Open** 4-7.30pm Mon; 9.30am-12.30pm, 4-7.30pm Tue-Sat.
Map p92 B3 ⑬
The only children's bookshop in Venice, Laboratorio Blu carries a good selection of books in English.

Mori & Bozzi

Cannaregio 2367, rio terà Maddalena (041 715 261). Vaporetto San Marcuola. **Open** *June-Aug, Nov-Mar* 9.30am-7.30pm Mon-Sat. *Apr, May, Sept-Oct* 9.30am-7.30pm Mon-Sat; 11am-7pm Sun. **Map** p92 C3 ⑭
Shoes for the coolest of the cool: whatever the latest fad – pointy or square – you'll find it here.

Nightlife

Do Fradei

Cannaregio 1974A, rio terà San Leonardo (338 944 6218). Vaporetto San Marcuola. **Open** 8am-2am Tue-Sun. No credit cards. **Map** p92 C3 ⑮
A great place to stop off for salads and snacks during the day, Do Fradei is busy till late with a mix of young Venetians and tourists who come for the live music on Wednesdays and Fridays.

Santo Bevitore

Cannaregio 2393A, campo Santa Fosca (041 717 560/www.ilsantobevitore pub.com). Vaporetto Ca' d'Oro or San Marcuola. **Open** 7am-midnight Mon-Fri; 9.30am-1am Sat. No credit cards. **Map** p92 C3 ⑯
This friendly pub-café is popular with locals who drop in for *cicheti* during the day or come to while away the evening over a beer or a glass of wine, enlivened by live jazz acts on Mondays.

Arts & leisure

Teatrino Groggia

Cannaregio 3150, Parco di Villa Groggia (041 524 4665/www.comune. venezia.it/teatrinogroggia). Vaporetto San Marcuola or Sant'Alvise. **Open**

Fondamenta della Misericordia p98

Box office 1hr before start.
Performances 9pm, days vary.
No credit cards. **Map** p92 B1 ⑰
This little space has earned a faithful following for its multimedia performances, experimental music and drama, and shows for children in the beautiful garden.

The North

If you're tired of the crowds, there's no better place to get away from it all than the north-western areas of Cannaregio. Built around three long parallel canals, this area has no large animated squares and no sudden surprises – just occasional views over the northern lagoon.

That's not to say it doesn't have its life and landmarks: fondamenta della Misericordia is a nightlife hub, as well as being home to the *vecchia* (old; 14th-century) and *nuova* (new; 16th-century) Scuole della Misericordia, the 'new' one being a huge building by Sansovino awaiting conversion – though it's not clear into what.

On the northernmost canal (rio della Madonna dell'Orto) are the churches of the **Madonna dell' Orto** and **Sant'Alvise**, as well as many fine *palazzi*. Opposite Santa Maria dell'Orto is the 15th-century Palazzo Mastelli, also known as Palazzo del Cammello because of its relief of a turbaned figure with a camel. The Arabic theme continues in the campo dei Mori ('of the Moors') across the bridge, named after the three stone figures set into the façade of a building, all wearing turbans.

Sights & museums

Madonna dell'Orto

Cannaregio, campo Madonna dell'Orto (041 275 0462/www.chorusvenezia. org). Vaporetto Orto. **Open** 10am-5pm Mon-Sat. **Admission** €2.50 (see also p12 Chorus). No credit cards. **Map** p93 D2 ⑱

The 'Tintoretto church' was originally dedicated to St Christopher, whose statue stands over the main door. However, a cult developed around a 'miraculous' statue of the Madonna and Child that stood in a nearby garden. In 1377 the sculpture was brought here (it's now in the Chapel of San Mauro), and the church's name was changed to Our Lady of the Garden. It was rebuilt between 1399 and 1473, with a beautiful Gothic façade. But it is Tintoretto's works that have made this church famous.

Two colossal paintings dominate the side walls of the chancel. On the left is *The Israelites at Mount Sinai*; some have seen portraits of Giorgione, Titian, Veronese and Tintoretto himself in the bearers of the Golden Calf. Opposite is a gruesome *Last Judgment*. Tintoretto's paintings in the apse include *St Peter's Vision of the Cross* and *The Beheading of St Paul*. On the wall of the right aisle is the *Presentation of the Virgin in the Temple*. The Contarini Chapel, off the

Madonna dell'Orto

left aisle, contains the artist's beautiful *St Agnes Reviving the Son of a Roman Prefect*, with swooping angels in dazzling blue vestments. Tintoretto, his son Domenico and artist-daughter Marietta are buried in a chapel off the right aisle.

When the Tintorettos get too much for you, take a look at Cima da Conegliano's masterpiece *Saints John the Baptist, Mark, Jerome and Paul* (1494-5) over the first altar on the right. The second chapel on the left contains a painting by Titian of *The Archangel Raphael and Tobias*. Beneath the bell tower is a small treasury.

Sant'Alvise

Cannaregio, campo Sant'Alvise (041 275 0462/www.chorusvenezia.org). Vaporetto Sant'Alvise. **Open** 10am-5pm Mon-Sat. **Admission** €2.50 (see p12 Chorus). No credit cards. **Map** p92 C2 ⓳
A simple 14th century Gothic building, whose interior was remodelled in the 1600s with extravagant, if not wholly convincing, trompe-l'oeil effects on the ceiling. On the inner façade is a *barco*, a hanging choir of the 15th century, formerly used by the nuns of the adjacent convent. Beneath are eight charmingly naïve 15th-century biblical paintings, attributed to Lazzaro Bastiani. On the right wall of the church are two paintings by Tiepolo, *The Crowning of Thorns* and *The Flagellation*. A livelier work by the same painter, *Road to Calvary*, hangs on the right wall of the chancel.

Eating & drinking

Anice Stellato

Cannaregio 3272, fondamenta della Sensa (041 720 744). Vaporetto Guglie or Sant'Alvise. **Meals served** 12.30-2pm, 7.30-10pm Wed-Sun. Closed 1wk Jan; 3wks Aug. **€€**. **Map** p92 B/C2 ⓴
This nouveau *bacaro* has become a fave with budget-conscious gourmets. The ambience is friendly, and the food good and fairly priced. A walk-around bar at the entrance fills up with snackers before lunch and evening meals. Tables

Venetian tipples

Perhaps the most famous of Venice's liquid offerings is the Bellini, the sparkling white wine and fresh peach juice combo dreamed up at that legendary watering hole, Harry's Bar. But it's a drink invented for visitors, and one that Venetians don't consider theirs.

Much more to their taste is the *spritz*, a drink probably brought here by Austrian occupiers but enthusiastically adopted and consumed in copious quantities. The perfect *spritz* consists of half a glass of white wine and a generous shot of some bitter-tasting *aperitivo* (Campari for the full experience, a low-alcohol fizz such as Aperol for a more steady-headed result), all topped up with super-fizzy seltzer (purists frown on the mineral water often substituted for this).

The sparkling dry white *prosecco* produced in the Veneto region is now popular as an *aperitivo* throughout Italy; so Venetians set themselves apart by drinking *prosecco spento* – the same wine but without the bubbles. The slightly musty aftertaste grows on you.

But far and away the most drunk Venetian tipple – consumed with almost religious regularity by home-bound workers – is the *ombra*: a glass of perfectly quaffable, unassuming local red or white. The *ombra* glass is tiny, so it's easy to lose count of how many of them you've had in your evening perambulations… by the time dinner comes round, you may already be babbling.

spill out from the simple interior to the canalside in summer. There are Venetian classics, plus more creative outings like tagliatelle with scampi and courgette flowers. Always book ahead.

Bea Vita

NEW *Cannaregio 3082, fondamenta delle Cappuccine (041 275 9347). Vaporetto Sant'Alvise or Tre Archi.* **Meals served** noon-2.30pm, 7.30-10.30pm Mon-Sat. **€€. Map** p92 A2 ㉑
This eaterie with rustic decor, ample portions and fair prices was a hit from day one. A creative menu includes herb tagliatelle with lamb ragôut and cherry tomatoes, and red mullet on a bed of papaya purée with mint vinaigrette. At lunch there's a good-value €11 two-course *menu fisso*.

Da Rioba

Cannaregio 2553, fondamenta della Misericordia (041 524 4379). Vaporetto Orto. **Meals served** noon-2.30pm, 7.30-10.30pm Tue-Sun. Closed 3wks Jan. **€€. Map** p92 C3 ㉒
Da Rioba is a pleasant place for lunch on warm days, when tables are laid out along the edge of the canal. The menu ranges from local standards like *schie con polenta* (polenta with shrimps) and *spaghetti alla busara* (in an anchovy sauce) to forays like halibut fillet in pistachio crust on a bed of artichokes and asparagus tips.

Shopping

Jesurum Outlet

Cannaregio 3219, fondamenta della Sensa (041 524 2540/www.jesurum.it). Vaporetto Guglie or San'Alvise. **Open** 10am-1pm, 1.30-5pm Tue-Sat. **Map** p92 B2 ㉓
Elegant embroidered linens, towels and fabrics from a lace company that has been going for more than 100 years. Be warned: quality costs.

Nightlife

Iguana

Cannaregio 2515, fondamenta della Misericordia (041 713 561). Vaporetto

San Marcuola. **Open** 6pm-2am daily. **Map** p93 D3 ㉔
With tacos, tequila and *tecate*, the Misericordia's Mexican swings to salsa sounds till late. The music comes live 7-9pm, usually on Tuesdays and/or Thursdays.

Paradiso Perduto

Cannaregio 2540, fondamenta della Misericordia (041 720 581). Vaporetto San Marcuola. **Open** 7pm-1am Tue-Thur; 11am-2am Fri-Sun. **Map** p93 D3 ㉕
Arty types of all ages take their places at long *osteria* tables for a mix of seafood and succulent sounds, which go live on Fridays and Sundays.

Arts & leisure

Remiera Canottieri Cannaregio

Cannaregio 3161, calle del Capitello (041 720 539). Vaporetto Sant'Alvise. **Open** 8.30am-12.30pm, 2.30-6pm Tue-Sun. No credit cards. **Map** p92 B1 ㉖
This boat club does beginners' Venetian rowing courses by arrangement. There's a good gym too.

The East

The areas of Cannaregio closest to the Rialto – the parishes of **Santi Apostoli** and **San Giovanni Crisostomo** – were among the first to be settled in Venice, before 1000. Development then spread along the Grand Canal, where splendid palaces such as the **Ca' d'Oro** would later appear.

Adventurer Marco Polo hailed from this end of Cannaregio, and some of the Veneto-Byzantine-style houses in the corte seconda del Milion would have been standing when he was born there in 1256. It was on the wellhead in the centre of the *corte* that Dirk Bogarde collapsed in Visconti's *Death in Venice*.

North-eastern Cannaregio is more intriguingly closed in, with many narrow alleys (including the Venetian record-holder, calle Varisco, which is 52 centimetres/20 inches wide at its narrowest point) and charming courtyards. Titian had a house here, with a garden extending to the lagoon; the courtyard where the house was located is named after the artist.

Sights & museums

Ca' d'Oro (Galleria Franchetti)

Cannaregio 3932, calle Ca' d'Oro (041 523 8790/www.artive.arti.beniculturali. it). Vaporetto Ca' d'Oro. **Open** 8.15am-2pm Mon; 8.15am-7.15pm Tue-Sun. **Admission** €5; €2.50 concessions (see also p12 State Museums). No credit cards. **Map** p93 D5 ㉗

When it was built, in 1421-31, the façade of this townhouse was light blue and burgundy, with 24-carat gold highlights. The colour has worn off, but the Grand Canal frontage of the Ca' d'Oro is still an elaborate example of the florid Venetian-Gothic style. Inside, little of the original decor has survived. The courtyard was reconstructed with its original 15th-century staircase and wellhead a century ago. The highlight of the collection of paintings, sculptures and coins exhibited on the first and second floors is Mantegna's *St Sebastian*. The rest is good in parts. A small medal of Sultan Mohammed II by Gentile Bellini is more impressive than faded frescoes by Titian and Giorgione. There are some small but vigorous plaster models by Bernini.

I Gesuiti

Cannaregio, campo dei Gesuiti (041 528 6579). Vaporetto Fondamente Nove. **Open** 10am-noon, 4-6pm daily. **Map** p93 F4 ㉘

This church, dating from 1715, leaves no room for half measures: you either love it or you hate it, and most people do the latter. The exterior is conventional enough; the interior is anything but. All that tassled, bunched, over-powering drapery is not the work of a rococo set designer gone berserk with brocade: it's green and white marble. The statues above the extravagant baldachin are by Giuseppe Torretti, as are the archangels at the corners of the crossing. Titian's *Martyrdom of St Lawrence* (1558-9), over the first altar on the left, came from an earlier church on this site.

San Giovanni Crisostomo

Cannaregio, campo San Giovanni Crisostomo (041 522 7155). Vaporetto Rialto. **Open** 8.30am-noon, 3.30-7pm Mon-Sat; 3.30-7pm Sun. **Map** p93 E5 ㉙

This small Greek-cross church by Mauro Codussi contains two great paintings. On the right-hand altar is *Saints Jerome, Christopher and Louis of Toulouse*, signed by Giovanni Bellini and dated 1513. On the high altar hangs *Saints John the Baptist, Liberale, Mary Magdalene and Catherine* (c1509) by Sebastiano del Piombo, who trained under Bellini but was also influenced by Giorgione. On the left-hand altar is *Coronation of the Virgin*, a fine relief (1500-2) by Tullio Lombardo.

Santa Maria dei Miracoli

Cannaregio, campo Santa Maria dei Miracoli (041 275 0462/www.chorus venezia.org). Vaporetto Fondamente Nove or Rialto. **Open** 10am-5pm Mon-Sat. **Admission** €2.50 (see also p12 Chorus). No credit cards. **Map** p93 E/F5 ㉚

Exquisite Santa Maria dei Miracoli was built in the 1480s to house a miraculous image of the Madonna. The building is the work of the Lombardo family, early Renaissance masons who fused architecture, surface detail and sculpture into a unique whole. There is a painterly approach to the use of multicoloured marble in the sides of the church. Inside, 50 painted ceiling panels by Pier Maria Pennacchi (1528) are almost impossible to distinguish. So focus on the church's true treasures: the delicate carvings by the Lombardo family on the columns, steps and balustrade.

Big nights out

Central Venice boasts just two tiny dancefloors – at the **Piccolo Mondo** and the **Round Midnight**. Otherwise, nightlife *alla veneziana* involves long evenings chatting in bars with or (usually) without live music. Or a hop across to the mainland.

The nearest club to Venice proper is Blu Paradise at **The BLV Rooms** in Marghera (via delle Industrie 29, 041 531 7357, www.blunotte.it), a short hop on the 2, 4 or 6 bus from piazzale Roma. Open on Saturday nights from September through April, it serves up hard-core house in the main room and a mix of commercial and revival in the other. On Thursday-Sunday evenings in May to September, the action shifts to nearby **Molo 5** (via dell'Elettricità 8, Marghera, 041 538 4983).

Also in Marghera, **Al Vapore** (via Fratelli Bandiera 8, 041 930 796, www.alvapore.it, closed Mon) has been putting on jazz, blues, soul and rock gigs for years. Jazz Buffet nights take place during the week, with funk and fusion DJ sets and a free buffet to go with *aperitivi*.

In the summer, you could combine a day on the beach at Lido di Jesolo with a Big Night Out in Jesolo's plethora of clubs. The Lido di Jesolo bus leaves from piazzale Roma, but it's more fun to get the double-decker *motonave* from San Zaccaria-Pietà on the riva degli Schiavoni to Punta Sabbioni and bus it from there. Regular boats make the return journey, with a change at Lido between 1am and 6am. (If you drop before dawn, you'll need a lift or taxi – call 0421 372 301, €40 approx – back to the boat stop at Punta Sabbioni as no buses link up with the boats between 12.30am and 5.10am.)

Recommended venues in Jesolo include the **Empire Music Hall** (via Fausta 279, Cavallino, nr Punta Sabbioni, 338 875 2823, www.soundgardencafe.com) for pop and rock during the week, and new wave and metal on Saturday; super-trendy **Il Muretto** (via Roma Destra 120, 0421 371 310, closed Mon & Tue) for serious house spun by highly respected resident DJs and guests; and **Terrazza Mare Teatro Bar** (vicolo Faro 1, 0421 370 012, www.terrazzamare.com), where the informal atmosphere attracts a mixed group of groovers.

Jesurum Outlet p101

Santi Apostoli

Cannaregio, campo Santi Apostoli (041 523 8297). Vaporetto Ca' d'Oro. **Open** 8.30am-noon, 5-7pm Mon-Sat; 4-7pm Sun. **Map** p93 E5

A seventh-century church here was replaced in the 17th century. The campanile (1672), crowned by an onion dome, is a Venetian landmark. The Corner Chapel by Mauro Codussi, off the right side of the nave, is a century older than the rest of the structure. On the altar is a splendidly theatrical *Communion of St Lucy* by Giambattista Tiepolo. The chapel to the right of the high altar has remnants of 14th-century frescoes, while the one to the left has a dramatically stormy painting of *The Guardian Angel* by Francesco Maffei.

Eating & drinking

Al Fontego dei Pescaori

Cannaregio 3711, sottoportego del Tagliapietra (041 520 0538). Vaporetto Ca' d'Oro. **Meals served** 12.30-2pm, 7.30-10pm Tue-Sun. **€€€**. **Map** p93 D4 ㉜

The menu in this spacious, soberly elegant restaurant sets itself apart from the herd by its insistence on fish and fresh veg or herb combos – as in the salad of shrimps and artichokes, or the spider crab with asparagus tips. There are also some meaty *secondi*. The excellent wine list has several by-the-glass options, and there's a pretty courtyard.

Algiubagiò

Cannaregio 5039, Fondamenta Nuove (041 523 6084), Vaporetto Fondamente Nove. **Open** 6.30am-11.30pm Mon, Wed-Sun. **Meals served** noon-3pm, 7-10.30pm Mon, Wed-Sun. Closed Jan. **€€€**. **Map** p93 F4 ㉝

This place has morphed from bar-pizzeria to full-on restaurant. There's no seafood on the eclectic menu, which ranges from meat, salad and cheese *antipasti* through pasta dishes like tagliolini with duck and autumn greens to the restaurant's speciality, Angus steak, prepared every which way. Vegetarians are well served, and there's a pizza menu too.

Alla Frasca

Cannaregio 5176, campiello della Carità (041 528 5433). **Meals served** July-Sept noon-2.30pm, 6.30-10pm Mon-Sat. Oct-June noon-2.30pm, 6.30-9pm

Mon, Wed-Sun. Closed 1wk Aug, 2wks Dec-Jan. **€€€**. No credit cards. **Map** p93 F4 ❸❹

It's not on the gastronomic cutting edge, but this pleasant trattoria ranks among Venice's most picturesque places to eat. *Primi* are based on home-made pasta, while main courses range from grilled fish to meatier options. There's a good-value €12 lunch menu.

Antica Adelaide

NEW *Cannaregio 3728, calle larga Doge Priuli (041 523 2629). Vaporetto Ca' d'Oro.* **Open** 7am-midnight daily. **Meals served** noon-2.30pm, 7.30-10.30pm daily. **€€**. **Map** p93 D4 ❸❺

This historic bar-*osteria* dates back to the 18th century. Abandoned for years, it was reopened in 2006 by dynamic restaurateur and wine buff Alvise Ceccato. It looks set to make a splash, with its unusual menu of revisited traditional dishes.

Boccadoro

Cannaregio 5405A, campiello Widman (041 521 1021/www.osteriaboccadoro ve.org). Vaporetto Fondamente Nove. **Meals served** 12.30-2.30pm, 8-11pm Tue-Sun. **€€€€**. **Map** p93 F5 ❸❻

This creative seafood restaurant with modern decor has slowly picked up business and plaudits. The cuisine is excellent, with a focus on fresh fish in dishes such as tuna tartare, or *tagliolini con alici e finocchietto selvaggio* (thin

pasta strips with anchovies and wild fennel). *Secondi* range from simple grilled fish to more adventurous seafood and vegetable pairings. In summer, there are tables outside on the *campo*.

Ca d'Oro (Alla Vedova)

Cannaregio 3912, ramo Ca' d'Oro (041 528 5324). **Meals served** 11.30am-2.30pm, 6.30-10.30pm Mon-Wed, Fri, Sat; 6.30-11pm Sun. Closed Aug. **€€**. No credit cards. **Map** p93 D4 ❸❼

This is one of the best-preserved traditional *bacari* in town, known to locals as *alla vedova* (the widow's place). The widow has now joined her husband, but her family still runs it, and her spirit marches on. Tasty pasta dishes like spaghetti in cuttlefish ink and *secondi* are served at tables (be sure to book); locals tend to snack at the bar on a range of classic *cicheti*, including some of the best *polpette* (meatballs) in Venice.

Da Alberto

Cannaregio 5401, calle Giacinto Gallina (041 523 8153). Vaporetto Fondamente Nove. **Meals served** noon-3pm, 6.30-9.30pm Mon-Sat. Closed mid July-early Aug. **€€**. **Map** p93 E5 ❸❽

The wide sit-down menu in this *bacaro* with charming trad decor centres on local specialities such as *granseola* (spider crab) and *seppie in umido* (stewed cuttlefish), along with plenty of seafood pastas and risottos. A favourite with

I Gesuiti p102

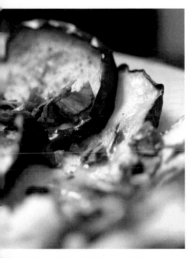

Antica Adelaide p105

young Venetians, Alberto's is always buzzing – so book ahead.

Fiaschetteria Toscana

Cannaregio 5719, salizada San Giovanni Grisostomo (041 528 5281/ www.fiaschetteriatoscana.it). Vaporetto Rialto. **Meals served** 7.30-10.30pm Tue, Wed; 12.30-2.30pm, 7.30-10.30pm Mon, Thur-Sun. Closed mid July-mid Aug. €€€€. **Map** p93 E5 ❸
Despite its name, the cuisine here is true to Venetian tradition, with favourites such as *schie con polenta* (with shrimps) and *fegato alla veneziana (*veal liver in onions). Pasta is not a strong point; better to leap from the fine *antipasti* to delicious *secondi* like grilled John Dory, or a renowned *fritto misto*. The decor is a little tired, and the service can be gruff, but Mamma Mariuccia's desserts are fabulous, and the wine list is extensive.

La Cantina

Cannaregio 3689, campo San Felice (041 522 8258). Vaporetto Ca' d'Oro. **Open** 11am-10pm Tue-Sat. Closed 2wks Jan; 2wks July-Aug. **Map** p93 D4 ❹
This is a wonderful bar in which to enjoy your *aperitivo*, yet the snack offerings are so substantial that a drink can easily turn into a full meal. The friendly staff will help you to order a plate piled high with mouth-watering *crostini*. Some 30 wines are available by the glass; there's a beer called Gaston brewed specially for the bar.

Un Mondo diVino

NEW *Cannaregio 5984A, salizada San Canciano (041 521 1093). Vaporetto Ca' d'Oro or Rialto.* **Open** 10am-3pm; 5.30-8pm Tue-Sun. **Map** p93 E5 ❹
Cora and Raffaele have recently opened what is fast becoming one of the most popular *bacari* in town. Over 40 fine wines are offered by the glass, and the large bar has a bewildering selection of *cicheti*.

Vini da Gigio

Cannaregio 3628A, fondamenta San Felice (041 528 5140/www.vinida gigio.com). Vaporetto Ca' d'Oro. **Meals served** noon-2.30pm, 7.30-10.30pm

Wed-Sun. Closed 3wks Jan-Feb; 3wks Aug-Sept. €€€. **Map** p93 D4 ❹
It's no longer a secret that this is one of the best-value restaurants in Venice, so book well in advance. Gigio is strong on Venetian *antipasti* such as *crocchette di baccalà* (breaded stockfish) and *canestrelli alla griglia* (grilled razor clams); there are also a number of good meat and game options. Wine is another forte. The only drawback here is the decidedly unhurried service.

Shopping

Vittorio Costantini

Cannaregio 5311, calle del Fumo (041 522 2265/www.vittoriocostantini.it). Vaporetto Fondamente Nove. **Open** 9.15am-1pm, 2.15-6pm Mon-Fri. **Map** p93 F4/5 ❹
Renowned as one of the most original Venetian lamp-made glass workers, Vittorio Costantini creates animals, insects, fish and birds.

Nightlife

Fiddler's Elbow Irish Pub

Cannaregio 3847, corte dei Pali già Testori (041 523 9930). Vaporetto Ca' d'Oro. **Open** 5pm-1am daily. **Map** p93 D4 ❹
Expats, locals and tourists of all ages prop up the bar in Venice's oldest Irish pub. Neighbours have put a stop to regular live music, but local bands still play at Hallowe'en and St Patrick's Day.

Arts & leisure

Teatro Malibran

Cannaregio 5873, calle dei Milion (041 786 603/www.teatrolafenice.it). Vaporetto Rialto. **Open** *Box office* HelloVenezia (p181); at venue 1hr before performances. *Performances* 7 or 8pm, days vary; 3.30pm Sat, Sun. **Map** p93 E5 ❹
Inaugurated in 1678, this 900-seater was built on the site where Marco Polo's family palazzo stood. It now shares the classical music, ballet and opera season with La Fenice and has its own chamber music season.

Rialto Market

San Polo & Santa Croce

Probably only postmen know where the boundary lies between these two *sestieri*, which nestle within the pear-shaped bulge of the upper loop of the Grand Canal. The eastern portion, tightly clustered around the Rialto market, is the city's ancient heart, and despite the invasion of trashy tourist trinkets, one can still feel its steady throb here. The western part was settled later and has a slightly more spacious feel; its fulcrum is the great religious complex of the Frari.

The South & East

'Rialto', most experts agree, derives from *rivoaltus* (high bank), and it was on this higher ground at the midpoint along the Grand Canal that one of the earliest settlements was founded, in the fifth century.

Near the foot of the **Rialto bridge**, the church of **San Giacomo di Rialto** (known affectionately as San Giacometto) is generally agreed to be the first of the city's churches – tradition has it that it was founded in 421.

The Rialto market district has been the commercial centre of the city since the market was established here back in 1097. Place names reflect the goods sold: Erberia was the vegetable centre, oranges were sold in the Naranzeria, cheese in the Casaria and spices in ruga degli Speziali.

Beyond the market extends a warren-like zone of medieval low-rent housing interspersed with proud *palazzi*.

From the Rialto bridge, a pedestrian route runs westward, more or less parallel to the Grand Canal, towards campo **San Polo** – the biggest square on this side of the Grand Canal and once used for bull-baiting, religious ceremonies and parades, as well as weekly markets – and on to the great Gothic bulk of Santa Maria Gloriosa dei Frari (aka **I Frari**), with the Tintoretto-filled *scuola* of **San Rocco** nearby.

Sights & museums

Casa di Carlo Goldoni

San Polo 2794, calle dei Nomboli (041 275 9325). Vaporetto San Tomà. **Open** *Apr-Oct* 10am-5pm Mon-Sat. *Nov-Mar* 10am-4pm Mon-Sat. **Admission** €2.50; €1.50 concessions. No credit cards. **Map** p110 C4/5 ❶
This museum, focusing on the works of 18th-century playwright Carlo Goldoni and theatre studies in general, appeals mostly to specialists, although the attractive Gothic courtyard, with its carved wellhead and staircase, is worth seeing. Goldoni transformed Italian theatre, introducing comedy based on realistic observation.

I Frari (Santa Maria Gloriosa dei Frari)

San Polo, campo dei Frari (041 522 2637). Vaporetto San Tomà. **Open** 9am-6pm Mon-Sat; 1-6pm Sun. **Admission** €2.50. No credit cards. **Map** p110 C4 ❷
The brick house of God that is known officially as Santa Maria Gloriosa dei Frari is one of the city's most significant artistic storehouses. The Franciscans were granted the land in about 1250; this church was completed just over a century later. At the entrance you are brought face-to-face with the long sweep of church leading up to Titian's glorious *Assumption*

found hanging above the high altar. (The artist is buried in the second bay in the right aisle).

In the right transept, to the right of the sacristy door, is the 15th-century tomb of the Blessed Pacifico (a companion of St Francis) – attributed to Nanni di Bartolo and Michele da Firenze with a splendidly carved canopy in the florid Gothic style. The third chapel on the right side of this transept has an altarpiece by Bartolomeo Vivarini, in its original frame. Next to the chancel, the Florentine chapel contains the only work by Donatello in the city: a striking wooden statue of a stark, emaciated St John the Baptist.

Commissioned by the Pesaro family, the sacristy contains one of Giovanni Bellini's greatest paintings: the *Madonna and Child with Saints Nicholas, Peter, Benedict and Mark* (1488), still in its original frame.

The high altar is dominated by Titian's *Assumption*, a visionary work that seems to open the church up to the heavens. The left wall of the chancel boasts one of the finest Renaissance tombs in Venice, the monument to Doge Niccolò Tron (1473), by Antonio Rizzo. In the centre of the nave stands the choir, with wooden stalls (1468) carved by Marco Cozzi, inlaid with superb intarsia decoration.

The third chapel in the left transept has an altarpiece by Bartolomeo Vivarini and Marco Basaiti; a slab on the floor marks the grave of composer Claudio Monteverdi.

Another magnificent Titian hangs to the right of the side door in the left aisle: the *Madonna di Ca' Pesaro*. This work was commissioned by Bishop Jacopo Pesaro in 1519 and celebrates a naval victory against the Turks, led by the bellicose cleric in 1502. The bishop is kneeling and waiting for St Peter to introduce him and his family to Mary. Behind, an armoured warrior leads Turkish prisoners. This work revolutionised altar paintings in Venice: Titian dared to move the Virgin from the centre of the composition, and

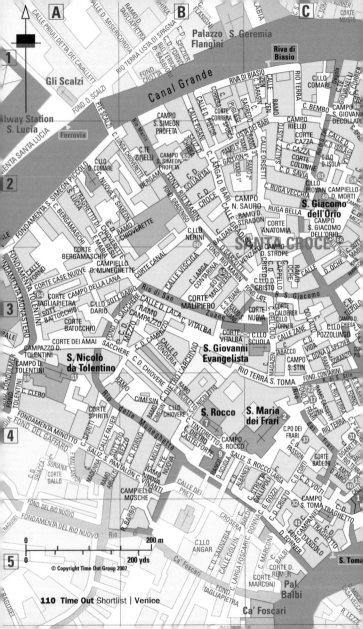

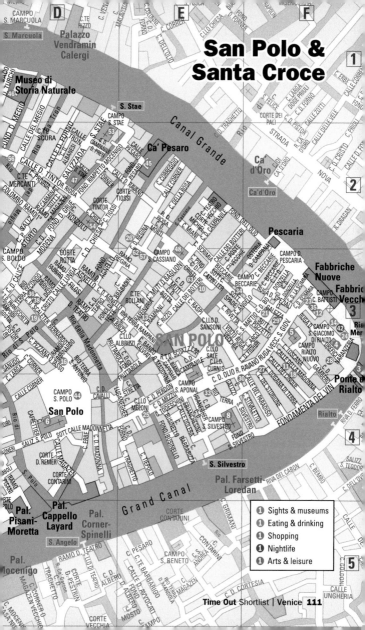

San Polo & Santa Croce

Sights & museums
Eating & drinking
Shopping
Nightlife
Arts & leisure

Cicheto etiquette

Venetians are inveterate snackers, and their grazing grounds of choice are the city's *bacari* – traditional Venetian wine bars.

Whereas bars in Turin only unveil their famous snack-buffets for evening *aperitivi*, Venetian *bacari* bring out their huge range of (large) bite-size *cicheti* from soon after the shutters go up in the morning until the last worker drags him- or herself away from the counter and heads back to the family – or even longer, if the bacaro is a late-opener.

The etiquette of *cicheti* is fairly straightforward. First, take up your position at the bar – not an easy task in the most popular *bacari*, where, if you hang back deferentially, you may never eat or drink anything. (Don't worry, you'll get the hang of inconspicuous ground-gaining quickly enough.)

Then, once you've ordered a glass of soave or cabernet (just pointing to the bottle you fancy should do the trick, though watch out in smarter places where some of the open bottles may contain very pricey wines indeed), reach for the snacks and start eating. It's considered polite to keep tabs on how many you've consumed, but even if you lose count, don't worry about it too much: you'll be amazed to find that that barman who hadn't seemed to register your existence has made a mental note of every morsel of food that's gone into your mouth.

For more on *cicheti*, see the Menu Glossary on p189.

introduced a rich humanity, from the beautifully portrayed family (with the boy turning to stare straight at us) to the Christ child, so active and alive.

The whole of the next bay, around the side door, is occupied by the mastodontic mausoleum of Doge Pesaro (died 1659). The penultimate bay harbours a monument to Canova, carved by his pupils in 1827.

Rialto bridge

Vaporetto Rialto. **Map** p111 F3 ❸
The Ponte di Rialto was built in 1588-92 to a design by Antonio Da Ponte. Until the 19th century it was the only bridge over the Grand Canal. It replaced a wooden one, which can be seen in Carpaccio's painting of *The Miracle of the True Cross* in the Accademia. After the decision was made to build it, 60 years passed, during the course of which designs by Michelangelo, Vignola, Sansovino and Palladio were rejected.

San Giacomo di Rialto

San Polo, campo San Giacomo (041 522 4745). Vaporetto Rialto. **Open** 9.30am-noon, 4-6pm Mon-Sat. **Map** p111 F3 ❹
The traditional foundation date for this church is that of the city itself: 25 March 421. San Giacomo has undergone several radical reconstructions since its foundation, the last in 1601, but the original Greek-cross plan was always preserved, as were the church's minuscule dimensions. The interior has columns of ancient marble with 11th-century Corinthian capitals.

San Giovanni Elemosinario

San Polo, ruga vecchia San Giovanni (041 275 0462). Vaporetto Rialto or San Silvestro. **Open** 10am-5pm Mon-Sat. **Admission** €2.50. No credit cards. **Map** p111 F3 ❺
This small Renaissance church was founded in the ninth or tenth century but rebuilt after a fire in 1514, probably by Scarpagnino. On the high altar is a painting by Titian of the titular saint, *St John the Alms Giver*. In the left aisle

is a fragment of sculptural relief (12th or 13th century) of the Nativity, which shows an ox and a donkey reverently licking the face of the Christ child.

San Polo

Campo San Polo (041 275 0462). Vaporetto San Silvestro or San Tomà. **Open** 10am-5pm Mon-Sat. **Admission** €2.50. No credit cards. **Map** p111 D4 ⑥

This Gothic church was given a neo-classical makeover in the 19th century. Paintings include a *Last Supper* by Tintoretto to the left of the entrance, and a Tiepolo: *The Virgin Appearing to St John of Nepomuk*. Giambattista Tiepolo's son Giandomenico painted the brilliant *Stations of the Cross* in the Oratory of the Crucifix (entrance under the organ) and the ceiling paintings at the age of 20. The campanile (1362) has two 12th-century lions at the base, one brooding over a snake and the other toying with a human head.

San Rocco

San Polo, campo San Rocco (041 523 4864). Vaporetto San Tomà. **Open** *Apr-Oct* 8am-12.30pm, 3-5pm daily.

Nov-Mar 8am-12.30pm Mon-Fri; 8am-12.30pm, 2-4pm Sat, Sun.
Map p110 B4 ⑦

Built in the Renaissance style by Bartolomeo Bon in 1489-1508, but radically altered by Giovanni Scalfarotto in 1725, the church has paintings by Tintoretto, or his school, on either side of the entrance door, between the first and second altar on the right, and on either side of the chancel. The best is probably *St Roch Cures the Plague Victims* (chancel, lower right).

San Silvestro

San Polo, campo San Silvestro (041 523 8090). Vaporetto San Silvestro. **Open** 7.30-11.30am, 4-6pm Mon-Sat. **Map** p111 E4 ⑧

This church was rebuilt in the neo-classical style between 1837 and 1843. A *Baptism of Christ* (c1580) painted by Tintoretto hangs over the first altar on the right. Opposite is *St Thomas à Becket Enthroned* (1520) by Girolamo da Santacroce, with the saint in startling white robes against a mountain landscape.

Rialto p108

VENICE BY AREA

I Frari p109

Scuola di San Rocco

San Polo 3054, campo San Rocco (041 523 4864). Vaporetto San Tomà. **Open** *Apr-Oct* 9am-5.30pm daily. *Nov-Mar* 10am-5pm daily. **Admission** €5.50; €4 concessions. **Map** p110 B4 ❾

The Archbrotherhood of St Roch was the richest of the six *scuole grandi* (p11) in 15th-century Venice. Its members came from the top end of mercantile and professional classes. It was dedicated to the French plague protector and dog lover St Roch/Rock/Rocco, whose body was brought here in 1485. The architecture, by Bartolomeo Bon and Scarpagnino, is far less impressive than the interior decoration, which was entrusted to Tintoretto in 1564 after a competition in which he stole a march on rivals by presenting a finished painting rather than the required sketch. In three intensive sessions over the following 23 years, Tintoretto went on to make San Rocco his epic masterpiece. The devotional intensity of his works can shade a touch too much into kitsch for the postmodern soul, but his feel for narrative structure is timeless. Filling up the whole of the far wall of the *albergo* (upstairs hall) is the mas-

sively complex *Crucifixion* (1565). Tintoretto began work on the larger upstairs room in 1575, with Old Testament stories on the ceiling and a *Life of Christ* cycle around the walls, experimenting relentlessly with form, lighting and colour. Below the canvases are late 17th-century wooden carvings, which include a caricature of Tintoretto. In the ground-floor hall the paintings (1583-7) reach a visionary pitch. The *Annunciation* and *Flight into Egypt*, with its verdant landscape, are among the painter's masterpieces.

Eating & drinking

Al Garanghelo

San Polo 1570, calle dei Botteri (041 721 721). Vaporetto Rialto or San Stae. **Meals served** noon-2.30pm, 6.30-9pm Mon-Sat. €€. **Map** p111 E3 ❿

This friendly new (but very authentic) *osteria-bacaro* serves good, cheap fare. The place is dominated by the long wooden bar counter, where you can perch and tuck into a cornucopia of *cicheti*. At mealtimes, grab one of the tables crammed into the tiny space and order from a small menu that might

include risotto with *funghi porcini* and langoustines, or *fegato alla veneziana*.

Alla Madonna

NEW *San Polo 594, calle della Madonna (041 522 3824/www.ristorantealla madonna.com). Vaporetto Rialto or San Silvestro.* **Meals served** noon-3pm, 7-10pm Mon, Tue, Thur-Sun. Closed Christmas-Jan. **€€€. Map** p111 F3 **⓫**
This big, bustling fish trattoria, with its friendly (though brisk) service and fair (though rising) prices, piles in loyal locals and clued-up tourists. The cooking wins no prizes, but Venetian favourites such as *granseola* and *anguilla fritta* are made competently. Bookings aren't taken: join the queue.

Al Mercà

San Polo 213, campo Cesare Battisti (393 992 4781). Vaporetto Rialto. **Open** 9am-3pm, 6-9pm Mon-Sat; 6-9pm Sun. Closed 1wk Christmas. No credit cards. **Map** p111 F3 **⓬**
With standing room only in the *campo*, this hole-in-the-wall bar has been serving Rialto market-goers since 1918. A recent change in ownership has brought young partners Gabriele, Marco and Giuseppe behind the counter. The tiny space has a snack-filled cabinet with meatballs, artichoke hearts and mini-sandwiches, in addition to a wide selection of wines by the glass. You can now buy bottles too.

Antiche Carampane

San Polo 1911, rio terà delle Carampane (041 524 0165/www. antichecarampane.com). Vaporetto San Silvestro. **Meals served** 12.30-2.30pm, 7.30-10.30pm Tue-Sat. Closed 1wk Jan; Aug. **€€€. Map** p111 E3 **⓭**
This trattoria probably wins the prize for the hardest-to-find restaurant in Venice. The inaccessibility is reinforced by a prickly attitude towards non-locals. But break the ice, and the Antiche Carampane will deliver a fine (though pricey) seafood meal of *recherché* local specialities like *spaghetti in cassopipa* (a spicy sauce of shellfish and crustaceans). Make sure you leave room for an unbeatable *fritto misto* (mixed seafood fry-up) and the most delicious desserts.

Bancogiro

San Polo 122, campo San Giacomo di Rialto (041 523 2061). Vaporetto Rialto. **Meals served** Sept-May noon-2.30pm, 7.30-10.30pm Tue-Sun. *June-Aug* noon-10.30pm Tue-Sun. **€€.** No credit cards. **Map** p111 F3 **⓮**
The back door of this updated *bacaro* gives access to a prime bit of Grand Canal frontage where outside tables give a ringside view. Downstairs, player-manager Andrea dispenses excellent wines to crowds of locals; above, at tables squeezed in under brick ceiling vaults, a light, creative menu is served, which might include turbot fillets with pumpkin and rosemary, or squid with radicchio and cinnamon. Service can be sluggish.

Bar Ai Nomboli

San Polo 2717C, rio terà dei Nomboli (041 523 0995). Vaporetto San Tomà. **Open** 7am-9pm Mon-Fri. Closed 3wks Aug; 1wk Christmas. No credit cards. **Map** p110 C4 **⓯**
This bar, much loved by Venice's student population, has expanded its impressive repertoire of sandwich combinations: try the Serenissima with tuna, peppers, peas and onions, or the Appennino, with roast beef, broccoli and pecorino cheese. Take a seat outside, even in bad weather, when the wide awning will keep you dry.

Birraria La Corte

San Polo 2168, campo San Polo (041 275 0570/www.birrarialacorte.it). Vaporetto San Silvestro or San Tomà. **Meals served** noon-2.30pm, 7-10.30pm daily. Closed 2wks Nov. **€ Pizzeria. €€ Restaurant. Map** p111 D3 **⓰**
The outside tables of this huge, no-nonsense pizzeria are a great place for people-watching – or for parents with small children, who can chase pigeons while mum and dad tuck into a pizza or some decent pasta options and grilled-meat *secondi*. Service can be slow at peak times.

Caffè dei Frari

San Polo 2564, fondamenta dei Frari (041 524 1877). Vaporetto San Tomà. **Open** 8am-9pm daily. Closed 2wks Aug. No credit cards. **Map** p110 C4 ⑰

This cosy bar has an even cosier mezzanine, which is often packed with students skipping lectures and lawyers from nearby offices. Comfy chairs and a good selection of *aperitivi* make it a fine place to recoup after visiting the Frari church or the Scuola Grande di San Rocco.

Caffè del Doge

San Polo 609, calle dei Cinque (041 522 7787/www.caffedeldoge.com). Vaporetto San Silvestro. **Open** 7am-7pm Mon-Sat; 7am-1pm Sun. No credit cards. **Map** p111 F3 ⑱

Italians scoff at the idea of drinking cappuccino after 11am, but rules like this go by the board at the Caffè del Doge, a temple to coffee culture. It's a bright, minimalist space designed to eliminate any distractions from the matter at hand: coffee. Two signature blends and ten single-origin coffees are available in various preparations.

Da Fiore

San Polo 2202, calle del Scaleter (041 721 308). Vaporetto San Stae. **Meals served** 12.30-2.30pm, 7.30-10.30pm Tue-Sat. Closed Christmas to mid Jan; Aug. €€€€. **Map** p111 D3 ⑲

The Michelin-starred Da Fiore is widely considered to be Venice's best restaurant. In the elegant, barge-like dining room, owner Maurizio Martin treats his guests – many of whom are visiting celebrities or local big shots – with egalitarian courtesy, while his wife Mara concentrates on getting the food right. Raw fish and seafood are key features of the excellent *antipasti*; *primi* are equally divided between pasta dishes like the classic *pennette* with scallops and broccoli and a series of faultless risottos. *Secondi* are all about bringing out the flavour of the fish: the *tagliata di tonno al rosmarino* is a case in point. In the end it's a good, rather than a superlative, dining experience; but that's Venice for you.

Da Ignazio

San Polo 2749, calle dei Saoneri (041 523 4852). Vaporetto San Tomà. **Meals served** noon-3pm, 7-10pm Mon-Fri, Sun. Closed 3wks July-Aug; 2wks Dec-Jan. €€. **Map** p111 D4 ⑳

The big attraction of this tranquil neighbourhood restaurant is its pretty, pergola-shaded courtyard. Don't expect any frills: the cooking is safe, traditional, homey Venetian.

Do Mori

San Polo 429, calle dei Do Mori (041 522 5401). Vaporetto Rialto or San Silvestro. **Open** 8.30am-8.30pm Mon-Sat. No credit cards. **Map** p111 F3 ㉑

The Do Mori, with its battery of copper pans hanging from the ceiling, claims to be the oldest *bacaro* in Venice, dating back to 1462. At peak times the bar is a heaving mass of bodies, all lunging for the excellent *francobolli* (mini-sandwiches) and the huge selection of fine wines. Don't point to a label at random, as prices can be in the connoisseur bracket.

Frary's

San Polo 2559, fondamenta dei Frari (041 720 050). Vaporetto San Tomà. **Meals served** noon-3.30pm, 6.30-10.30pm Mon, Wed-Sun. Closed 2wks Aug. €€. **Map** p110 C4 ㉒

A friendly, reasonably priced restaurant specialising in Arab cuisine, though there are some Greek and Kurdish dishes as well. Couscous comes with a variety of sauces; the *mansaf* (Bedouin rice with chicken, almonds and yoghurt) is tasty. At lunch there's a two-course menu for €10.

Muro Vino e Cucina

San Polo 222, campo Cesare Battisti (041 523 7495). Vaporetto Rialto. **Open** 9am-3.30pm, 5pm-1am Mon-Sat. **Meals served** noon-3pm, 7.30-11pm Mon-Sat. €€€. **Map** p111 F3 ㉓

Sleek, modern Muro hosts not only a buzzing bar but also one of the city's most interesting new restaurants. German chef Jozef Klostermaier ('Beppe') plays fast and loose with the local tradition in dishes like *caserecce*

Birraria La Corte p115

(homemade pasta) with *radicchio di Treviso* and pear in gorgonzola sauce, or chamoix meatballs in barbera d'Asti sauce with puréed potatoes and red cabbage. There's a serious grill for barbecued fish or steak and a select wine list that is strong on the Veneto, Friuli and Alto Adige. The lunch menu is simpler, and cheaper.

Naranzaria

San Polo 130, Erbaria (041 724 1035/ www.naranzaria.it). Vaporetto Rialto. **Open** *Apr-mid Nov* noon-2am Tue-Sun. *Mid Nov-Mar* noon-3pm, 6pm-2am Tue-Sun. **Meals served** noon-3pm, 7-11pm Tue-Sun. Closed 2wks Jan. €€€. **Map** p111 F3 ㉔

This relative newcomer on the eating and drinking scene offers fine wines, many of them produced in the neighbouring Friuli region by Narazaria's co-owner Brandino Brandolini, plus a small but interesting menu that ranges from local specialities to couscous, sushi and sashimi. There are a few tables upstairs beneath the brick-arched ceiling, but it's the handful of tables out by the Grand Canal that makes this place truly special.

Rizzardini

San Polo 1415, campiello dei Meloni (041 522 3835). Vaporetto San Silvestro. **Open** 7am-8.30pm Mon, Wed-Sun. Closed Aug. No credit cards. **Map** p111 E4 ㉕

When owner Paolo is behind the counter of this bar-*pasticceria*, there's never a dull moment. It's good for traditional Venetian pastries, cookies and *frittelle* during Carnevale… anything, if you can manoeuvre up to the counter and place your order. The coffee's great too.

Vecio Fritolin

Santa Croce 2262, calle della Regina (041 522 2881/www.veciofritolin.com). Vaporetto San Stae. **Meals served** noon-2.30pm, 7-10.30pm Tue-Sun. €€€. **Map** p111 E2 ㉖

Wooden beams, sturdy tables and a long bar at the back of the main dining room set the mood; but the menu is more creative than one might expect, with a scallop and courgette-flower risotto, or a main course of *branzino* (sea bass) with *porcini* mushrooms. Service can be a little uncertain, but prices are reasonably contained by Venice standards.

Shopping

Aliani Gastronomia

*San Polo 654, ruga Rialto/ruga
vecchia San Giovanni (041 522 4913).
Vaporetto San Silvestro.* **Open** 8am-
1pm, 5-7.30pm Tue-Sat. **Map** p111
F3 ㉗

This traditional grocery stocks a selection of cold meats and cheeses from
every part of Italy. Also on offer is an
assortment of prepared dishes and
roast meats.

Attombri

*San Polo 74, sottoportego degli Orafi
(041 521 2524/www.attombri.com).
Vaporetto Rialto or San Silvestro.*
Open 9.30am-1pm, 2.30-7pm Mon-Sat.
Map p111 F3 ㉘

Jeweller brothers Stefano and Daniele
Attombri create intricate, unique
pieces combining metal wire and delicate antique Venetian glass beads, or
beads designed by and made for them.
There's another small outlet at San
Marco 2668A, campo San Maurizio
(041 521 0789).

Drogheria Mascari

*San Polo 381, ruga degli Spezieri (041
522 9762). Vaporetto San Silvestro.*
Open 8am-1pm, 4-7.30pm Mon-Sat. No
credit cards. **Map** p111 F3 ㉙

This is the best place in the city to find
exotic spices, nuts, dried fruit and
mushrooms, as well as oils and wines
from different regions in Italy.

Francis Model

*San Polo 773A, ruga Rialto/ruga del
Ravano (041 521 2889). Vaporetto
San Silvestro.* **Open** 9.30am-7.30pm
Mon-Sat; 10.30am-6.30pm Sun. **Map**
p111 E4 ㉚

Handbags and briefcases are produced
in this tiny *bottega* by a father-and-son
team that has been in the business for
more than 40 years.

Gilberto Penzo

*San Polo 2681, calle II dei Saoneri
(041 719 372/www.veniceboats.com).
Vaporetto San Tomà.* **Open** 9.30am-
12.30pm, 3-6pm Mon-Sat. **Map** p110
C4 ㉛

Gilberto Penzo creates models of gondolas, *sandolos* and *topi* as well as
remarkable reproductions of *vaporetti*.
Inexpensive kits are also on sale if you
want to do it yourself.

Guarinoni

*San Polo 2862, calle del Mandoler
(041 522 4286). Vaporetto San Tomà.*
Open 7am-noon, 3-7pm Mon-Sat.
Map p110 C5 ㉜

An assortment of antique furnishings
that date from as early as the 16th
century is sold here.

Hibiscus

*San Polo 1060-1061, ruga Rialto/
calle dell'Olio (041 520 8989).
Vaporetto San Silvestro.* **Open** 9.30am-
7.30pm Mon-Sat; 11am-7pm Sun.
Map p111 E4 ㉝

Viaggio nei colori – a voyage into
colour – is the Hibiscus motto; it is
demonstrated in clothing, jewellery,
handmade scarves, bags and ceramics
with an ethnic flair.

Interpress Photo

*San Polo 365, campo delle Beccarie
(041 528 6978). Vaporetto San
Silvestro.* **Open** 9am-12.30pm, 3.30-
7.30pm Mon-Sat. **Map** p111 E3 ㉞

This is one of the cheapest – and best –
places in Venice for film development.
A small selection of authentic Murano
glass is on sale alongside sunglasses.

Kirei

*San Polo 219, campo Cesare Battisti
(041 522 8158). Vaporetto San
Silvestro.* **Open** 10am-12.30pm, 4-
7.30pm Mon-Sat. **Map** p111 F3 ㉟

This elegant kitchenware shop sells
exquisite accessories, from Versace
dinner services to Riedel glassware.

Laberintho

*San Polo 2236, calle del Scaleter (041
710 017/www.laberintho.it). Vaporetto
San Stae or San Tomà.* **Open** 9.30am-
1pm, 2.30-7pm Tue-Sat. **Map** p111 D3 ㊱

A group of young goldsmiths runs this
tiny *bottega* hidden away behind
campo San Polo. They specialise in
inlaid stones, in one-of-a-kind rings,
earrings and necklaces.

Alive and pretty well

Daniele Bianchi's *Untitled*

Venice may host the world's longest-running contemporary art fest – the Biennale – but it's not their peers that artists working here today find themselves up against: contemporary artists in the lagoon city have to vie with Titian and Tiepolo for attention.

But despite labouring in the shadow of these Old Masters, the Venetian art scene, though not exactly thriving, is alive and pretty well. The Biennale may not have sparked a mass of artistic production, but it has attracted some international artists, and inspired a few talented locals.

Though young Venetian artists tend to use more conventional methods than their YBA counterparts (paint is often the preferred medium), they still succeed in creating new and exciting work.

Carolina Antich (Giudecca 710C, fondamenta del Ponte Piccolo, 041 241 1131, www.carolina antich.com) exhibited in the Italian pavilion at the 2005 Biennale, though she is Argentinian born and bred. Now happily ensconced in Venice, Antich brings events and moments from childhood to her work. In her paintings we see how children often unwittingly become witnesses and protagonists of everyday life. There is a sense of silence in her work, the children often depicted as small figures clutched together or alone against a backdrop of muted colour.

Another outsider who chose Venice as her base is Milanese artist Maria Morganti (Cannaregio 4842, fondamenta Sartori, 041 522 7738, www.italianarea.it). Already well established both in her adopted hometown and New York, Morganti concentrates on the development of colour. Each work is meticulously constructed with layer upon layer of paint. Leaving a corner or a strip from each stratum in view, Morganti offers a hint of what the painting may once have been, demonstrating how a seemingly simple, bold work is the result of a persistent and painstaking research.

Local lad Daniele Bianchi (Santa Croce 2006, calle del Modena, 041 710 247, www.danielebianchi.com) has been producing great art for over 15 years. Moving from his more abstract and ephemeral work at the end of the 1980s through to the more personal figurative work at the beginning of the noughties, what stands out is his sublime use of light and shadow. Often working with brown tones illuminated by gold or silver light, Bianchi creates art that is both atmospheric and romantic.

For an overview of contemporary Italian art, see www.italianarea.it.

Caffè del Doge
p116

Çaffè

San Tomà. **Open** 10am-7pm daily.
Map p110 C4 ⑩
A spellbinding collection of mytho-
logical masks, Harlequins, Columbines
and Pantaloons, as well as 18th-
century dandies and ladies.

VizioVirtù

*San Polo 2898A, calle del Campaniel
(041 275 0149/www.viziovirtu.com).
Vaporetto San Tomà.* **Open** 10am-
7.30pm daily (with variations in July).
Closed Aug. **Map** p111 C5 ⑪
Witness chocolate being made before
your very eyes while sipping an iced
chocolate drink or nibbling on a spicy
praline. This cornucopia of cocoa has
delights such as blocks of chocolate
parmesan, and cocoa *tagliatelle*.

Nightlife

See also p116 **Muro Vino e
Cucina** and p117 **Naranzaria**.

Al Pesador

*San Polo 125-126, campo San
Giacometto di Rialto (041 523 9492).
Vaporetto Rialto.* **Open** 10pm-2am
Tue-Sun. No credit cards. **Map** p111
F3 ⑫
This *bacaro*-style bar was where fruit
and veg were weighed for the local market (the scales are still here). Crowds of
students cram inside or hang out at the
back door overlooking the Grand Canal
to swill *spritz* into the small hours.

Da Baffo

*San Polo 2346, campiello Sant'Agostin
(041 520 8862). Vaporetto San Stae or
San Tomà.* **Open** 7.30am-2am Mon-
Sat. No credit cards. **Map** p111 C3 ⑬
This is one of the hippest hangouts in
Venice: locals, students and their profs
all come to sample the wide selection
of Italian wines, international beers
and single malts.

Arts & leisure

Arena di Campo San Polo

*Campo San Polo (041 524 4347).
Vaporetto San Silvestro or San Tomà.*
Season 6wks late July-early Sept. No
credit cards. **Map** p111 D4 ⑭

Legatoria Polliero

*San Polo 2995, campo dei Frari (041
528 5130). Vaporetto San Tomà.*
Open 10.30am-1pm, 3.30-7.30pm Mon-
Sat; 10am-1pm Sun. **Map** p110 C4 ㊲
This bookbinding workshop sells
leather-bound diaries, frames and photograph albums.

Monica Daniele

*San Polo 2235, calle Scaleter (041 524
6242/www.monicadaniele.com).
Vaporetto San Silvestro or San Stae.*
Open 9am-12.30pm, 3-6.30pm, 9.30pm-
midnight Mon-Sat. **Map** p111 D3 ㊳
This odd little shop specialises in
tabarri (traditional Venetian cloaks)
and hats, from panamas to stylish creations by the shop's owner.

Sabbie e Nebbie

*San Polo 2768A, calle dei Nomboli (041
719 073). Vaporetto San Tomà.* **Open**
10am-12.30pm, 4-7.30pm Mon-Sat.
Map p111 D4 ㊴
A beautiful selection of Italian ceramics, as well as refined Japanese works.

Tragicomica

*San Polo 2800, calle dei Nomboli (041
721 102/www.tragicomica.it). Vaporetto*

This vibrant square is home to Venice's second most important cinematic event of the year. Around 1,000 cinema-goers a night brave the mosquitoes to fill this open-air arena for re-runs of the previous season's blockbusters, with the odd preview thrown in.

The North & West

Yellow signs pointing to 'Ferrovia' mark the zigzagging north-western route from the Rialto past the fish market, through campo **San Giacomo dell'Orio**.

Many of the most important sights face on to the Grand Canal, including **Ca' Pesaro**, home to both the contemporary art museum and the oriental museum; the 18th-century church of **San Stae**; and the Fondego dei Turchi, home to the city's **Museo di Storia Naturale**.

In the far north-west, the rather forlorn Giardino Papadopoli, a small park with Grand Canal views, stands on the site of the church and convent of Santa Croce. The name survives as that of the *sestiere*, but all that remains of the church is a chunk of crenellated wall. Beyond the garden there is little but the carbon-monoxide kingdom of piazzale Roma and the multi-storey car parks. One last curiosity is the complex of bridges across the rio Novo known as Tre Ponti (three bridges); there are, in fact, five interlocking bridges.

Sights & museums

Ca' Pesaro

Galleria d'Arte Moderna *Santa Croce 2076, fondamenta Ca' Pesaro (041 524 0695/www.museicivici veneziani.it)*.
Museo Orientale *Santa Croce 2070, fondamenta Ca' Pesaro (041 524 1173/www.museiciviciveneziani.it)*. *Vaporetto San Stae*. **Open** *Apr-Oct* 10am-6pm Tue-Sun. *Nov-Mar* 10am-5pm Tue-Sun. **Admission** €5.50; €3 concessions. No credit cards.
Map p111 E2 ⑮

This grandiose palazzo was built in the second half of the 17th century to a design by Baldassarre Longhena. The interior still has some of the original fresco decorations. The palazzo's last owner, Felicita Bevilacqua La Masa, bequeathed it to the city.

Into one section went the city's collection of modern art. The museum now covers a century of mainly Italian art, from the mid-19th century to the 1950s, including a monumental *Eve* by Francesco Messina, a bronze *Cardinal* by Giacomo Manzù and pieces by Gustav Klimt, Giorgio Morandi, Giorgio De Chirico and Vassily Kandinsky.

Another wing of the palazzo is home to the Museo Orientale – an odd attraction for such a monocultural city as Venice, though if you come here after the Palazzo Ducale and the Museo Correr, all this ceremonial paraphernalia will seem oddly familiar. The collection features parade armour, decorative saddles and case upon case of curved samurai swords. There is a dwarf-sized gilded lady's litter, and lacquered picnic cases. The final rooms have musical instruments and eastern miscellanea.

Museo di Storia Naturale (Natural History Museum)

Santa Croce 1730, salizada del Fondego dei Turchi (041 275 0206). *Vaporetto San Stae*. **Open** 9am-1pm Tue-Fri; 10am-4pm Sat, Sun. **Admission** free. **Map** p111 D1 ⑯

This museum is undergoing a very leisurely restoration. At this time, just two rooms are open to the public: the Acquario delle Tegnue, devoted to the aquatic life of the northern Adriatic, and the Sala dei Dinosauri, a state-of-the-art exhibition chronicling an expedition to Niger in 1973 that unearthed the previously unknown fossil *Auronosaurus nigeriensis*. The museum is housed in the Fondego dei Turchi, a building that was leased to the Turks in the 17th century as a residence and warehouse; the present edifice is a 19th-century reconstruction.

Palazzo Mocenigo

Santa Croce 1992, salizada San Stae (041 721 798/www.museicivici veneziani.it). Vaporetto San Stae. **Open** *Apr-Oct* 10am-5pm Tue-Sun. *Nov-Mar* 10am-4pm Tue-Sun. **Admission** €4; €2.50 concessions. No credit cards. **Map** p111 D2 ㊼

The interior of Palazzo Mocenigo gives a fine illustration of the sort of furniture and fittings an 18th-century Venetian noble family liked to surround itself with. Frescoes by late 18th-century artists such as Jacopo Guarana and Gian Battista Canal glorify the Mocenigo family's achievements. There are also examples of 18th-century Venetian dress.

San Cassiano

San Polo, campo San Cassiano (041 721 408). Vaporetto San Stae. **Open** 9am-noon Tue-Sat. **Map** p111 E2/3 ㊽

This church has a dull exterior and a heavily decorated interior. The chancel contains three major Tintorettos: *Crucifixion, Resurrection* and *Descent into Limbo*. A painting by Antonio Balestra looks at first glance like a dying saint surrounded by *putti*; on closer inspection, it transpires that the chubby children are, in fact, hacking the man to death. It represents *The Martyrdom of St Cassian*, a teacher who was murdered by his pupils with their pens, which, of course, makes him the patron saint of schoolteachers.

San Giacomo dell'Orio

Santa Croce, campo San Giacomo dell'Orio (041 275 0462). Vaporetto Riva di Biasio. **Open** 10am-5pm Mon-Sat. **Admission** €2.50. No credit cards. **Map** p110 C2 ㊾

Delightful campo San Giacomo dell'Orio is dominated by this church, with its plump apses and stocky 13th-century campanile. The interior is a mix of styles. Most of the columns have 12th- or 13th-century Veneto-Byzantine capitals, and there's a fine

Hibiscus p118

14th-century ship's-keel roof. The five gilded compartments on the ceiling have paintings by Veronese: an *Allegory of the Faith* surrounded by four Doctors of the Church. Francesco Bassano's *St John the Baptist Preaching* includes a portrait of Titian (in the red hat). Behind the high altar is a *Madonna and Four Saints* by Lorenzo Lotto. In the St Lawrence Chapel in the left transept are an altarpiece by Veronese and two fine early works by Palma il Giovane.

San Giovanni Decollato

Santa Croce, campo San Giovanni Decollato (041 524 0672). Vaporetto Riva di Biasio. **Open** 10am-noon Mon-Sat. **Map** p110 C1 ㊿

The church of Saint John the Headless, or San Zan Degolà in Venetian dialect, is a good building to visit if you want a relief from baroque excesses and ecclesiastic clutter. It preserves much of its 11th-century appearance. The interior has Greek columns with Byzantine capitals supporting ogival arches, and an attractive ship's-keel roof. The right apse has a splendidly heroic 14th-century fresco of Michael the Archangel; the left apse has some of the earliest frescoes in Venice,

Veneto-Byzantine works of the early 13th century. The church is used for Russian Orthodox services.

San Nicolò da Tolentino

Santa Croce, campo dei Tolentini (041 710 806). Vaporetto Piazzale Roma. **Open** 8.30am-noon, 4.30-6.30pm Mon-Sat; 4.30-6.30pm Sun. **Map** p110 A4 ⑤

This church (1591-5), usually known as I Tolentini, was planned by Vincenzo Scamozzi. Its unfinished façade has a massive Corinthian portico (1706-14) added by Andrea Tirali. The interior is a riot of baroque decoration. On the wall outside the chancel to the left is *St Jerome Succoured by an Angel* by Flemish artist Johann Liss. Outside the chapel in the left transept is *The Charity of St Lawrence* by Bernardo Strozzi, in which the hoary old beggar in the foreground upstages the wimpish saint. In the chancel hangs an *Annunciation* by Neapolitan Luca Giordano and opposite is a splendidly theatrical monument to 17th-century patriarch Francesco Morosini (1678) by Filippo Parodi.

San Simeone Profeta

Santa Croce, campo San Simeone Profeta (041 718 921). Vaporetto Ferrovia. **Open** 8am-noon, 5-6.30pm Mon-Sat. **Map** p110 B2 ㉒

More commonly known as San Simeone Grande, this small church of possibly tenth-century foundation underwent numerous alterations in the 18th century. The interior preserves its ancient columns with Byzantine capitals. To the left of the entrance is a *Last Supper* by Tintoretto, with the priest who commissioned the painting standing to one side, a spectral figure in white robes. The other major work is the stark statue of a recumbent St Simeon, with an inscription dated 1317 attributing it to an otherwise unknown Marco Romano.

San Stae

Santa Croce, campo San Stae (041 275 0462). Vaporetto San Stae. **Open** 10am-5pm Mon-Sat. **Admission** €2.50. No credit cards. **Map** p111 D2 ㉝

Stae is the Venetian version of Eustachio, or Eustace, a martyr saint who was converted to Christianity by the vision of a stag with a crucifix between its antlers. This church on the Grand Canal has a dramatic late baroque façade (1709) by Domenico Rossi. On the side walls of the chancel, all the leading painters operating in Venice in 1722 were asked to pick an apostle. The finest of these are: Domenico Tiepolo's *Martyrdom of St Bartholomew* (left wall, lower row); Sebastiano Ricci's *Liberation of St Peter* (right wall, lower row); and Piazzetta's *Martyrdom of St James*.

Santa Maria Mater Domini

Santa Croce, calle della Chiesa (041 721 408). **Open** 10am-12.30pm, 3.30-6pm Tue, Fri; 10am-noon, 3.30-6pm Wed; 10am-noon Thur. **Map** p111 D2 ㉞

Set off the *campo* of the same name, this church was built in the first half of the 16th century to a project by either Giovanni Buora or Mauro Codussi. The façade is attributed to Jacopo Sansovino; the harmonious Renaissance interior alternates grey stone with white marble. The *Vision of St Christine* on the second altar on the right is by

Kirei p118

Vincenzo Catena, a spice merchant who painted in his spare time. In the left transept hangs *The Invention of the Cross*, a youthful work by Tintoretto.

Eating & drinking

Alaska Gelateria-Sorbetteria

Santa Croce 1159, calle larga dei Bari (041 715 211). Vaporetto Riva de Biasio. **Open** *Apr-Oct* 11am-midnight daily. *Nov, Feb-Mar* noon-9pm daily. Closed Jan, Dec. No credit cards. **Map** 110 B2 ⑤⑤

Carlo Pistacchi is passionate about making ice-cream, and experiments with new flavours using only the freshest natural ingredients. Sample the seasonally changing exotic flavours such as artichoke, celery, fennel, asparagus or ginger.

Alla Zucca

Santa Croce 1762, ponte del Megio (041 524 1570/www.lazucca.it). Vaporetto San Stae. **Meals served** 12.30-2.30pm, 7-10.30pm Mon-Sat. €€. **Map** p111 D2 ⑤⑥

This was one of the first of Venice's 'alternative' trattorias, and it's still one of the best – and best-value. The menu at the Pumpkin is divided between meat (lamb roasted with fennel and pecorino cheese; ginger pork with pilau rice) and vegetables (*penne* with aubergine and feta; pumpkin and seasoned ricotta quiche). Lone women will feel at home in this predominantly female-staffed eaterie.

Al Nono Risorto

Santa Croce 2338, sottoportico di Siora Bettina (041 524 1169). Vaporetto San Stae. **Meals served** noon-2.30pm, 7-11pm Mon, Tue, Fri-Sun; 7-11pm Thur. Closed 2wks Jan, 1wk Aug. € **Pizzeria**. €€ **Restaurant**. No credit cards. **Map** p111 E3 ⑤⑦

This is the place to hang out over a tasty pizza margherita in a shady garden courtyard with Venice's bright young things. It also does traditional Venetian trattoria fare, at traditional Venetian trattoria prices.

Al Prosecco

Santa Croce 1503, campo San Giacomo dell'Orio (041 524 0222). Vaporetto San Stae. **Open** *Feb-July, Sept-Dec* 8am-10pm Mon-Sat. Closed Jan, Aug. No credit cards. **Map** p110 C2 ⑤⑧

Prosecco – whether sparkling or still – is second only to *spritz* in terms of daily Venetian consumption, and this bar is a good place for consuming it. Exceptional wines are served by the glass, with a great choice of cheeses, cold meats, marinated fish and oysters to accompany them. Shady outside tables are a great vantage point for observing life in the *campo*.

Da Lele

Santa Croce 183, campo dei Tolentini (no phone). Vaporetto Piazzale Roma. **Open** 6am-2pm, 4-8pm Mon-Fri; 6am-2pm Sat. No credit cards. **Map** p110 A4 ⑤⑨

Gabriele's (Lele's) tiny place is the first authentic *osteria* for those arriving in Venice; look out for the two barrels outside, and you've found it. There are local wines from Piave, Lison and Valdobbiadene, and the fresh rolls are made to order with simple meat and/ or cheese fillings.

Gilda Vio

Santa Croce 784, fondamenta Rio Marin (041 718 523). Vaporetto Riva di Biasio. **Open** 6.30am-8.15pm Mon, Tue, Thur-Sun. Closed Aug. No credit cards. **Map** p110 B2 ⑥⓪

Gilda Vio's delicious pastry shop offers a world of choice, and a selection of sizes. Individual portions can be consumed with a coffee or drink at one of the tables along the *rio*. Treats such as tiramisu or a creation with cream and fresh fruit can be purchased in family-size portions to take away.

Il Refolo

Santa Croce 1459, campiello del Piovan (041 524 0016). Vaporetto Riva di Biasio or San Stae. **Meals served** *Apr-Oct* 7-11pm Tue; noon-3.30pm, 7-11pm Wed-Sun. Closed Nov-Mar. €€ **Pizzeria**. €€€ **Restaurant**. **Map** p110 C2 ⑥①

San Giovanni Decollato p122

The 'Sea Breeze' has tables outside (and only outside) in one of Venice's prettiest squares. Set up by a scion of the Da Fiore dynasty (p116), it is Venice's most luxurious pizzeria – a status that is reflected in the prices. As well as excellent pizzas, there is also a small international-style menu. Book ahead.

Shopping

Ceramiche La Margherita

Santa Croce 2345, sottoportico della Siora Bettina (041 723 120/www. lamargheritavenezia.com). Vaporetto San Stae. **Open** 9.30am-1pm, 3.30-7pm Mon-Sat. **Map** p111 E3 ❷
A wonderful collection of hand-painted terracotta designed by the English-speaking owner.

L'Erbania

San Polo 1735, calle dei Botteri (041 723 215). Vaporetto San Silvestro or San Stae. **Open** 10am-1.30pm, 3.30-7.30pm Tue-Sat. **Map** p111 E3 ❸
A quaint shop near the Rialto where a herbalist will mix up concoctions for you. Alternatively, choose from a variety of prepared creams and perfumes.

Mare di Carta

Santa Croce 222, fondamenta dei Tolentini (041 716 304/www.maredi carta.com). Vaporetto Piazzale Roma. **Open** 9am-1pm, 3.30-7.30pm Mon-Sat. **Map** p110 A3 ❻
A must for boat lovers, this nautical bookshop carries publications in English as well as Italian, as well as posters and charts. The bulletin board has boats for sale.

Nightlife

Ai Postali

Santa Croce 821, fondamenta Rio Marin (no phone). Vaporetto Riva di Biasio or San Tomà. **Open** 7.30pm-2am Mon-Sat. Closed Aug. No credit cards. **Map** p110 B3 ❻
This long-established and late-opening *osteria* is a firm Venetian favourite. Locals moor their boats beneath the outside terrace and linger into the small hours.

Bagolo

Santa Croce 1584, campo San Giacomo dell'Orio (041 717 584). Vaporetto San Stae. **Open** 7.30am-1am Mon-Fri; 8am-1am Sat; 9am-1am Sun. No credit cards. **Map** p110 C2 ❻
Laid-back Bagolo, with its Murano glass sconces, attracts a more mature crowd who sit up at the high stools inside or sink into an armchair outside and explore the selection of excellent Friulian grappas.

Giudecca Canal's Zattere p130

Dorsoduro

Dorsoduro stretches along Venice's southern flank from the western docks to the magnificent church of the Salute. It is home to a varied social mix; the eastern areas around the Salute exude international affluence, while Santa Marta in the west is salt-of-the-earth working class. In between these social and geographical extremes is the wholly democratic campo Santa Margherita, an area that is Dorsoduro's largest square and nightlife hub.

Western Dorsoduro

This was one of the first areas in the lagoon to be settled, initially by fisherfolk. The church of **San Nicolò dei Mendicoli** ('of the beggars' – this was never a top-income-bracket zone) was founded as early as the seventh century. Fishing was superseded as a source of employment long ago by the port, and subsequently by the Santa Marta cotton mill – now converted into the stunning Istituto Universitario di Architettura di Venezia, the architecture university.

Moving westwards, the atmosphere remains unpretentious around the churches of **Angelo Raffaele** and **San Sebastiano**, with its splendid decoration by Paolo Veronese.

Sights & museums

Angelo Raffaele

Dorsoduro, campo Angelo Raffaele (041 522 8548). Vaporetto San Basilio. **Open** 8am-noon, 3-5pm Mon-Sat; 9am-noon Sun. **Map** p128 A3 ❶

Tradition relates that this church was founded by St Magnus in the eighth century, but the current building dates from the 17th century. The ceiling has a lively fresco by Gaspare Diziani of *St Michael Driving out Lucifer*, with Lucifer apparently tumbling out of the heavy stucco frame. There are matching Last Suppers on either side of the organ (by Bonifacio de' Pitati on the left and a follower of Titian on the right). But the real jewels are on the organ loft, where five compartments by Giovanni Antonio Guardi recount the story of *Tobias and the Angel* (1750-3). They are works of dazzling luminosity, quite unlike anything else done in Venice at the time.

San Nicolò dei Mendicoli

Dorsoduro, campo San Nicolò (041 275 0382). Vaporetto San Basilio or Santa Marta. **Open** 10am-noon, 4-6pm Mon-Sat; 4-6pm Sun. **Map** 128 A3 ❷

San Nicolò is one of the few Venetian churches to have maintained its 13th-century Veneto-Byzantine structure. During restoration in 1971-7, traces of the original foundations were revealed, confirming the church's seventh-century origins. Film buffs will recognise this as the church from Nicolas Roeg's dwarf-in-Venice movie *Don't Look Now*. The 15th-century loggia at the front originally served as a shelter for the homeless. The interior contains no major works of art, but a marvellous mishmash of architectural and decorative styles. The gilded statues of the apostles are 16th century, the paintings mainly 17th. There are also some fine wooden sculptures, including a large statue of San Nicolò by the Bon studio.

San Sebastiano

Dorsoduro, fondamenta di San Sebastiano (041 275 0462/www.chorus venezia.org). Vaporetto San Basilio. **Open** 10am-5pm Mon-Sat. **Admission** €2.50 (see also p12 Chorus). No credit cards. **Map** p128 A3 ❸

The brilliantly colourful interior of this is mostly the work of one man: Paolo Veronese, who is buried here. One of Veronese's earliest commissions in

Venice was *The Coronation of the Virgin* and the four panels of the Evangelists in the sacristy (1555). Between 1556 and 1565 he did the rest. The ceiling paintings, depicting scenes from the life of Esther, are full of sumptuous pageantry and splendidly shimmering effects. Huge canvases in the chancel depict *The Martyrdom of St Sebastian* (right) and *St Sebastian Encouraging St Mark and St Marcellan* (left). Other paintings in the church include *St Nicholas*, a late painting by Titian, in the first altar on the right.

Eating & drinking

Pane, Vino e San Daniele

Dorsoduro 1722, campo dell'Angelo Raffaele (041 523 7456). Vaporetto San Basilio. **Meals served** noon-2.30pm, 7-10.15pm Mon, Tue, Thur-Sun. Closed 2wks Jan. €€. **Map** p128 A3 ❹

This *nouvelle osteria* belongs to a chain specialising in the wine and ham of the Friuli region. But dishes like *gnocchetti alla San Daniele in cestino di frico croccante* (little gnocchi in white sauce with San Daniele ham, served in a crunchy cheese basket) vie with others that reflect the chef's Sardinian roots: *coniglio al mirto* (rabbit baked with myrtle) or *porcheddu* (roasted piglet). The single table down in the cellar is a romantic hideaway that you'll need to book well in advance. The place functions as a bar from 9am to 11pm.

Central Dorsoduro

At the heart of central Dorsoduro is long, irregular-shaped *campo* Santa Margherita. The morning market (Mon-Sat) is a non-stop bustle of shopping housewives, hurrying students and scavenging pigeons. In the evening, the bars and cafés are invaded by hordes of Venice's under-30s, much to the irritation of local residents.

In the middle of the square is the isolated Scuola dei Varoteri (school

Dorsoduro

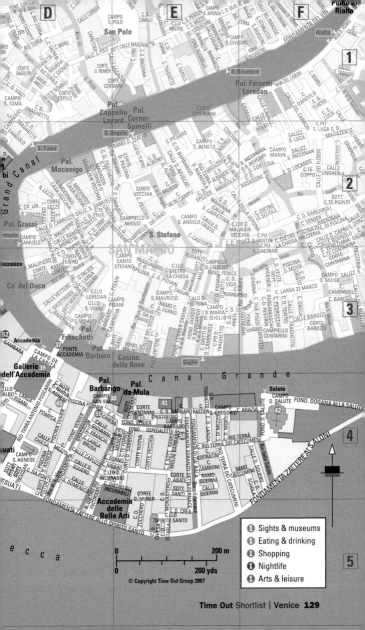

D   **E**   **F**   Ponte di Rialto

1

2

3

4

5

①	Sights & museums
①	Eating & drinking
①	Shopping
①	Nightlife
①	Arts & leisure

0   200 m
0   200 yds

© Copyright Time Out Group 2007

of the tanners). At the north end is the former church of Santa Margherita; St Margaret's dragon features on the campanile, and the sculpted saint also stands triumphant on the beast between the windows of a house at the north end of the square. A miraculous escape from the dragon's guts for some reason makes her the patron saint of pregnant women.

Leaving the *campo* to the south you reach the picturesque rio di San Barnaba, with the entrance to the swaggering **Ca' Rezzonico** at its eastern end. The middle of the three bridges across the canal is ponte dei Pugni, with white marble footprints indicating that punch-ups between rival factions – the *nicolotti*, from the western quarters of the city, and the *castellani*, from the east – were held here. Until a particularly bloody bout in 1705, these free-for-alls were tolerated by the authorities, who saw them as a chance for the working classes to let off steam. Nearby is the world's most photographed greengrocer's: a barge moored in the canal.

By the church of **San Trovaso**, is a picturesque *squero*, which is one of the few remaining yards where gondolas are made.

On the southern shore is the widest stretch of the Zattere. This promenade bordering the Giudecca Canal is named after the *zattere* (rafts) that used to moor here, bringing wood and other materials across from the mainland. The paved quayside was created in 1519. The promenade fills with sun-worshipping locals in good weather.

Sights & museums

Ca' Rezzonico (Museo del Settecento Veneziano)

Dorsoduro 3136, fondamenta Rezzonico (041 241 0100/www.museicivici veneziani.it). Vaporetto Ca' Rezzonico.

San Sebastiano p127

Open *Apr-Oct* 10am-6pm Mon, Wed-Sun. *Nov-Mar* 10am-5pm Mon, Wed-Sun. **Admission** €6.50; €4-€4.50 concessions (see also p12 Musei Civici Veneziani). No credit cards.
Map p128 C3 ⑤

The Museum of 18th-Century Venice is dedicated to the art of the twilight years of the Republic, but the paintings on display are perhaps less impressive than the palazzo itself, an imposing Grand Canal affair designed by Baldassarre Longhena in 1667. Giambattista Tiepolo was called upon to commemorate the 1758 marriage of Ludovico Rezzonico into the noble Savorgnan family on the ceiling of the *sala del trono*. Giovanni Battista Crosato's ceiling frescoes in the ballroom have aged less well but, together with the Murano chandeliers and the intricately carved furniture, they provide an accurate record of the lifestyles of the rich and famous at the time. There are canvases by Giovanni

Battista Piazzetta and Antonio Diziani, plus some detached frescoes, recently restored, of *pulcinellas* (ancestors of the English character, Punch) by Giandomenico Tiepolo. There are some good genre paintings by Pietro Longhi, and a series of portraits by Rosalba Carriera. On the third floor is the picture gallery, with mainly Venetian works, and a reconstruction of an 18th-century city pharmacy. The Mezzanino Browning is where the poet Robert Browning died in 1889.

San Pantalon

Dorsoduro, campo San Pantalon (041 523 5893). Vaporetto San Tomà. **Open** 8-10am, 4-6pm Mon-Sat. **Map** p128 C1/2 **6**

The dedicatee of this church is St Pantaleon, court physician to Emperor Galerius, who was tortured and beheaded by Diocletian. His story is depicted inside the church in one of the most extraordinary ceiling paintings in Italy – a huge illusionist work by the Cecil B De Mille of the 17th century, Gian Antonio Fumiani. It took him 24 years (1680-1704) to complete it, after which he fell from the scaffolding to his death. Veronese depicts the saint in less melodramatic fashion in the second chapel on the right, in *St Pantaleon Healing a Child*. To the left of the chancel is the Chapel of the Holy Nail. The nail, supposedly from the Crucifixion, is preserved in a richly decorated Gothic altar. On the right wall is a fine *Coronation of the Virgin* by Antonio Vivarini and Giovanni d'Alemagna.

Santa Maria dei Carmini

Dorsoduro, campo dei Carmini (041 522 6553). Vaporetto Ca' Rezzonico or San Basilio. **Open** 8am-noon, 2.30-6.30pm Mon-Sat; 2.30-6.30pm Sun. **Map** p128 B3 **7**

The church officially called Santa Maria del Carmelo is richly decorated, with 17th-century gilt wooden statues over the arcades of the nave and, above, a series of baroque paintings illustrating the history of the Carmelite order. The best works in the church are

a *Nativity* by Cima da Conegliano on the second altar on the right and *St Nicholas of Bari* by Lorenzo Lotto opposite; the latter has a dreamy landscape containing tiny figures of St George and the dragon. To the right of the Lotto painting is a *Holy Family* by Veronese. In the chapel to the right of the high altar is a graceful bronze relief of *The Lamentation Over the Dead Christ* by the Sienese sculptor, painter and inventor Francesco di Giorgio.

San Trovaso

Dorsoduro, campo San Trovaso (041 522 2133). Vaporetto Zattere. **Open** 8-11am, 3-6pm Mon-Sat. **Map** p128 C4 **8**

San Trovaso was built on the border of areas of the city controlled by the rival *nicolotti* and *castellani* factions; in the event of a wedding between members of the two sides, each party could make its own sweeping entrance and exit from one of the two identical doors. There are five works by the Tintoretto family in the church; three are probably by the son, Domenico, including the two on either side of the high altar. In the left transept is a small *Last Supper* by Tintoretto *padre*; the tavern setting is strikingly realistic. In the chapel to the left of the high altar is *The Temptations of St Anthony the Abbot*. On the side wall of this same chapel is a charming painting in the International-Gothic style by Michele Giambono, *St Chrisogonus on Horseback* (c1450). Marble reliefs of angels in the right transept date from around 1470.

Scuola dei Carmini

Dorsoduro 2617, campo dei Carmini (041 528 9420). Vaporetto Ca' Rezzonico or San Basilio. **Open** *Apr-Oct* 10am-5pm daily. *Nov-Mar* 10am-4pm daily. **Admission** €5; €2 concessions. No credit cards. **Map** p128 B3 **9**

Begun in 1670 to plans by Baldassarre Longhena, this gives a good idea of what an early 18th-century Venetian confraternity HQ looked like, from the elaborate Sante Piatti altarpiece downstairs to the staircase with its gilded cherubs. On the upper floor is one of the most impressive of Giambattista Tiepolo's Venetian ceilings: the panels (1740-3) recount the complex tale of a celestial donation that took place in Cambridge, where Simon Stock received the scapular (the badge of the Carmelite order) from the Virgin. In the two adjoining rooms are wooden sculptures by Giacomo Piazzetta and a dramatic *Judith and Holofernes* by his more gifted son Giovanni Battista.

Eating & drinking

Ai Do Draghi

Dorsoduro 3665, calle della Chiesa (041 528 9731). Vaporetto San Tomà. **Open** *Apr-Oct* 7.30am-2am daily. *Nov-Mar* 7.30am-11pm daily. No credit cards. **Map** p128 C2 ❿

Throngs of cheerful drinkers cram into the tiny *calle* off campo Santa Margherita, where the entrance to Ai Do Draghi is located – and also on to its numerous tables on the square – to enjoy draught beers, strong *spritz* and some 40 wines by the glass. The indoor seating is intimate and snug.

Al Chioschetto

Dorsoduro 1406A, fondamenta delle Zattere (348 396 8466). Vaporetto Zattere. **Open** *June-Sept* 7.30am-2am daily. *Oct-May* 7.30am-6pm daily. No credit cards. **Map** p128 C4 ⓫

A much-loved spot – not only for scrumptious panini and nibbles, but also for the tranquillity of sitting outside by the Giudecca Canal with a sweeping view from the industrial Marghera to Palladian San Giorgio Maggiore. Seating is strictly outside, so take advantage of any sunny day.

Casin dei Nobili

Dorsoduro 2765, sottoportego del Casin dei Nobili (041 241 1841). Vaporetto Ca' Rezzonico. **Meals served** noon-11pm Tue-Sun. **€**. **Map** p128 C3 ⓬

Just off campo San Barnaba, this large pizzeria-restaurant with an artsy-rustic decor and a garden out back

serves up pizzas to a mainly student clientele. There is the usual range of *primi* and *secondi* (€€) on offer as well, but you'll eat better, and more cheaply, if you just stick to the pizza.

Gobbetti

Dorsoduro 3108B, rio terà Canal (041 528 9014). Vaporetto Ca' Rezzonico. **Open** 7am-8pm daily. No credit cards. **Map** p128 C3 ⓭

Gobbetti produces some of Venice's most delicious cakes. The sought-after chocolate mousse is its best-known delight and is snapped up soon after the day's batch is displayed. If you're not after a whole cake, sample a single serving with a coffee.

La Bitta

Dorsoduro 2753A, calle lunga San Barnaba (041 523 0531). Vaporetto Ca' Rezzonico. **Meals served** 6.30-11pm Mon-Sat. Closed Jan; 2wks. No credit cards. **Map** p128 C3 ⓮

Warm and rustic, with a courtyard out back, this restaurant stands out by having virtually no fish on the menu. Veneto mainland dishes like *straccetti di pollo ai finferli* (chicken strips with chanterelle mushrooms) or *oca in umido* (stewed goose) make a welcome change from all that seafood. They also have a good by-the-glass wine choice.

L'Avogaria

Dorsoduro 1629, calle dell'Avogaria (041 296 0491/www.avogaria.com). Vaporetto San Basilio. **Meals served** 12.30-3pm, 7.30pm-midnight Mon, Wed-Sun. Closed 2wks Jan; 2wks Aug. **€€€**. **Map** p128 B3 ⓯

L'Avogaria is neither as pretentious nor as expensive as its cutting-edge appearance might at first suggest. At lunch you can eat a light two-course meal with wine for around €15 a head; the pricier dinner menu is a little more elaborate. The cuisine is *pugliese*, from the heel of Italy. Pasta courses include home-made *cavatelli* pasta with carpet shells and beans, followed by baked lamb and potatoes, or *burrata* (a half-liquid mozzarella) with grilled vegetables.

Race for the Punta

The question of what to do with the huge, decaying 19th-century bonded warehouses on the Punta della Dogana, east of the Salute church, has been open for decades. Nearby neighbour the Peggy Guggenheim Collection tried hard – but unsuccessfully – to expand into the premises at the end of the 20th century. An invitation for tenders to redevelop the Punta was issued in 2006. Even before bids were opened in December of that year, it was clear it was a two-horse race.

In the end, it was French magnate François Pinault – owner of Gucci, Yves Saint Laurent, FNAC, Christie's... and, since 2005, the Palazzo Grassi on the Grand Canal – who had this massive pile revamped by Japanese architect-superstar Tadao Ando; it reopened in 2006 with a show of selected pieces – some Rothkos, Damian Hirst's dissections and a couple of Koons among others – from Pinault's own legendary collection of post-war works.

But also making a strong showing in the race for the Punta was a consortium comprising the Guggenheim Foundation, the Veneto regional council and local impresarios. Responsible for drafting the consortium's makeover plan was Anglo-Iranian architect Zaha Hadid.

As this guide went to press, a final decision had not been taken. So bewildered was the deciding committee, that in January 2007 it even went so far as to suggest that the two bidders might like to share the space; a Pinault aide scoffed at this, saying they needed a space three times that size for the Frenchman's collection alone.

Whoever wins in the end, it's clear that by transforming these neglected warehouses into an exhibition venue, city hall is making the *sestiere* of Dorsoduro into a hub with a concentration of art unequalled anywhere else on the planet. With the Gallerie dell'Accademia, the Peggy Guggenheim Collection, the petite Fondazione Cini and the modern and contemporary selection to be installed at the Punta della Dogana, this quiet, prosperous corner of the lagoon city will become a world-class mecca for art fans.

Pane, Vino e San Daniele p127

coffee is exceptional. On Sundays the place fills up with locals buying sweet offerings to take to lunch.

Shopping

3856

Dorsoduro 3749, calle San Pantalon (041 720 595). Vaporetto San Tomà. **Open** 10am-7.45pm Tue-Sat. **Map** p128 C1/2 ⑱
Popular with fashion-conscious students, 3856 fits a lot into a small space. Jewellery, scarves and bags are tucked in alongside clothes and Georgina Goodman shoes.

Annelie

Dorsoduro 2748, calle lunga San Barnaba (041 520 3277). Vaporetto Ca' Rezzonico. **Open** 9.30am-1pm, 4-7.30pm Mon-Sat. **Map** p128 C3 ⑲
This delightful shop has a beautiful selection of sheets, tablecloths, curtains, shirts and baby clothes, plus antique lace at reasonable prices.

Antichità

Dorsoduro 1195, calle Toletta (041 522 3159). Vaporetto Accademia. **Open** 9.30am-1pm, 3.30-7pm Mon-Sat. No credit cards. **Map** p128 C3 ⑳
Hand-painted antique glass beads can be purchased here – individually or made into jewellery. There's also a good selection of antiques and lace.

Arras

Dorsoduro 3235, campiello Squellini (041 522 6460/www.arrastessuti. com). Vaporetto Ca' Rezzonico. **Open** 9am-1pm, 3.30-7.30pm Mon-Sat. **Map** p128 C2 ㉑
Hand-woven fabrics are created in a vast range of colours using silk, wool and cotton. They are then worked into bags, clothing and scarves. Customised designs can be ordered.

Ca' Macana

Dorsoduro 3172, calle delle Botteghe (041 520 3229/www.camacana.com). Vaporetto Ca' Rezzonico. **Open** 10am-6pm daily. **Map** p128 C3 ㉒
This workshop is packed with trad papier-mâché masks. Explanation of

Oniga

Dorsoduro 2852, campo San Barnaba (041 522 4410/www.oniga.it). Vaporetto Ca' Rezzonico. **Meals served** noon-2.30pm, 7-10.30pm Mon, Wed-Sun. Closed 3wks Jan; 1wk Aug. €€€. **Map** p128 C3 ⑯
With tables outside on bustling campo San Barnaba, Oniga has a friendly, local feel. The menu is Venetian – though Hungarian chef Annika also does an great goulash. The pasta is excellent: try the pumpkin gnocchi with prawns and *broccoletti*, or the spaghetti with veal and chicken ragoût. *Secondi* have a meaty slant. Annika's husband Marino will guide you through the select wine list. At lunchtime, a two-course meal costs €15. By the second dinner sitting (from 8.30pm on), the menu can be reduced as ingredients are used up.

Tonolo

Dorsoduro 3764, calle San Pantalon (041 523 7209). Vaporetto San Tomà. **Open** 7.45am-8pm Tue-Sat; 7.45am-1pm Sun. Closed Aug. No credit cards. **Map** p128 C1 ⑰
This Venice institution has been operating in the same spot, since 1953. The

the mask-making process is enthusiastically given by the artist in residence.

Faggiotto

Dorsoduro 1078, fondamenta Sangiantoffetti (041 241 0386). Vaporetto Accademia. **Open** 10.30am-1.30pm, 2.30-7.30pm Tue-Fri; 9.30am-1pm, 3-7.30pm Sat, Sun. Closed 2wks Aug. **Map** p128 C3 ㉓

Giuseppe Faggiotto's choc delights range from 100% cocoa slabs for fundamentalists, to white-chocolate novelty football boots. In colder weather, the hot chocolate (made following an old recipe using water rather than milk) is a must.

Genninger Studio

Dorsoduro 2793A, calle del Traghetto (041 522 5565/www.genningerstudio. com). Vaporetto Ca' Rezzonico. **Open** 10am-1.30pm, 2.30-7pm Mon-Sat. **Map** p128 C3 ㉔

Leslie Ann Genninger designs the flame-worked and blown jewellery, knick-knacks, lighting and mirrors on offer in this Grand Canal-side shop.

L'Angolo

Dorsoduro 2755, calle lunga San Barnaba (041 277 7895). Vaporetto Ca' Rezzonico. **Open** 10am-12.30pm, 4-7.30pm Mon-Sat. **Map** p128 C3 ㉕

L'Angolo has bags, hats and scarves in rich, colourful fabrics and unique styles. There's also jewellery and a selection of clothing.

Libreria Toletta, Toletta Studio & Toletta Cube

Dorsoduro 1214, calle Toletta (041 523 2034). Vaporetto Accademia. **Open** *Sept-June* 9.30am-7.30pm Mon-Sat; 3.30-7.30pm Sun. *July, Aug* 9.30am-1pm, 3.30-7.30pm Mon-Sat. **Map** p128 C3 ㉖

These three neighbouring stores stock well-priced books ranging from Italian classics, children's books, and art, history and cooking titles to works on architecture in the Studio and photography in Cube.

Madera

Dorsoduro 2762, campo San Barnaba (041 522 4181/www.maderavenezia.it).

Vaporetto Ca' Rezzonico. **Open** 10.30am-1pm, 3.30-7.30pm Tue-Sat. **Map** p128 C3 ㉗

Fusing minimalist design with traditional techniques, the architect and craftswoman behind Madera creates unique objects in wood. She also sells lamps, ceramics, jewellery and textiles by other European artists.

MondoNovo

Dorsoduro 3063, rio terà Canal (041 528 7344/www.mondonovomaschere. it). Vaporetto Ca' Rezzonico. **Open** 10am-6pm Mon-Sat. **Map** p128 C3 ㉘

Venice's best-known *mascheraio* offers an enormous variety of masks, both traditional and modern. His sculptures can be seen at the restored Fenice.

Signor Blum

Dorsoduro 2840, campo San Barnaba (041 522 6367/www.signorblum.com). Vaporetto Ca' Rezzonico. **Open** 10am-7pm daily. **Map** p128 C3 ㉙

Mr Blum's colourful, handmade wooden puzzles of Venetian *palazzi*, gondolas and animals make great gifts for children and adults alike.

Nightlife

Café Blue

Dorsoduro 3778, calle della Scuola (041 710 227). Vaporetto San Tomà. **Open** 8pm-2am daily. **Map** p128 C1 ㉚

This pub-style boozer near campo Santa Margherita is packed with students and an older international set. Homesick Scots can enjoy a wee dram in the Whiskeria, while lounge lovers can chill out to the occasional DJ set.

Café Noir

Dorsoduro 3805, crosera San Pantalon (041 710 925/www.cafenoirvenezia.it). Vaporetto San Tomà. **Open** 8am-2am Mon-Sat; 7pm-2am Sun. No credit cards. **Map** p128 C1 ㉛

Warm, intimate Café Noir is a winter favourite among the university and twentysomething crowd, who can be found whiling away their days over panini and hot chocolate. It livens up later for *spritz* and alcopops.

Expanding Accademia

A diligent trawl through the wonders of Venetian art from the 14th to the 18th centuries displayed in the Gallerie dell'Accademia will leave all but the most dedicated art-craver gasping for breath. But this abundance is only part of the story: clued-in visitors with a consuming passion for grand masters queue patiently on Saturdays and Sundays for a peek at the Accademia's Quadreria – the massive storehouse of masterpieces for which there is no space in the gallery proper.

By late in 2007 – if all goes to plan – many of those hidden gems will take their places on the walls of what will be known as the Grandi Gallerie dell'Accademia (the Great Accademia Galleries). Since 2005, in fact, this enormous art repository has been an obstacle race of builders' clutter, as work goes ahead to double exhibition space to 12,000 square metres (393,700 square feet). But the first crucial step on the way to the new-look gallery was taken two years before that,

when the Scuola delle Belle Arti (fine-arts school) was ousted from these premises where it had been installed by Napoleon in 1807. With the school's departure to the former Ospedale degli Incurabili on the Zattere, great spaces opened up in the Accademia complex – in the former convent of the Lateran canons, a building on which Palladio worked 1551-60; and in the former church of La Carità, an area that will become a venue for temporary exhibitions when work is complete. Also being integrated into the complex is Palladio's gracious inner courtyard, hidden from public view for decades.

The new-look gallery will have a café and a bookshop, and the wheelchair access that is so conspicuously lacking now. Lighting, security, temperature and humidity will be controlled by state-of-the-art technology, and restoration facilities will be expanded and improved. And the walls of the Grandi Gallerie will have 650 works hanging on them, as opposed to the 'mere' 400 on display until now.

Il Caffè

*Dorsoduro 2963, campo Santa
Margherita (041 528 7998). Vaporetto
Ca' Rezzonico.* **Open** 7am-1am Mon-
Sat. No credit cards. **Map** p128 B/C2 ㉜
Whether for its red exterior or for the
political leanings of its clientele, the
campo's oldest bar is universally
known as *Caffè Rosso* (red café).
Relaxed and bohemian, it attracts a
mixed crowd of all ages to sip a *spritz*
in the campo or to choose from the
impressive wine list. Excellent live
music, usually on Thursdays.

Impronta Café

*Dorsoduro 3815, crosera San Pantalon
(041 275 0386). Vaporetto San Tomà.*
Open 7am-2am Mon-Sat. **Closed** 3wks
Aug. **Map** p128 C1/2 ㉝
Modern and minimalist, Impronta is
packed with students until the wee
small hours in winter, and busy
throughout the year with anyone looking for an affordable bite to eat, cool
cocktails, or a night cap.

Orange

NEW *Dorsoduro 3054A, campo Santa
Margherita (041 523 4740). Vaporetto
Ca' Rezzonico.* **Open** 7.30am-2am Mon-
Sat; 5pm-2am Sun. No credit cards.
Map p128 C3 ㉞

Creative cocktails, sleek design and
friendly staff have made this newest
and coolest kid on the *campo* a roaring
success with a hip young locals.

Round Midnight

*Dorsoduro 3102, fondamenta dei
Pugni (041 523 2056). Vaporetto Ca'
Rezzonico.* **Open** midnight-4am Wed-
Sat. Closed July-Sept. **Admission** free.
No credit cards. **Map** p128 C2/3 ㉟
This tiny DJ bar behind campo Santa
Margherita has disco sounds that keep
its minuscule dancefloor busy with
bouncing students.

Arts & leisure

Cristina Gemin Zanchi

*Dorsoduro 3707, campo San Pantalon
(041 528 6154). Vaporetto San Tomà.*
No credit cards. **Map** pp128 C2 ㊱
If your energy channels are blocked
after traipsing up and down bridges all
day, qualified shiatsu practitioner
Cristina Gemin will put you to rights
for another cultural onslaught.

Eastern Dorsoduro

The eastern reaches of Dorsoduro,
between the Accademia and the
Salute, is an area of elegant

VENICE BY AREA

Orange

prosperity, home to many artists and would-be artists, writers and wealthy foreigners.

There's a huge concentration of great art here, from works by Old Masters at the **Gallerie dell'Accademia**, Venice's most important picture gallery, to the modern art extravaganza at the **Peggy Guggenheim Collection**.

On Sunday mornings, campo San Vio becomes some corner of a foreign land, as British expatriates home in on the Anglican church of St George (services 10.30am). Further west, in campiello Barbaro, stands pretty, lopsided Ca' Dario which is rumoured, after a series of sudden deaths of owners over the centuries, to be cursed.

The colossal magnificence of Longhena's church of **Santa Maria della Salute** brings the residential area to an end. Once, you could stroll on past the church to the old Dogana di Mare (Customs House) on the tip of Dorsoduro, but scaffolding and administrative foot-dragging stopped that some

years ago. Now, however, an end to the long-raging debate about redeploying this empty space appears to be at hand (see box p133). Crowning the corner tower of the Dogana, a 17th-century weathercock figure of Fortune perches daintily on top of a golden ball.

At the eastern end of Dorsoduro, the southern Zattere promenade is generally quiet, with the occasional flurry of activity: around the vast 14th-century salt warehouses, now used by rowing clubs; at the grimly-named 16th-century Ospedale degli Incurabili, recently converted to house the Accademia di Belle Arti (fine-arts school); and by the church of **I Gesuati**, where Venetians flock on warm evenings to savour ice-cream or sip drinks at canalside tables.

Sights & museums

Accademia Bridge

Map p129 D3 ③⑦

The first bridge on this spot was built by the Austrian occupiers in 1854.

In 1932 that iron Ponte dell'Accademia was found to be unstable and was replaced by a 'temporary' wooden one. When this was discovered to be on the point of collapse in 1984, the Venetians had grown too fond of it, so it was rebuilt exactly as before.

Galleria Cini

Dorsoduro 864, piscina del Forner (041 521 0755/www.cini.it). Vaporetto Accademia. **Open** *during exhibitions only* 10.30am-1pm, 3-6.30pm Tue-Sun. **Admission** €6.50; €5.50 concessions. No credit cards. **Map** p129 D/E4 ❸❻
This small collection of Ferrarese and Tuscan art was put together by industrialist Vittorio Cini. There are one or two gems, such as the unfinished Pontormo double *Portrait of Two Friends* on the first floor, and Dosso Dossi's *Allegorical Scene* on the second. There is also a 14th-century wedding chest decorated with chivalric scenes.

Gallerie dell'Accademia

Dorsoduro 1050, campo Carità (041 522 2247/www.artive.arti.beni culturali.it). Vaporetto Accademia. **Open** 8.15am-2pm Mon; 8.15am-7.15pm Tue-Sun. **Admission** €6.50; concessions €3.25 (see also p12 State Museums). No credit cards. **Map** p129 D3 ❸❾
The Accademia is one of the world's greatest art treasure houses. Until late 2007 at the very earliest, it is also a building site (see box p136).

The Accademia's collection was made possible by Napoleon, who confiscated art works from hundreds of suppressed churches and convents, and moved the city's fine-arts school here, so that students could learn from these extraordinary examples.

In its current layout, the collection opens with a group of 14th- and 15th-century devotional works by Paolo Veneziano and others – stiff figures against gold backdrops, still firmly in the Byzantine tradition. Rooms 2 and 3 have devotional paintings and altarpieces by Carpaccio, Cima da Conegliano and Giovanni Bellini (a fine *Enthroned Madonna with Six Saints*).

Rooms 4 and 5 have Renaissance gems such as Mantegna's *St George* and Giorgione's mysterious *Tempest*. Three greats of 16th-century Venetian painting – Titian, Tintoretto and Veronese – appear in Room 6. But the battle of the giants gets under way in earnest in Room 10, where Tintoretto's ghostly *Transport of the Body of St Mark* vies for attention with Titian's moving *Pietà* – his last painting – and Veronese's huge *Christ in the House of Levi*. Room 11 has canvases by Tintoretto (the exquisite *Madonna dei Camerlenghi*), Bernardo Strozzi and Tiepolo. The series of rooms beyond brings the plot up to the 18th century, with Canaletto, Guardi, Longhi and soft-focus portraits by female superstar Rosalba Carriera.

Rooms 19 and 20 return to the 15th century; the latter has the *Miracle of the Relic of the Cross* cycle, a collaborative effort by Gentile Bellini, Carpaccio and others, which is packed with telling social details.

An even more satisfying cycle has Room 21 to itself. Carpaccio's *Life of St Ursula* (1490-5) tells the story of the legendary Breton princess who embarked on a pilgrimage to Rome with her betrothed so that he could be baptised into the true faith. All went swimmingly until Ursula and the 11,000 virgins accompanying her were massacred by the Huns in Cologne (the initial 'M' for martyr in one account was mistaken as the Roman numeral for 1,000, causing the multiplication of maidens from 11 to 11,000). More than the legend, it's the architecture, ships and pageantry in these paintings that grab the attention.

In Room 23 are devotional works by Vivarini and the Bellinis. Room 24 contains the only work in the gallery that is in its original site: Titian's *Presentation of the Virgin*.

I Gesuati

Dorsoduro, fondamenta Zattere ai Gesuati (041 275 0462/www. chorusvenezia.org). Vaporetto Gesuati. **Open** 10am-5pm Mon-Sat.

Admission €2.50 (see also p12 Chorus). No credit cards. **Map** p129 D4 ⓴

The official name of this church is Santa Maria del Rosario, but it is always known as the Gesuati, after the order that owned the previous church on the site. It's a great piece of teamwork by a trio of rococo masters: architect Giorgio Massari (he of Palazzo Grassi on the Grand Canal), painter Giambattista Tiepolo and sculptor Giovanni Morlaiter.

The façade has statues with typically 18th-century histrionic flamboyance. Plenty more theatrical sculpture is to be found inside, all by Morlaiter. On the magnificent ceiling by Tiepolo are three frescoes on obscure Dominican themes. Tiepolo also painted the surrounding grisailles, which, at first sight, look like stucco reliefs.

On the first altar on the right is Tiepolo's extravagant *Virgin and Child with Saints Rosa, Catherine and Agnes*. Giovanni Battista Piazzetta's painting of three Dominican saints on the third altar on the right is more sober.

Peggy Guggenheim Collection

Dorsoduro 701, fondamenta Venier dei Leoni (041 520 6288/www. guggenheim-venice.it). Vaporetto Accademia or Salute. **Open** 10am-6pm Mon, Wed-Sun. **Admission** €10; €5-€8 concessions. **Map** p129 D4 ⓳

This remarkable establishment, tucked behind a high wall, was founded by the most colourful of Venice's expat residents, Peggy Guggenheim, who turned up in Venice in 1949 looking for a home for her already sizable art collection. A short-sighted curator at London's Tate Gallery had described her pile of surrealist and modernist works as 'non-art'. Venice was less finicky, and Peggy found a perfect, eccentric base in Palazzo Venier dei Leoni, a truncated 18th-century Grand Canal building.

There are big European names in the collection, including Brancusi, Picasso, Duchamp, Giacometti and Max Ernst, plus a few Americans such as Calder and Jackson Pollock. Highlights include the enigmatic *Empire of Light* by Magritte and Giacometti's disturbing *Woman with Her Throat Cut*. But perhaps the most startling exhibit of all is the rider of Marino Marini's *Angel of the City*, out on the Grand Canal terrace, who thrusts his manhood towards passing *vaporetti*. Another wing has been given over to futurist works.

The gallery also has a charming garden, best surveyed from the terrace of the café-restaurant.

Santa Maria della Salute

Dorsoduro, campo della Salute (041 522 5558). Vaporetto Salute. **Open** 9am-noon, 3-5.30pm daily. **Map** p129 F4 ⓴

This magnificent baroque church queening it over the entrance of the Grand Canal was built between 1631 and 1681 in thanksgiving for the end of Venice's last bout of the plague, which had wiped out at least a third of the population.

The competition called for a church that was colossal but inexpensive; there was to be an unimpeded view of the high altar on entrance; the light was to be evenly distributed; and the whole building should *creare una bella figura* – show itself off to good effect. Baldassarre Longhena, aged 26, succeeded brilliantly in satisfying all these requisites. Longhena said he chose the circular shape with the reverent aim of offering a crown to the Madonna. She stands on the lantern above the cupola. Beneath her, on the great scroll-brackets around the cupola, are statues of the apostles. Inside the church, at the centre of the mosaic floor, amid a circle of roses, is an inscription, *Unde origo inde salus* ('from the origin comes salvation') – a reference to the legendary birth of Venice under the Virgin's protection.

The three chapels on the right have paintings by Luca Giordano, a prolific Neapolitan who brought a little southern brio to the art of the city in the mid-17th century, when most painting had become limply derivative.

On the opposite side is a clumsily restored *Pentecost* by Titian. The high altar has a dynamic sculptural group by Giusto Le Corte, the artist responsible (with assistants) for most of the statues inside and outside the church. This group represents *Venice Kneeling Before the Virgin and Child*, while the plague, in the shape of a hideous old hag, scurries off to the right, prodded by a tough-looking putto. In the midst of all this marble hubbub is a calm Byzantine icon of the *Madonna and Child*, brought from Crete in 1669.

The best paintings – including Tintoretto's *Marriage at Cana* (1551) – are in the sacristy (admission €1.50). On the altar is a very early Titian of *Saints Mark, Sebastian, Roch, Cosmas and Damian*; the painting was created during the plague outbreak of 1509-14. Three later works by Titian are on the ceiling: *The Sacrifice of Abraham, David Killing Goliath* and *Cain and Abel*. These works established the conventions for all subsequent ceiling paintings in Venice; Titian chose an oblique viewpoint, as if observing the action from the bottom of a hill. More Old Testament turbulence can be seen in works by Salviati (*Saul Hurling a Spear at David*) and Palma il Giovane (*Samson and Jonah* – in which the whale is represented mainly by a vast lolling rubbery tongue).

Santa Maria della Visitazione

Dorsoduro, fondamenta Zattere ai Gesuati (041 522 4077). Vaporetto Zattere. **Open** *Apr-Sept* 8am-12.30pm, 2.30-7pm Mon-Sat. *Oct-Mar* 8am-12.30pm, 2.30-6pm Mon-Sat. **Map** p128 C4 **43**

Confusingly, this Church has the same name as the Vivaldi church on the riva degli Schiavoni – though the latter is usually known as La Pietà. Designed by Tullio Lombardo or Mauro Codussi and built in 1423, has an attractive early Renaissance façade. All that remains after Napoleonic looting is the original coffered ceiling, its 58 compartments adorned with portraits of

Santa Maria della Salute

saints and prophets by a painter of Luca Signorelli's school, one of the few examples of central Italian art in Venice. To the right of the façade is a lion's mouth for secret denunciations.

Eating & drinking

Ai Gondolieri

Dorsoduro 336, fondamenta Ospedaletto (041 528 6396/www.ai gondolieri.com). Vaporetto Accademia or Salute. **Meals served** noon-3pm, 7-10pm Mon, Wed-Sun. €€€€. **Map** p129 E4 **44**

If you're looking to splash out, Ai Gondolieri offers a creative menu that belies its ultra-traditional decor. Unusually for Venice, it's fish-free. The attractively presented dishes include a warm salad of venison with blueberries; *panzerotti* (pasta parcels) filled with Jerusalem artichokes in Montasio cheese sauce; and rack of lamb with

Barolo and radicchio. Truffles invade the menu in autumn (be sure to ask about the price before you order).

Da Gino

Dorsoduro 853A, calle Nuova Sant' Agnese (041 528 5276). Vaporetto Accademia. **Open** 6am-7.30pm Mon-Sat. Closed Aug; 2wks Dec-Jan. No credit cards. **Map** p129 D4 ⓸⑧

You'll always be greeted with a smile by the Scarpa family, whether it's your first visit or your 100th to this delightful bar. Tables outside along the *calle* make excellent viewpoints for watching the flow of gallery-goers between the Accademia and the Guggenheim Collection. Gino's serves some of the best made-to-order panini around.

Gelateria Lo Squero

Dorsoduro 989-990, fondamenta Nani (347 269 7921). Vaporetto Accademia or Zattere. **Open** 11am-9pm daily. No credit cards. **Map** p128 C4 ⓸⑥

Simone Sambo makes of some of the finest ice-cream in Venice. His changing repertoire is determined by the freshest ingredients available. His mousse series is marvellously light and creamy.

Il Cantinone (già Schiavi)

Dorsoduro 992, fondamenta Nani (041 523 0034). Vaporetto Accademia or Zattere. **Open** 8am-8.30pm Mon-Sat; 9am-1pm Sun. Closed 1wk Aug. No credit cards. **Map** p128 C4 ⓸⑦

Two generations of the Gastaldi family work here, filling glasses, carting cases of wine, and preparing huge panini with mortadella or more delicate crostini with creamy tuna spread with leeks or parmesan and figs. When the bar is full, you'll be in good company on the steps of the bridge outside.

Shopping

Cartoleria Accademia

Dorsoduro 1044, campiello Calbo (041 520 7086). Vaporetto Accademia. **Open** *Sept-July* 8am-1pm, 3.30-7pm Mon-Fri; 8am-1pm Sat. *Aug* 9am-1pm Mon-Sat. No credit cards. **Map** p129 D4 ⓸⑨

This small but well-stocked store behind the Accademia, carries a wide range of artists' supplies. In business since 1810, it must be doing something right. **Other locations**: Dorsoduro 2928, campo Santa Margherita (041 528 5283).

Il Pavone

Dorsoduro 721, fondamenta Venier dei Leoni (041 523 4517). Vaporetto Accademia. **Open** 9.30am-1.30pm, 2.30-6.30pm daily. **Map** p129 E4 ⓸⑨

Il Pavone stocks handmade paper with floral motifs in a variety of colours, plus picture frames, key chains and other quality products at decent prices.

Le Forcole di Saverio Pastor

Dorsoduro 341, fondamenta Soranzo de la Fornace (041 522 5699/www.forcole.com). Vaporetto Salute. **Open** 8.30am-12.30pm, 2-6pm Mon-Fri. **Map** p129 E4 ⑤⓿

This is the place to come when you need a new *forcola* (rowlock) or pair of oars for your gondola. Saverio Pastor is one of only three recognised *marangon* (oar-makers) in Venice. Non-rowing visitors may be more interested in the postcards, and books (in English) on Venetian boat-making.

Marina & Susanna Sent

Dorsoduro 669, campo san Vio (041 520 8136). Vaporetto Accademia. **Open** 10am-6pm daily. **Map** p129 D4 ⑤①

Venice's best contemporary glass jewellery is created by the Sent sisters. There's also a good selection from the design house Arcade.

Nightlife

Piccolo Mondo

Dorsoduro 1056, calle Contarini-Corfù (041 520 0371). Vaporetto Accademia. **Open** 10.30pm-4am daily. **Map** p129 D3 ⑤②

This 'small world' is one of the few places to dance in Venice proper. On its dancefloor you'll find ageing medallion men, lost tourists and foreign students so desperate to dance, they'll dance anywhere.

Molino Stucky p144

La Giudecca & San Giorgio

Immediately south of Venice 'proper', and divided from it by the Giudecca canal and the bacino di San Marco, the islands of San Giorgio and La Giudecca are quite different in feel. The former is dominated by its church and monastery, and the erudition of the Fondazione Cini headquartered there. While La Giudecca has a more artsy feel, with a creative community that mixes happily with the workers from the boatyards on the southern side of the island.

La Giudecca

This gondola-shaped island, the honorary seventh *sestiere*, has a strong character all of its own.

Some claim that the name 'Giudecca' derives from an early community of Jews; others point to the fact that the island was a place of exile for troublesome nobles, who had been *giudicati*, judged.

In fact, many people chose to exile themselves in what was, until not so long ago, a rural retreat. Michelangelo moped here when he was banished from Florence in 1529. Three centuries later, during his torrid love affair with George Sand, Alfred de Musset wrote in praise of the meadows of 'la Zuecca'.

During the 19th century the city authorities made use of the numerous abandoned convents and monasteries, converting them into factories and prisons. Two prisons

Industrial splendour

From mill wheels to conference halls

You can't miss the Molino Stucky. Built in 1896, this turreted, crenellated neo-Gothic brick pile, designed by Ernest Wullekopf, was (and remains) the largest building on the lagoon, and it milled an impressive 125 tons of flour a day.

By the 1920s the business, founded by Italo-Swiss industrialist Giovanni Stucky, was in decline; in 1955 the mill closed its doors definitely. Thereafter this Teutonic eyesore impressed only by its desolation, an oppressive reminder of the city's industrial torpor.

It wasn't until the 1990s that a solution was presented for the Stucky. The Acqua Marcia company began work on the old mill in 2002. In its reborn form, the mill is to include a luxurious 308-room hotel – managed by the Hilton International group – smart apartments and conference facilities for 2,000. A rooftop pool will compete with a rooftop restaurant for the title of cushiest place from which to enjoy sweeping lagoon views.

It's all a far cry, of course, from the industry that brought the Stucky family its fortune. But then again, that's Venice all over: a victim of its own unique beauty, La Serenissima's only hope for survival is as a conference centre to the world.
- www.hilton.com
- www.acquamarcia.it

(one for drug offenders, the other for women) are still operating.

Some factories remain abandoned. A few have been converted into new residential complexes. The most conspicuous one, the massive **Molino Stucky** (see box), is due to open as a luxury hotel in spring 2007.

With their splendid views across to San Marco, the *palazzi* along the northern *fondamenta* attract well-heeled outsiders: Elton John and Giorgio Armani have holiday homes here. Venice's most expensive hotel, the Cipriani, stands at the eastern end.

The main sights of the Giudecca are all on this *fondamenta*: **Santa Eufemia**, and the Palladian churches of Le Zitelle ('the spinsters': the convent ran a hospice where poor girls were trained as lace-makers; the church is nearly always closed) and **Il Redentore**.

Near Le Zitelle is the neo-Gothic Casa De Maria. The Bolognese painter Mario De Maria built it for himself from 1910 to 1913. Its patterned brickwork mirrors that of the Doge's Palace across the way.

On the fondamenta Rio della Croce (No.149, close to the Redentore) stands Palazzo Munster, once an infirmary for English sailors.

On the southern side of the island is Parco Savorgnan – a small public garden with benches looking out over the islands. Take calle San Giacomo, turn left along calle degli Orti, then right; it's at the end.

Sights & museums

Il Redentore

Giudecca, campo del Redentore (041 275 0462/www.chorusvenezia.org). Vaporetto Redentore. **Open** 10am-5pm Mon-Sat. **Admission** €2.50. No credit cards. **Map** p146 B2 ❶

Il Redentore ('the redeemer') was built to celebrate deliverance from plague in 1575-7. Architect Andrea Palladio designed an eye-catching building with a prominent dome that appears to rise directly behind the Greek-temple façade. The solemn, harmonious interior has a single nave lit by large 'thermal' windows. The austere Capuchin monks to whom the building was entrusted were not pleased by its grandeur; so Palladio mollified them by designing very plain choir stalls. The best paintings are in the sacristy (rarely open); they include a *Virgin and Child* by Alvise Vivarini and a *Baptism* by Veronese.

Santa Eufemia

Giudecca, fondamenta Santa Eufemia (041 522 5848). Vaporetto Santa Eufemia. **Open** 8am-noon, 3-5pm Mon-Sat; 3-7pm Sun. **Map** p145 C2 ②
This church has a 16th-century Doric portico along its flank (currently *in restauro*). Inside, the nave and aisles are essentially 11th century, with Veneto-Byzantine columns and capitals, while the decoration consists mainly of 18th-century stucco and

paintings. Over the first altar on the right is *St Roch and an Angel* by Bartolomeo Vivarini (1480; being restored as this guide went to press).

Eating & drinking

Alla Palanca

Giudecca 448, fondamenta del Ponte Piccolo (041 528 7719). Vaporetto Palanca. **Open** 7am-8.30pm Mon-Sat. **Meals served** noon-2.30pm Mon-Sat. €€. No credit cards. **Map** p146 A2 ③
One of the cheapest meals with a view in Venice is on offer at this friendly bar-trattoria on the main Giudecca quay. It's a lunch-only place – the rest of the day it operates as a bar. Sit at one of the outside tables and order from a good-value menu that includes some surprisingly gourmet options like swordfish in an orange and lemon marinade.

Harry's Dolci

Giudecca 773, fondamenta San Biagio (041 522 4844/www.cipriani.com).

Vaporetto Sant'Eufemia. **Meals served** *Apr-Oct* noon-3pm, 7-10.30pm Mon, Wed-Sun. *Bar*-pasticceria 10.30am-11pm. Closed Nov-Mar. €€€€. **Map** p145 C1 ④

Arrigo Cipriani's second Venetian stronghold (his first is Harry's Bar) is open only when the weather allows outdoor diners to enjoy the stupendous views across the Giudecca Canal. The cuisine is supposedly lighter than *chez* Harry, but in fact many dishes are identical. But prices at Harry II are less than two-thirds of those at the mother ship (though that's still a big dent in the average wallet). Outside of mealtimes you can order a coffee and a delectable pastry at the bar-*pasticceria*.

Mistrà

Giudecca 212A, fondamenta del Ponte Lungo (041 522 0743). Vaporetto Palanca or Redentore. **Meals served** noon-3.30pm Mon; noon-3.30pm, 7.30-10.30pm Wed-Sun. Closed 3wks Jan; 3wks Aug. €€€. **Map** p146 A3 ⑤

The unvisited southern side of the Giudecca conceals one of the city's most unlikely gourmet treats. Amid boatyards, a fire-escape staircase leads up to this trat on the first floor of a warehouse with marvellous views over the southern lagoon. Mistrà has become a word-of-mouth success among local foodies for its excellent fish menu (octopus and potato salad, or baked fish with potatoes, cherry tomatoes and olives) and range of Ligurian specialities; they also do good steaks. Lunch is cheap and worker-oriented, dinner more ambitious and expensive.

Shopping

Fortuny Tessuti Artistici

Giudecca 805, fondamenta San Biagio (041 522 4078). Vaporetto Palanca. **Open** 9am-noon, 2-5pm Mon-Fri. **Map** p145 B1 ⑥

This pared-back factory showroom space glows with the exquisite colours and patterns of original Fortuny prints.

1 La Giudecca & San Giorgio 2

© Copyright Time Out Group 2007

At an across-the-board price of €300 a metre, you may not be tempted to buy, but it's worth the trip just to see it.

Arts & leisure

Centro Zitelle Culturale Multimediale CZ95

NEW *Giudecca 95, sottoportego della Croce (041 528 9833/www.cz95.org). Vaporetto Zitelle.* **Open** 5.30-11pm Mon-Sat. **Admission** free. No credit cards. **Map** p147 D2 **❼**

This cultural centre behind the youth hostel has a media library and internet point. It hosts exhibitions, film projections, live music (usually jazz) and the occasional party.

Teatro Junghans

NEW *Giudecca 494, campo Junghans (041 241 1974/www.teatrojunghans.it). Vaporetto Palanca.* **Open** *Box office* 1hr before performances. *Performances* 8.30pm, days vary. No credit cards. **Map** p146 A2 **❽**

Opened in 2005 in what was once a storehouse for World War II bomb fuses, Venice's newest theatre is an intimate venue that hosts dance and experimental drama productions, as well as puppet shows.

Isola di San Giorgio

The island of San Giorgio realised its true potential under architect extraordinaire Andrea Palladio, whose church of **San Giorgio Maggiore** is one of Venice's most recognisable landmarks. Known in the early days of the city as the *Isola dei Cipressi* (Cypress Island), it soon became an important Benedictine monastery and centre of learning – a tradition that is carried on today by the **Fondazione Giorgio Cini**, which runs an artistic and musical research centre and craft school in the monastery's buildings.

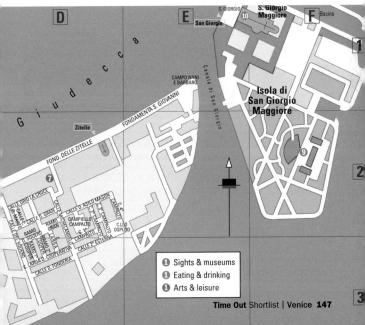

❶ Sights & museums
❶ Eating & drinking
❶ Arts & leisure

San Giorgio Maggiore

Sights & museums

Fondazione Giorgio Cini & Benedictine Monastery

(041 524 0119/www.cini.it). Vaporetto
San Giorgio. **Open** Monastery 10am-
4.30pm, with guided tours
every hour. **Admission** €12; €10
concessions. No credit cards.
Map p147 F2 ⑨

There has been a Benedictine monastery
on this island since 982. The city authorities often used the island as a luxury
hotel for prestigious visitors, such as
Cosimo de' Medici in 1433. Cosimo had
a magnificent library built here; it was
destroyed in 1614, to make way for a
more elaborate affair by Longhena (now
open only to bona fide scholars).

In 1800 the island hosted the conclave
that elected Pope Pius VII, after the car-
dinals had been expelled from Rome by
Napoleon. In 1806 the French got their
own back, suppressing the monastery
and sending its chief artistic treasure –
Veronese's *Marriage Feast at Cana* –
off to the Louvre, where it still hangs.
For the rest of the century, the
monastery served as a barracks.

In 1951, industrialist Vittorio Cini
bought the island. The Fondazione
Giorgio Cini uses the monastery buildings for its artistic and musical
research. A portion of the complex was
given back to the Benedictines.

The monastery has two beautiful
cloisters – one by Giovanni Buora
(1516-40), the other by Palladio (1579);
an elegant library and staircase by
Longhena (1641-53); and a magnificent
refectory by Palladio (1561). The tour
includes the monastery's garden.

San Giorgio Maggiore

041 522 7827. Vaporetto San Giorgio.
Open 9.30am-12.30pm, 2.30-6pm Mon-
Sat; 2-6.30pm Sun. **Admission** Church
free. *Campanile* €3, concessions €2.
No credit cards. **Map** p147 E1 ⑩

This unique spot cried out for an architectural masterpiece, and Andrea
Palladio provided it. In what was his
first solo church, he developed the system of superimposed temple fronts
with which he had experimented in the
façade of San Francesco della Vigna.

Over the first altar is an *Adoration of
the Shepherds* by Jacopo Bassano, with
startling lighting effects. The altar to
the right of the high altar has a
Madonna and Child with Nine Saints
by Sebastiano Ricci.

On the side walls of the chancel hang
two vast compositions by Tintoretto, a
Last Supper and the *Gathering of
Manna*. Tintoretto combines almost
surreal visionary effects (angels
swirling out from a lamp's eddying
smoke) with touches of domestic realism (a cat prying into a basket, a
woman stooping over her laundry).
Tintoretto's last painting, a moving
Entombment, hangs in the Cappella dei
Morti (often closed); the artist has been
identified as the bearded man gazing
at Christ's face. In the left transept is a
painting by Jacopo and Domenico
Tintoretto of the *Martyrdom of St
Stephen*, above an altar containing the
saint's remains.

En route from the left transept to the
campanile stands the huge statue of an
angel that crowned the bell tower until
it was struck by lightning in 1993. To
the left of the statue, a corridor leads to
the lift up to the bell tower. The view
from the top is extraordinary.

Busa alla Torre p158

Lido & Lagoon

Venice lies more or less in the centre of a salt-water lagoon, protected from the open sea by the two slender barriers of the Lido and Pellestrina. While other Italian towns defended themselves with monumental bastions and circling walls, Venice relied on her lagoon for protection.

Over the centuries Venetians have devoted their energies to strengthening these natural defences. In the 18th century the *murazzi* were created – a barrier of great blocks of stone and marble all the way down the seafront. Nowadays, the threat is seen as coming from the three *bocche di porto* (the lagoon's openings to the sea) between the Lido and Cavallino, the Lido and Pellestrina, and Pellestrina and Chioggia. Work has started on creating the highly controversial mobile dyke system known as MOSE.

Venice is by no means the only island (or island-cluster) in the lagoon. There are 34 islands, most of them uninhabited, containing only crumbling masonry, home to seagulls and lazy lizards. The lagoon itself covers some 520 square kilometres (200 square miles) – the world's biggest wetland.

It's in this wild, fragile environment that Venetians take refuge from the tourist hordes, escaping by boat for picnics on deserted islands, or fishing for bass and bream. Others set off to dig up clams at low tide, or organise hunting expeditions for duck. Many just head out after work, at sunset, to row.

Head above water

'Venice sinking!' makes great headlines, but the news is rather stale. Ever since mainlanders fleeing barbarian hordes hid out here in the fifth century, the inhabitants of this inhospitable wetland have been engaged in a battle for survival against the tides.

The two main weapons in their armoury have been protective sea walls at the *bocche di porto* – the openings between the lagoon and the Adriatic – and raising the street level in Venice proper when high tides encroached too far too often.

But in more recent decades – and especially since the early 20th-century development of the Mestre-Marghera industrial hub on the mainland – the good work of some has been stymied by the disastrous actions of many others. Aside from the immense quantities of serious pollutants sluiced into the lagoon by short-sighted manufacturers, the exponential growth of these mainland settlements has lowered the water table dramatically, making subsidence a major problem. Sludge dredged from the lagoon bottom has been used to create new land masses in the lagoon (Sant'Elena, Tronchetto, Sacca Fisola) and historical flood basins have been filled, meaning that water flowing into the lagoon simply has less space to occupy – except, of course, the deep-water channels hacked through the lagoon in 1952 and 1969 to allow deep-hulled vessels such as liners and tankers to dock here, but these merely encourage a greater volume of water to enter the lagoon. Given all this – plus the fact that the world's seas are all rising at an alarming rate – it's rather amazing that this doughty old lady of the sea has survived until now.

Initiatives to keep Venice afloat include the patient – and largely unsung – canal-dredging and pavement-raising of Insula (www.insula.it). And, of course, there is the much noisier MOSE: the idea of building mobile dams – pontoons that lie on the sea bed at the *bocche* but can be pumped full of air to raise them to block incoming high tides – was first floated in the 1980s, to a chorus of protest from environmentalists who predicted further damage to this fragile ecosystem. Since then, it has been a stop-go process, but with astronomic sums already spent on research and prototypes, it's now doubtful whether they can afford *not* to go ahead with it.

The Lido

The Lido is the northernmost of the two strips of land that separate the lagoon from the open sea. It is no longer the playground for wealthy aesthetes that fans of *Death in Venice* might come in search of. These days Venice-by-the-sea is a placidly residential suburb, complete with supermarkets and cars, where pale young boys in sailor-suits are in very short supply.

Things perk up in summer, when buses are full of city sunbathers and tourists staying in the Lido's overspill hotels. But the days of all-night partying and gambling are long gone. In January 2001 the Lido Casinò closed. Now the only moment when the place stirs to anything like its former vivacity is at the beginning of September, when the film festival rolls into town with its bandwagon of stars, directors, PR people and sleep-deprived, caffeine-driven journalists.

The Lido has few tourist sights. Only the church of San Nicolò (opening times vary) – founded in 1044 – on the riviera San Nicolò can claim any great antiquity. Inside is the tomb of Nicola Giustiniani, a Benedictine monk who was forced to leave holy orders in 1172 to assure the future of his illustrious family, of which he was the sole heir. He married the doge's daughter, had lots of kids, then went back to being a monk. After his death he was beatified for his spirit of self-sacrifice.

Fans of art nouveau and deco have plenty to look at on the Lido. On the Gran Viale there are two gems: the tiled façade of the Hungaria Hotel (No.28), with its Beardsley-esque nymphs; and Villa Monplaisir at No.14, from 1906. For full-blown turn-of-the-century exotica, though, it's hard to beat the Hotel Excelsior on lungomare Marconi, a neo-Moorish party piece, complete with minaret.

Getting around

The main Santa Maria Elisabetta stop on the Lido is served by frequent boats from Venice and the mainland. The San Nicolò stop to the north is served by the No.17 car ferry from Tronchetto.

Bus routes are confusing but cover the whole island fairly well, including the popular Alberoni beach at the southern tip of the island. Bike is a good way of getting around the pancake-flat Lido; there are a number of bike-hire outlets along the Gran Viale.

Tourist information

There's a tourist information office at Gran Viale 6A (041 526 5721/fax 041 529 8720), open June-Sept 9.30am-1pm, 3-6.30pm daily.

La Favorita p152

Eating & drinking

La Favorita

Via Francesco Duodo 33, Lido (041 526 1626). Vaporetto Lido. **Meals served** 7.30-10.30pm Tue; 12.30-2.30pm, 7.30-10.30pm Wed-Sun. Closed Jan. **€€€**.

This is the best restaurant on the Lido, and has a lovely vine-shaded pergola. It's an old-fashioned, reassuring sort of place that does textbook exemplars of Venetian seafood. Service is professional, and the wine list has a fine selection from the north-east.

The northern lagoon

San Michele

Halfway between Venice and Murano, San Michele is the city's cemetery (open Apr-Sept 7.30am-6pm daily, Oct-Mar 7.30am-4pm daily). It's not a morbid spot, but an elegant city of the dead, with more than one famous resident – Ezra Pound, Sergei Diaghilev, Igor Stravinsky, Joseph Brodsky, to name but a few.

Burano lace p153

The island was originally just a Franciscan monastery, but during the Napoleonic period the grounds were seconded for burials to stop unhygienic Venetians digging graves in the *campi* around parish churches.

Venice's first Renaissance church, **San Michele in Isola** (open 7.30am-12.15pm, 3-4pm daily) was designed by Mauro Codussi in the 1460s. Turn left after the entrance to the cemetery and pass through the fine cloisters. Next to the church is a dignified archway marked by a 15th-century bas-relief of St Michael slaying a dragon with one hand and holding a pair of scales in the other. In the cloisters, staff hand out maps of the cemetery, which are indispensable for celebrity hunts.

Murano

After San Michele, the number 41 or 42 vaporetto continues to Murano (lines LN and 13 also stop here, but only at the Faro stop). In the 16th and 17th centuries, when it was a world centre of glass production and a decadent resort for pleasure-seeking Venetians, Murano had a population of more than 30,000. Now fewer than 5,000 people live here. Many of the glass-workers commute from the mainland.

In 1291, glass furnaces were transferred here because of fear of fire in the city centre. The secrets of glass were jealously guarded: any glass-maker leaving Murano was proclaimed a traitor. Even today, there is no official glass school, and the delicate skills of blowing and flame work are only learned by apprenticeship.

At first sight Murano looks close to being ruined by glass tourism. Dozens of 'guides' swoop on visitors as they pile off the ferry, to whisk them off on tours of furnaces.

Fondamenta dei Vetrai is a snipers' alley of shops selling glass knick-knacks, most of which are made far from Murano. But there *are* some serious glass-makers on the island, and even the tackiest showroom usually has one or two gems.

There's more to Murano, however, than glass. The 14th-century parish church of **San Pietro Martire** holds important works of art, the **Museo dell'Arte Vetraria** inside 17th-century Palazzo Giustinian is the best place to learn about the history of glass, while the 12th-century basilica of **Santi Maria e Donato** is an architectural jewel.

Burano & Mazzorbo

Mazzorbo, the long island before Burano, is a haven of peace, rarely visited by tourists. The view across the lagoon to Venice from the long wooden bridge that connects Mazzorbo to Burano is stunning.

Mazzorbo is a lazy place of small farms with a pleasant walk to the 14th-century Gothic church of Santa Caterina (opening times vary), whose wobbly looking tower still has its original bell dating from 1318 – one of the oldest in Europe.

The adjective 'picturesque' might have been invented to describe **Burano**, famed for its lace and its multicoloured houses. The street leading from the main quay throbs with souvenir shops selling lace, lace and more lace – much of it machine-made in the Far East.

Lace was first produced in Burano in the 15th century, originally by nuns, but then by fishermen's wives and daughters. So skilful were the local lace-makers that in the 17th century many were paid handsomely to work in the Alençon lace ateliers in Normandy. Today most work is done on commission, though interested parties will have to get

to know one of the lace-makers in person, as the co-operative that used to represent the old ladies closed down in 1995.

Fishing is the island's other mainstay: fishermen have lived here since the seventh century. According to local lore, they painted their houses different colours so that they could recognise them when fishing out on the lagoon – though, in fact, only a tiny proportion of the island's houses can be seen from the lagoon.

The busy main square of Burano is a good place for sipping a glass of *prosecco*. Across from the **Scuola dei Merletti** lace museum is the church of San Martino (open 8am-noon, 3-7pm daily), containing an early Tiepolo *Crucifixion* and three small paintings by the 15th-century painter Giovanni Mansueti; the *Flight into Egypt* presents the Holy Family amid an imaginative menagerie of beasts and birds. There's a lively morning fish market (Tue-Sat) on the fondamenta della Pescheria.

San Francesco del Deserto

From behind the church of San Martino on Burano there is a view across the lagoon to the idyllic monastery island of San Franceso del Deserto (041 528 6863, www.isola-sanfrancescodeldeserto.it, open 9-11am, 3-5pm Tue-Sat; 3-5pm Sun). The island, with its 4,000 cypress trees, is inhabited by a small community of Franciscan monks. Getting there can be a challenge. Expect to pay at least €50 for a water taxi from Burano. Local fishermen are usually willing to ferry tourists across for around €25 for the return trip. HelloVenezia offices (p181) can arrange tours.

The monk who shepherds visitors around will tell how the island was St Francis's first stop

VENICE BY AREA

Museo dell'Estuario p154

in Europe on his journey back from the Holy Land in 1220. He planted his stick, it grew into a pine tree and birds flew in to sing for him.

Torcello

Torcello is a sprawling, marshy rural backwater with a resident population of less than 20. It's hard to believe that in the 14th century more than 20,000 people lived here. This was the first settlement in the lagoon, founded in the fifth century by the citizens of Altino on the mainland, driven here in waves by Barbarian invasions – first by Attila and his Huns, then in the seventh century, by the Lombards. But Torcello's dominance of the lagoon did not last: Venice itself was found to be more salubrious (malaria was rife on Torcello) and more easily defendable. But past decline is present charm, and rural Torcello is a great antidote to the pedestrian traffic jams around San Marco.

From the ferry jetty, the **campanile** can already be made out; to get there, follow the main canal through the island. Halfway along is the ponte del Diavolo, one of only two ancient bridges in the lagoon without a parapet.

Torcello's main square has some souvenir stalls, a small but interesting **Museo dell'Estuario**, a battered stone seat known rather arbitrarily as Attila's throne, and two extraordinary churches.

The 11th-century church of Santa Fosca (open Apr-Oct 10.30am-5.30pm daily, Nov-Mar 10am-5pm daily, free) is more Byzantine than European with its Greek-cross plan and external colonnade; its bare interior allows the perfect geometry of the space to come to the fore. Next door is the imposing cathedral of **Santa Maria Assunta**. A combination ticket for the basilica, campanile and the Museo dell'Estuario is available at the sights themselves and costs €8 (€5.50 groups) or €5.50 (€3 groups). No credit cards are accepted.

The ferry (line T) from Burano to Torcello leaves every half hour during the day; the crossing takes five minutes.

Sant'Erasmo & Vignola

Sant'Erasmo (served by vaporetto 13) is the best-kept secret of the lagoon: it is larger than Venice itself, but with a tiny population that grows most of the vegetables eaten in *La Serenissima* – on Rialto market stalls, the sign '*San Rasmo*' is a mark of quality. Venetians refer to the islanders of Sant'Erasmo as *i matti* ('the crazies') because of their legendarily shallow gene pool. The islanders don't think much of the Venetians either. The island lacks a policeman, a doctor, a pharmacy and a high school, but there is a supermarket, a primary school and two restaurants: Ca' Vignotto (via Forti 71, 041 528 5329, €€, closed Tue and mid Dec-mid Jan), where bookings are essential, and a fishermen's bar-trattoria called Ai Tedeschi (open 9am-11pm daily) on a beach by the Forte Massimiliano. This moat-surrounded Austrian fort occasionally hosts exhibitions by local painters.

The main attraction of the island lies in the beautiful country landscapes and lovely walks past traditional Veneto farmhouses, through vineyards and fields of artichokes and asparagus. Bicycles can be hired from the guesthouse Lato Azzurro (041 523 0642), a ten-minute walk southwards from the vaporetto stop Capannone.

By the main vaporetto stop (Chiesa) is a 20th-century church, on the site of an earlier one founded before 1000 (opening hours vary). Hanging above the entrance door is a gruesome painting, attributed to Domenico Tintoretto, of the martyrdom of St Erasmus, who had his intestines wound out of his body on a windlass. The resemblance of a windlass to a capstan resulted in St Erasmus becoming the patron saint of sailors.

Opposite the Capannone vaporetto stop is the tiny island of Lazzaretto Nuovo. Get off here at the weekend, shout across, and with luck a boat might row over to get you. In the 15th century the island was fortified as a customs deposit and military prison; during the 1576 plague outbreak, it became a quarantine centre. More recently, it has become a research centre for the Archeo Club di Venezia, which is excavating its ancient remains, including a church that may date back to the sixth century.

The number 13 vaporetto also stops at the smaller island of Vignole, where there is a medieval chapel dedicated to St Erosia.

Sights & museums

Campanile di Torcello

Torcello (041 730 119). **Open** *Apr-Oct* 10.30am-5pm daily. *Nov-Mar* 10am-4.15pm daily. **Admission** €3. No credit cards.
The view of the lagoon from the campanile is quite breathtaking, as is the climb up steep ramps (there's no lift) to the top.

Museo dell'Arte Vetraria

Fondamenta Giustinian 8, Murano (041 739 586). Vaporetto Museo.

Torcello's wild abandon p154

Open *Apr-Oct* 10am-5pm Mon, Tue,
Thur-Sun. *Nov-Mar* 10am-4pm Mon,
Tue, Thur-Sun. **Admission** €4; €2.50
concessions (see also p12 Musei Civici
Veneziani). No credit cards.

Housed in the late 17th-century Palazzo
Giustinian, the museum has a huge collection of Murano glass. As well as the
famed chandeliers, there are ruby-red
beakers, opaque lamps and delicate
Venetian *perle* – glass beads that were
used in trade and commerce all over
the world. One of the earliest pieces is
the 15th-century Barovier marriage
cup. In one room is a collection of 17th-
century oil lamps in the shapes of
animals, some of which are uncannily
Disney-like.

Museo dell'Estuario

*Palazzo del Consiglio, Torcello (041 730
761).* **Open** *Apr-Oct* 10.30am-5pm Tue-
Sun. *Nov-Mar* 10am-4.30pm Tue-Sun.
Admission €3. No credit cards.

A small collection of sculptures and
archaeological finds from the cathedral and other sites in Torcello.
Among the exhibits on the ground
floor are late 12th-century fragments
of mosaic from the apse of Santa Maria
Assunta. Upstairs you'll find Graeco-
Byzantine icons, painted panels and
pottery fragments, as well as an
exquisite carved ivory statuette of an
embracing couple from the beginning
of the 15th century.

San Pietro Martire

*Fondamenta dei Vetrai, Murano
(041 739 704). Vaporetto Colonna
or Faro.* **Open** 9am-noon, 3-6pm Mon-
Sat; 3-6pm Sun.

Behind its unspectacular façade, San
Pietro Martire conceals an important
work by Giovanni Bellini, backed by
a marvellous landscape: *The Virgin
and Child Enthroned with St Mark,
St Augustine and Doge Agostino
Barbarigo*. There is also a Tintoretto
Baptism, two works by Veronese and
assistants (mainly the latter) and an
ornate altarpiece (*Deposition*) by
Salviati. The sacristy (€1.50) contains
remarkable wood carvings from the
17th century and a small museum.

Santa Maria Assunta

Torcello (041 270 2464). **Open** *Apr-
Oct* 10.30am-5.30pm daily. *Nov-Mar*
10am-4.30pm daily. **Admission** €3
(€1 for audioguide). No credit cards.

Dating from 638, this basilica is the
oldest building on the lagoon. The
interior has an elaborate 11th-century
mosaic floor. But the main draws of
this church are the vivid mosaics on the
vault and walls, which range in date
from the ninth century to the end of the
12th. The apse has a simple but stunning mosaic of a *Madonna and Child*
on a plain gold background, while
the other end of the cathedral is dominated by a huge mosaic of the *Last
Judgement* (a good audioguide in
English gives a detailed explanation).

Santi Maria e Donato

*Campo San Donato, Murano (041 739
056). Vaporetto Museo.* **Open** 8.30am-
noon, 4-6pm Mon-Sat; 4-6pm Sun.

Though altered by overenthusiastic
19th-century restorers, the exterior of
this church is a classic of the Veneto-
Byzantine style, with an ornate blind
portico on the rear of the apse. Inside
is a richly coloured mosaic floor, laid
down in 1140 at the same time as the
floor of the Basilica di San Marco.
Above, a Byzantine apse mosaic of the
Virgin looms out of the darkness in a
field of gold.

Scuola di Merletti

*Piazza B Galuppi, Burano 187 (041
730 034). Vaporetto LN.* **Open** *Apr-
Oct* 10am-5pm Mon, Wed-Sun. *Nov-
Mar* 10am-4pm Mon, Wed-Sun.
Admission €4; €2.50 concessions
(see also p12 Musei Civici Veneziani).
No credit cards.

In a series of rooms are cases full of
elaborate examples of lace work from
the 17th century onwards; aficionados
will have fun spotting the various
stitches, such as the famous *punto burano*. Many of the older exhibits change
every few months for conservation reasons. There are fans, collars, parasols
and paper pattern-sheets. Unfortunately,
the school that gives the museum its
name is now virtually defunct.

Celluloid rivalry

For a few days at the end of August 2006, things almost got nasty. On the eve of the first Venice film festival since Rome's announcement of a rival cinema extravaganza – to be held less than two months later, in mid October – festival director Marco Müller was quoted by a RAI news reporter as saying 'the Rome festival is being put together out of Venice's cast-offs'.

Müller later claimed that he had never actually used the word 'cast-offs' (*scarti*) – what he'd really said was 'the films Venice doesn't want.' For some reason, this new version still didn't go down too well back in Rome, where festival supremo Giorgio Gosetti and chief programmer Mario Sesti reacted angrily, calling Müller's statement 'an incredible offence to cinema'.

The spat was soon patched up, and the two festivals put their films where their mouths were. When the dust had settled on the Rome fest, it was clear that Müller's unguarded statement contained more than a grain of truth. Though Rome managed to attract some muscular red-carpet films and stars, from Nicole Kidman to Leonardo di Caprio, these five or six big out-of-competition titles acted as a smokescreen for a competition selection (always the litmus test of a film festival) that was decidedly minor league.

But with the same level of funding as its northern cousin, it can only be a matter of time before Rome stops shopping at the Venice reject store and gets some nice new clothes of its own… at which time Venice can begin to get worried.

Rossana e Rossana p159

Eating & drinking

Antica Trattoria Valmarana
Fondamenta Navagero 31, Murano (041 739 313). Vaporetto Navagero. **Meals served** noon-3pm daily. Closed 3wks Jan. €€€.

With its Murano chandeliers and stuccoed interior, this is a good lunch option. The kitchen does refined versions of seafood classics like *risotto alla pescatora*, as well as more creative fare. Grilled fish star among the *secondi*, but there are also a number of meat and vegetarian dishes. In summer, there are two alfresco options: outside by the canal, or in the quiet garden out the back. They also do bar snacks.

Busa alla Torre
Campo Santo Stefano 3, Murano (041 739 662). Vaporetto Faro. **Meals served** noon-3.30pm daily. €€€.

This is a perfect place for refuelling after resisting the hard sell at the island's glass workshops. In summer, tables spill out on to a pretty square. The service is professional; the cuisine is reliable, no-frills seafood cooking. The jovial owner, Lele, is a giant of a man and a real character. Note the lunch-only opening.

Locanda Cipriani
Piazza Santa Fosca 29, Torcello (041 730 150/www.locandacipriani.com). Vaporetto LN to Torcello. **Meals served** noon-3pm, 7-9pm Mon, Wed-Sun. Closed Jan. €€€€.

There is a lot to like about the high-class Locanda Cipriani, which was a haunt of Hemingway. The setting is idyllic, with tables spread over a vine-shaded terrace. And although there is nothing especially adventurous about the food, it's good in an old-fashioned way. Specialities such as *risotto alla torcellana* (with seasonal vegetables) or *filetti di San Pietro alla Carlina* (John Dory fillets with capers and tomatoes) are done to perfection, and the desserts are tasty treats.

Shopping

Alfredo Barbini
Fondamenta Venier 44-48, Murano (041 739 270). Vaporetto Venier. **Open** 8am-noon, 2-6pm Mon-Fri; by appointment Sat, Sun.

If you're lucky, you'll find master glass-maker Alfredo (he's in his 90s) holding court in this showroom, where many of his classic designs are still on show, alongside more modern ones by his son Flavio.

Berengo Fine Arts
Fondamenta dei Vetrai 109A, Murano (041 739 453/www.berengo.com). Vaporetto Colonna or Faro. **Open** 10am-5.50pm daily.

Adriano Berengo commissions international artists to design brilliantly coloured scuptures in glass.

VENICE BY AREA

Cesare Toffolo

Fondamenta dei Vetrai 67A, Murano (041 736 460/www.toffolo.com). Vaporetto Colonna. **Open** 10am-6pm daily. Closed Jan.

Cesare Toffolo uses glass sticks and a gas flame to create miniatures of Venetian classic designs: cups, vases and even chandeliers.

Davide Penso

Shop and workshop: riva Longa 48, Murano; gallery: riva Longa 4 (041 527 4634/www.artstudiomurano.com). Vaporetto Museo. **Open** 9.30am-1.30pm, 2.30-5.30pm daily. Closed Jan.

Davide Penso makes and shows exquisite glass work. He uses simple, clean lines, and is often inspired by ethnic jewellery.

Fratelli Barbini

Calle Bertolini 36, Murano (041 739 777). Vaporetto Colonna or Faro. **Open** 8am-6pm Mon-Fri.

There's only one *fratello* (brother), Guido, left now to carry on his family craft: mirror-making. In this workshop he silvers, engraves and mounts them.

Luigi Camozzo

Fondamenta Venier 3, Murano (041 736 875). Vaporetto Museo or Venier. **Open** 10am-6pm Mon-Fri; by appointment Sat, Sun.

Luigi Camozzo carves, sculpts and inscribes wonderfully soft, natural bas-reliefs into glass.

Manin 56

Fondamenta Manin 56, Murano (041 527 5392). Vaporetto Colonna or Faro. **Open** 10am-6pm daily. Closed Jan.

This shop sells modern (though staid) lines in glassware and vases from prestigious houses.

Marina e Susanna Sent

Fondamenta Serenella 20, Murano (041 527 4665). Vaporetto Colonna. **Open** 10am-5pm Mon-Fri.

The Sent sisters create modern glass jewellery in interesting counterpoise with innovative pieces in other materials. It's always best to call ahead and make an appointment.

Murano Collezioni

Fondamenta Manin 1C/D, Murano (041 736 272). Vaporetto Colonna or Faro. **Open** 10.30am-5.30pm Mon-Sat. Closed 1wk Jan.

This shop sells pieces by some of the lagoon's most respected producers, including Carlo Moretti, Barovier e Toso, and Venini.

Rossana e Rossana

Riva Lunga 11, Murano (041 527 4076/www.ro-e-ro.com). Vaporetto Museo. **Open** 10am-6pm daily.

Traditional Venetian glass, from fili-gree pieces to models popular in the early years of last century, by master glass-maker Davide Fuin.

Seguso Viro

Fondamenta Venier 29, Murano (041 527 5353/www.segusoviro.com). Vaporetto Venier or Museo. **Open** *May-Oct* 10.30am-5.30pm Mon-Sat. *Nov-Apr* 11am-4pm Mon-Sat.

Giampaolo Seguso comes from a long line of Venetian glass-makers. His blown-glass collections experiment with Murano traditions.

Venini

Fondamenta dei Vetrai 47-50, Murano (041 273 7204/www.venini.com). Vaporetto Colonna. **Open** 9.30am-5.30pm Mon-Sat. Closed 2wks Aug.

Venini was *the* biggest name in Murano glass for much of the 20th century. Classic designs are joined by some more innovative pieces.

The southern lagoon

The lagoon south of Venice has 14 small islands, a few of which are still inhabited, though most are out of bounds to tourists.

La Grazia was for years a quarantine hospital, but the structure has now been closed. Huge **San Clemente**, originally a lunatic asylum and later a home for stray cats, has been turned into one of the lagoon's plushest hotels.

San Servolo and **San Lazzaro** are both served by vaporetto 20 and well worth visiting. From the 18th century until 1978, San Servolo was Venice's mental hospital; it is now home to Venice International University. In May 2006 the **Museo del Manicomio di San Servolo** (San Servolo Asylum Museum) was inaugurated and can be visited on a guided tour. The museum reveals the different ways in which mental diseases have been treated over the years; there are not only examples of the more or less brutal methods of restraint (chains, strait-jackets, handcuffs), but early examples of such treatment as hydromassage and electrotherapy. The tour ends in the reconstructed 18th-century pharmacy, which relied partly on medicines obtained from some of the exotic plants grown on the island. After the tour, you can visit the island's extensive, charming gardens.

A further five minutes on the number 20 will take you to the island of **San Lazzaro degli Armeni**, where there are guided tours every afternoon for visitors arriving on the 3.10pm boat from San Zaccaria.

Originally a leper colony, in 1717 the island was presented by the doge to an Armenian abbot called Mekhitar. There had been an Armenian community in Venice since the 11th century, centring on the tiny Santa Croce degli Armeni church, just round the corner from piazza San Marco, but the construction of this church made Venice a world centre of Armenian culture; it's still a global point of reference for Armenia's Catholic minority. The monastery was the only one in the whole of Venice to be spared the Napoleonic axe that did away with so many other religious establishments: the emperor had a soft spot for Armenians and claimed this was an academic, rather than a religious institute.

A black-cloaked Armenian priest meets the boat and leads visitors around the **Monastero Mechitarista**. Near the entrance stand the printing presses that helped to distribute Armenian literature all over the world for 200 years. Sadly, they are now silent, with the monastery's charmingly retro line in dictionaries and school and liturgical texts farmed out to a modern press.

The tour takes in the cloisters and the church, rebuilt after a fire in 1883. The museum and the modern library contain 40,000 priceless books and manuscripts, and a bizarre collection of gifts donated over the years by visiting Armenians, ranging from Burmese prayer books to an Egyptian mummy.

The island's most famous student was Lord Byron, who used to take a pause from his more earthly pleasures in Venice and row over three times a week to learn Armenian (as he found that his 'mind wanted something craggy to break upon') with the monks. He helped the monks to publish an Armenian-English grammar, although by his own confession he never got beyond the basics of the language. You can buy a completed version of this, plus a number of period maps and an illustrated children's Armenian grammar, in the shop just inside the monastery gate.

Sights & museums

San Lazzaro degli Armeni – Monastero Mechitarista

041 526 0104. **Open** 3.30-5pm daily for guided visits. **Admission** €6; €3 concessions. No credit cards.

San Servolo – Museo del Manicomio

NEW *041 524 0119.* **Open** weekends for guided visits; booking essential. **Admission** free.

Essentials

La Calcina p177

Hotels

After several years of post-9/11, post-recession slump, tourism in *La Serenissima* is thriving once again. Every year, over three million visitors spend at least one night in Venice.

The city has always been well supplied with places to stay in all categories. But just when you thought that Venice had reached hotel saturation point, 2005/2006 saw a spate of openings, ranging from high-profile hotels supplying lashings of luxury to charming guesthouses offering value for money and personal service.

Particularly significant over the past few years has been the increase in small hotels, guesthouses and B&Bs.

One constant is the fact that, in *La Serenissima*, a bargain is a relative concept, and prices remain as high as – indeed, often higher than – than anywhere else in Italy.

Location

Choosing your location carefully will enhance your enjoyment of the city.

Plush hotels are centred around St Mark's square and the riva degli Schiavoni, but so is the camera-touting tourist action. If you want a quieter setting without sacrificing creature comforts, make for the other side of the Grand Canal where, in the *sestieri* of Dorsoduro, Santa Croce and San Polo, chic little hideaways are springing up for those who are looking for style without grandeur.

What to expect

Price category and star rating reflect a hotel's facilities rather than its character, so it's difficult to judge a place on paper. Also remember that mod cons don't necessarily go hand in hand with Venetian magic.

For a city with no cars, Venice is surprisingly noisy; echoes bouncing off the walls of narrow *calli* can be very loud if the alley happens to be an important thoroughfare. Light sleepers should request a room out back.

Any kind of watery vista will push up the price of your room. You might be offered a room with a view of a canal, but this covers a multitude of sins: check just how much of a view it is before paying a huge surcharge.

By and large, most hotels will exchange currency (at an unfavourable rate) and, for an extra charge, organise babysitting, laundry and dry-cleaning. Expect to pay an extra 20 to 40 per cent on top of the room price for a baby cot or extra bed.

Facilities for the disabled are shamefully lacking in Venetian hotels, though this is partly due to the nature of the buildings. A surprising number of smaller establishments do not have lifts.

Italy's anti-smoking legislation means that you cannot smoke in any public space unless it has the legally required ventilation and special doors. This includes hotel rooms: you can smoke only in officially designated bedrooms. The majority of hotels have simply banned smoking altogether.

Breakfast is usually included in the price of the room; if it's not, head to the local bar or *pasticceria*.

Last-minute options

It's never a good idea to turn up in Venice without a pre-booked hotel room. However, if this should happen, staff at AVA (Venetian Hoteliers Association) bureaux at the railway station, piazzale

ESSENTIALS

B&B ai bareteri

price and quality

1 block from san marco's square

unique style

great comfort

spacious rooms

a nice breakfast

Roma or the airport will help you find somewhere to stay.

The cheaper hotels in the area around the station will often have rooms – though they may not be the cleanest. Then there's always Mestre on the mainland – by no means a bad bet if you're travelling by car; hotels are usually cheaper here, and it's a ten-minute hop across to Venice by train or bus. But it very definitely isn't Venice.

For last-minute bookings from home, AVA has an online booking service at www.veniceinfo.it. On the www.venicehotel.com site is a large directory of hotels, B&Bs and campsites that can be booked online.

Cutting costs

The best way to cut hotel costs in Venice is to visit off season (August; November to Carnevale with the exception of Christmas and New Year). Check hotel websites for special midweek offers.

For extended stays, renting an apartment will often work out to be cheaper. Check websites www.viewsonvenice.com and www.veniceapartment.com if you fancy a more residential approach to the city.

Our choice

The hotels listed below have been selected for their location, value for money or simply because they are great places to stay.

Those in the deluxe category (€€€€) feature opulence, multifarious facilities and utter luxury; a standard double in high season is likely to set you back anywhere from €400 and up. Those in the middle and upper price ranges (€€-€€€) will be smaller, often housed in lovely old palazzi and will, on the whole, offer more character but fewer services. Expect to pay between €120 and €250 for a moderately priced hotel,

and anywhere from €250 to €400 for an expensive room. Budget and low-cost hotels (€-€€) will cost up to €120 per night and may or may not include breakfast and a private bathroom in the room rate. Unless otherwise stated, rates quoted are for rooms with bathrooms and include breakfast.

San Marco

Bauer, Il Palazzo & Casa Nova

San Marco 1459, campo San Moisè (041 520 7022/fax 041 520 7557/ www.bauerhotels.com). Vaporetto Giglio. €€€€.

The Bauer offers several accommodation options, all of them luxurious. Choose between the main hotel, which occupies an ugly 1940s building on campo San Moisè; the more opulent, antique style of the adjacent Il Palazzo (the classiest choice, in our opinion); or the service apartments at Casa Nova, ideal if you want a bit of independence. Or whizz across the lagoon to the Giudecca and Il Palladio, the Bauer's newly inaugurated hotel and spa housed in an ex-church complex.

Casa de' Uscoli

San Marco 2818, campo Pisani (041 241 0669/fax 041 241 9659/ www.casadeuscoli.com). Vaporetto Accademia or Giglio. €€.

Two of the bedrooms in Casa de' Uscoli, the eclectic home of Spanish nobleman and classical-music buff Alejandro Suarez Diaz de Bethencourt, have the added appeal of overlooking the Grand Canal. The palazzo is grand in size but laid-back in atmosphere and attracts a suitably arty crowd. Slightly faded antiques rub shoulders with huge contemporary pieces and quirky modern art.

Do Pozzi

San Marco 2373, via XXII Marzo (041 520 7855/fax 041 522 9413/ www.hoteldopozzi.it). Vaporetto Giglio. €€.

ESSENTIALS

Locanda del Ghetto p173

A homely, friendly hotel in a very central location, the Do Pozzi is appealing in spite of some rather cramped rooms and tiny bathrooms. Located down a little alleyway and off the main tourist track, it fronts on to a lovely courtyard where guests can eat breakfast or relax with a book.

Flora

San Marco 2283A, calle Bergamaschi (041 520 5844/fax 041 522 8217/ www.hotelflora.it. Vaporetto Vallaresso. €€.

Book well in advance if you want to stay at the perennially popular Flora. Situated at the bottom of a cul-de-sac near piazza San Marco and complete with a charming garden, it offers a dreamy, tranquil stay and very helpful staff. The bedrooms vary significantly from the quite opulent to the relatively spartan and some are tiny. The decor is classic, olde-worlde Venetian.

Gritti Palace

San Marco 2467, campo Santa Maria del Giglio (041 794 611/fax 041 520

0942/www.luxurycollection.com/gritti palace). Vaporetto Giglio. €€€€.

A studied air of old-world charm and nobility pervades this 15th-century palazzo, former home of Doge Andrea Gritti. Refined and opulent, each room is uniquely decorated. If you want a canal or *campo* view, specify when booking: disappointingly, some rooms overlook a dingy courtyard. Guests can use the Starwood Group's sports facilities on the Lido. An *aperitivo* on the vast canal terrace is a must.

Hotel Monaco & Grand Canal

San Marco 1332, calle Vallaresso (041 520 0211/fax 041 520 0501/www.hotel monaco.it). Vaporetto Vallaresso. €€€€.

This Benetton-owned Grand Canal hotel is a curious hybrid. The lobby and bar area are a fussy mix of classic and modern, while the rooms in the main building are untouched by the design revolution. More charmants are the ethnic-Mediterranean rooms in the Palazzo Selvadego residence. Even if you are not staying here, pop in for a look at the extraordinary 17th-century Teatro Ridotto, Venice's first gambling hall.

Locanda Art Deco

San Marco 2966, calle delle Botteghe (041 277 0558/fax 041 270 2891/ www.locandaartdeco.com). Vaporetto San Samuele or Sant'Angelo. €€.

This friendly little hotel is situated off campo Santo Stefano on a busy street that is lined with antiques shops. The simple but stylish bedrooms are dotted with original pieces of 1930s and '40s furniture and other deco details. There's a tiny breakfast area on a mezzanine floor.

Locanda Fiorita

San Marco 3457, campiello Nuovo (041 523 4754/fax 041 522 0843/www. locandafiorita.com). Vaporetto Sant'Angelo. €€.

This cosy, family-run hotel has a pretty, vine-covered entrance and nine smartly refurbished rooms (two with bathrooms in the corridor) with beamed ceilings. The reception area and breakfast room have been smartened up and enlarged, and a nearby annexe houses more upmarket (and pricier) rooms.

Locanda Novecento

San Marco 2683-2684, calle del Dose (041 241 3765/fax 041 521 2145/ www.novecento.biz). Vaporetto Giglio. €€.

It's a real pleasure to return to this cosy home-from-home after a hard day's sightseeing, especially when it's warm enough to chill out in the delightful little garden. Friendly, helpful staff, ethnic textiles and Indonesian furniture in the sitting rooms and highly individual bedrooms combine with mellow background sounds to make this a very special place to stay.

Locanda Orseolo

San Marco 1083, corte Zorzi (041 520 4827/fax 041 523 5586/www.locanda orseolo.com). Vaporetto Rialto or Vallaresso. €€.

Palazzo Abadessa p173

This hard-to-find *locanda* is an old Venetian house in miniature, with beamed ceilings and painted wood panelling. An exceptionally generous breakfast is served in the dinky ground-floor breakfast room, while upstairs, the bedrooms are immaculate. The young staff are unfailingly helpful.

Luna Hotel Baglioni

San Marco 1243, calle larga dell' Ascensione (041 528 9840/fax 041 528 7160/www.baglionihotels.com). Vaporetto Vallaresso. €€€€.

Little period decor remains to suggest this hotel's 15th-century origins. Kilometres of shiny marble, swathes of rich fabric and lots of Murano glass provide the backdrop for luxurious bedrooms and communal areas. Views from the rooms are of the Giardinetti Reali, the lagoon and San Giorgio Maggiore.

Palazzo Sant'Angelo sul Canal Grande

San Marco 3878B, fondamenta del Teatro a Sant'Angelo (041 241 1452/ fax 041 241 1557/www.palazzosant angelo.com). Vaporetto Sant'Angelo. €€€€.

Palazzo Sant'Angelo may be rather lacking in soul, but it boasts a stunning Grand Canal location and luxurious red and gold bedrooms, all with whirlpool baths. Even if you are not up for the hefty canal-view supplement, you can watch the gondolas drift by from the ground-floor sitting room and bar area.

San Samuele

San Marco 3358, salizada San Samuele (tel/fax 041 522 8045/www.albergo sansamuele.it). Vaporetto San Samuele or Sant'Angelo. €.

This friendly little hotel has recently been given a lick of paint and general smarten up; the spotlessly clean rooms have a simple, sunny aspect, and you will get a warm welcome. The San Samuele offers great prices and an excellent central location, but several rooms have bathrooms in the corridor. No breakfast is served.

ESSENTIALS

Saturnia & International

San Marco 2398, via XXII Marzo (041 520 8377/fax 041 520 7131/ www.hotelsaturnia.it). Vaporetto Vallaresso. €€€.

An old-fashioned, friendly atmosphere pervades this bustling hotel, which is housed in a 14th-century building. The majority of bedrooms are done out in fairly traditional Venetian style, but five have been given a more contemporary makeover in the retro style of Ca' Pisani (under the same ownership; p176). There's a pleasant roof terrace.

Castello

B&B San Marco

Castello 3385L, fondamenta San Giorgio degli Schiavoni (041 522 7589/ 335 756 6555/www.realvenice.it/ smarco). Vaporetto San Zaccaria. €.

Marco Scurati's homely B&B lies just behind San Giorgio degli Schiavoni. Three cosy, antiques-filled bedrooms share a bathroom; there's also an apartment that sleeps four. Self-service breakfast is taken in Marco's own kitchen, and guests are treated as part of the family.

Ca' dei Conti

Castello 4429, fondamenta del Remedio (041 277 0500/fax 041 277 0727/ www.cadeiconti.com). Vaporetto San Zaccaria. €€€.

In a historic palazzo situated on a quiet canal between Santa Maria Formosa and San Marco, this small, elegant hotel has all the comforts you'd expect from a four-star place. The rooms are tastefully decorated in Venetian style, with particular attention paid to fabrics. There's a wonderful little terrace from which to survey the surrounding rooftops too.

Ca' del Dose

Castello 3801, calle del Dose (tel/fax 041 520 9887/www.cadeldose.com). Vaporetto Arsenale or San Zaccaria. €.

This friendly guesthouse just off the busy riva degli Schiavoni has simple,
stylish rooms on three floors. Book ahead for the one at the top with its own little roof terrace; there is no extra charge. In the morning, the wherewithal for a simple breakfast is supplied in the rooms.

Casa Fontana

Castello 4701, campo San Provolo (041 522 0579/fax 041 523 1040/ www.hotelfontana.it). Vaporetto San Zaccaria. €€.

It's all very well being in the thick of things, but it's a relief to leave the confusion of campo San Provolo behind you and enter this family-run hotel with its rather olde-worlde decor. Some rooms at the top have a view over the Romanesque campanile of San Zaccaria.

Casa Linger

Castello 3541, salizada Sant'Antonin (041 528 5920/fax 041 528 4851/ www.hotelcasalinger.com). Vaporetto Arsenale. €.

A steep, narrow flight of stairs leads up to this unassuming little hotel with a clutch of spacious and airy bedrooms. The bathrooms have recently been refurbished, though four rooms are still not en suite. It's a bit of a hike from the nearest vaporetto stop, and rates don't include breakfast.

Casa per Ferie

Castello 3701, calle della Pietà (041 244 3639/fax 041 241 1561/ www.pietavenezia.org). Vaporetto San Zaccaria. €.

The building that houses this clean, bright hostel is part of the sprawling Pietà complex, where Antonio Vivaldi once taught. It is spacious, sunny and spotlessly clean, with around 40 beds, mostly in multi-bedded rooms. The bathrooms are all shared. The hostel is at the top of the building, so there are some great views.

Casa Querini

Castello 4388, campo San Giovanni Novo (041 241 1294/fax 041 241 4231/www.locandaquerini.com). Vaporetto San Zaccaria. €€.

Beautiful B&Bs

B&B San Marco p168

The major low-cost competition for Venice's traditional – and traditionally exorbitant – hotels comes in the form of B&Bs, of which there are now over 200 in the city. These range from simple, yet clean rooms in relatively modern apartments to sumptuous spreads in glorious antiques-filled *palazzi*.

Prices reflect position and facilities. Some rooms can be quite spartan, so check when booking whether, for example, your room has a bathroom. Technically speaking, a B&B can have no more than three guest bedrooms, and there must be at least one bathroom exclusively for guests' use. Anything larger than this officially falls into another category, but many larger places call themselves B&Bs anyway, simply because it's cool.

As well as the establishments included in our main listings (B&B San Marco, Casa de' Uscoli, Palazzo dal Carlo), a couple of other places caught our eye.

Ca' Miani (San Marco 2865, calle del Frutarol, 041 241 1868) was one of Venice's very first B&Bs and surely the only accommodation option where you can get an in-house hairdo (Pascal, the French owner, is a hairdresser).

The prize for Venice's most unusual B&B experience goes to Boat & Breakfast, a lovely 1930s yawl called *Shaula* that is moored on the southern side of the Giudecca (Giudecca 212A, 335 666 6241, www.realvenice.it/shaula). There are three double berths, and cruises around the lagoon, complete with on-board meals, can be arranged.

The APT tourist office (p187) has a complete list of B&Bs in Venice. Alternatively, check out the excellent www.bed-and-breakfast.it website, which covers the whole of Italy region by region.

ESSENTIALS

Imagine...

Your next event in
Venice's Newest Landmark

Aromi Restaurant and Terrace

The upscale yet intimate **Aromi Restaurant** offers you the opportunity
to experience Executive Chef Franco Luise's signature dishes based on
fresh local ingredients and accompanied by a great selection of
Italian wines.
The outdoor **terrace**, open in good weather, enriches your dining
experience with enchanted views across the Giudecca Canal to Zattere.

Opening hours
Lunch	12:30am to 3pm	A la carte menu
Dinner	7pm to 11pm	A la carte menu

Adjacent to our signature restaurant, the **Aromi Bar** will delight you with
an exclusive range of martinis, cocktails, fruit juices and speciality
coffees, in a luxurious, yet relaxed atmosphere.

Opening hours
11am to midnight

TAKE ME TO THE HILTON
For the best rates, visit **hilton.com**

Hilton
Molino Stucky, Venice

Venice Pre-opening Office
Giudecca, 753 -30133 Venezia
Tel./Fax 041 522 1267
info.venice@hilton.com

Other Hiltons in Italy: Hilton Milan +39 02 69831 • Hilton Florence Metropole • +39 055 78711 • Rome Cavalieri Hilton +39 06 35091 • Hilton Rome Airport
+39 06 65258 • Hilton Sorrento Palace +39 081 8784141 • Hilton Nova Yardinia +39 099 8204901 • Villa Igiea Hilton Palermo +39 091 6312111
Coming soon: Hilton Portorosa • Des Palmes Hilton Palermo • Excelsior Hilton Palermo

This friendly hotel has a pretty little terrace area shaded by big umbrellas on a quiet *campo* that lies between bustling campo Santa Maria Formosa and St Mark's. The six comfortable bedrooms all are spacious; try and secure one with a view of the square.

Casa Verardo
Castello 4765, calle della Sacrestia (041 528 6138/fax 041 523 2765/ www.casaverardo.it). Vaporetto San Zaccaria. €€.

Tucked away at the end of a narrow calle a few minutes from piazza San Marco, Casa Verardo exudes cool and calm. Rooms are comfortable 'traditional' Venetian. There is a pretty courtyard at the back of the building and another terrace off the elegant salon where tables are laid for breakfast.

Danieli
Castello 4196, riva degli Schiavoni (041 522 6480/fax 041 520 0208/www.star woodhotels.com/italy). Vaporetto San Zaccaria. €€€€.

Take a twirl through the wonderful old revolving door of this Venetian classic to gawp at the magnificent Gothic reception hall. The Danieli is split between a 1940s building and the more atmospheric 14th-century Palazzo Dandolo. Rooms are sumptuous, but some are quite small and looking a trifle frayed around the edges. Views from the roof-top restaurant are spectacular. Guests can use the Starwood Group's sports facilities and beach on the Lido.

La Residenza
Castello 3608, campo Bandiera e Moro (041 528 5315/fax 041 523 8859/ www.venicelaresidenza.com). Vaporetto Arsenale. €€.

Offering great value for money and occupying two floors of a grand, if rather faded, Gothic palazzo, La Residenza lies on a quiet *campo* and possesses a genteel old-fashioned air, especially in the vast salon where breakfast is served. The bedrooms have all been pleasantly (although blandly) refurbished.

Locanda La Corte
Castello 6317, calle Bressana (041 241 1300/fax 041 241 5982/www. locandalacorte.it). Vaporetto Fondamente Nove. €€.

Housed within a small 16th-century palazzo down the side of the church of Santi Giovanni e Paolo, La Corte is far from the noisy tourist trails. Bedrooms are decorated in restful greens, and there is a lovely little courtyard for breakfast and *aperitivi*.

Londra Palace
Castello 4171, riva degli Schiavoni (041 520 0533/fax 041 522 5032/ www.hotelondra.it). Vaporetto San Zaccaria. €€€€.

No fewer than 100 of this hotel's bedroom windows face the Palladio's church of San Giorgio Maggiore across the lagoon. Today, the Londra Palace is elegant but restrained, offering traditional-style rooms furnished with antiques and paintings. It was here that Tchaikovsky wrote his fourth symphony in 1877

Metropole
Castello 4149, riva degli Schiavoni (041 520 5044/fax 041 522 3679/ www.hotelmetropole.com). Vaporetto San Zaccaria. €€€.

Of all the grand hotels that crowd this part of the *riva*, the Metropole is arguably the most characterful. The owner is a passionate collector; his antiques and curios are dotted throughout the sumptuous public spaces and the elegant, varied bedrooms (which come with lagoon views for a hefty supplement). In winter, tea is served in the red velvet-draped *salone*, while in summer, guests take refuge in the gorgeous, peaceful garden.

Palazzo Soderini
Castello 3611, campo Bandiera e Moro (041 296 0823/fax 041 241 7989/ www.palazzosoderini.it). Vaporetto Arsenale. €€.

Standing on the same charming *campo* as La Residenza (see above), Palazzo Soderini's blinding white minimalism represents the ultimate relief from

Oltre il Giardino p175

Venetian glitz, if you like that kind of thing. Its biggest asset is the delightful walled garden complete with lily pond and a pretty patio area where alfresco breakfasts are served.

Savoia & Jolanda
Castello 4187, riva degli Schiavoni (041 520 6644/041 522 4130/fax 041 520 7494/www.hotelsavoiajolanda.com). Vaporetto San Zaccaria. €€€.
A hotel of two different – but equally lovely – halves, the Savoia offers rooms with views across the watery expanse of the Bacino di San Marco in one direction, or facing back towards the glorious façade of San Zaccaria in the other. The decor manages to be pleasantly luxurious without going over the top.

Cannaregio

Ca' Dogaressa
Cannaregio 1018, calle del Sotoportego Scuro (041 275 9441/fax 041 275 7771/www.cadogaressa.com). Vaporetto Guglie or Tre Archi. €€.

This friendly, family-run hotel overlooking the Cannaregio canal offers a squeaky-clean modern take on 'traditional' Venetian decor, with modern marble bathrooms, very comfortable beds and air-con. Breakfast is served on the canalside on fine days, and there is also a roof terrace with wonderful open views.

Eden
Cannaregio 2357, campiello Volto Santo (041 524 4003/fax 041 720 228/www.htleden.com). Vaporetto San Marcuola. €€.
Situated on a tiny campiello just off busy rio terà della Maddalena, the Eden offers a genuinely friendly welcome, quiet and pretty rooms, and good value for money. One double has a (private) bathroom in the corridor. There is a cheerful breakfast room, but you can order breakfast in your room free of charge.

Locanda ai Santi Apostoli
Cannaregio 4391A, strada Nuova (041 521 2612/fax 041 521 2611/www. locandasantiapostoli.com). Vaporetto Ca' d'Oro. €€.

A pair of handsome dark green doors leads through the courtyard of this palazzo (situated on the Grand Canal). Once on the third floor, the atmosphere is discreet and understated; it feels like an elegant private apartment. The two best bedrooms look over the Canal and are a relative bargain. Overlooking the water, the comfortable sitting room is filled with antiques, books and magazines.

Locanda del Ghetto

Cannaregio 2892-2893, campo del Ghetto Nuovo (041 275 9292/fax 041 275 7987/www.locandadelghetto.net). Vaporetto Guglie or San Marcuola. €€.
Situated on the quiet, rather melancholy campo del Ghetto Nuovo, this stylish guesthouse occupies a 15th-century building; several of the light and airy bedrooms have original decorated wooden ceilings, and two have small terraces on the *campo*. The small ground-floor breakfast room overlooks the canal.

Palazzo Abadessa

Cannaregio 4011, calle Priuli (041 241 3784/fax 041 521 2236/www.abadessa. com). Vaporetto Ca' d'Oro. €€.
A beautiful, shady walled garden is laid out in front of this privately owned 16th-century palazzo, which is filled with family antiques, paintings and silver. A magnificent double stone staircase leads to the 12 impressive rooms, some of which are truly vast. Beware, however; the low-ceilinged doubles on the mezzanine floor are rather cramped.

Rossi

Cannaregio 262, calle delle Procuratie (041 715 164/fax 041 717 784/ www.hotelrossi.ve.it). Vaporetto Ferrovia. €.
Located at the end of a quiet alley, this very reasonable one-star hotel is quite a find for the area around the railway station, which is, as a rule, best avoided. The basic rooms are acceptably clean, and all have air-con. New bathrooms have been added recently; only four rooms are now without.

San Polo & Santa Croce

Ai Due Fanali

Santa Croce 946, campo San Simeon Grande (041 718 490/fax 041 244 8721/www.aiduefanali.com). Vaporetto Riva di Biasio. €€.
Housed in what was once the annexe of the church of San Simeon Grande next door, this hotel has a smart little terrace at the front where tables are set out under big white umbrellas. The 16 bedrooms are quite small but have good, modern bathrooms. Views from the top floor breakfast room and altana (terrace) are stunning.

Al Ponte Mocenigo

Santa Croce 2063, fondamenta Rimpetto Mocenigo (041 524 4797/fax 041 275 9420/www.alpontemocenigo. com). Vaporetto San Stae. €€.
Located on a quiet canal near San Stae, this delightful little hotel has to be one of Venice's best-value accommodation options. It boasts tastefully decorated mod-Venetian rooms and good bathrooms, and there's a pretty courtyard garden. The genuinely charming owners manage to be warm and laid-back in just the right proportions.

Casa Peron

Santa Croce 84, salizada San Pantalon (041 710 021/fax 041 711 038/ www.casaperon.com). Vaporetto San Tomà. €.
Casa Peron is a simple, clean, family-run hotel located in the bustling university area, near campo Santa Margherita. Two rooms at the top of the house have the benefit of private terraces; all have showers, though three are without toilets. All in all, an excellent budget choice.

Falier

Santa Croce 130, salizada San Pantalon (041 710 882/fax 041 520 6554/www.hotelfalier.com). Vaporetto Piazzale Roma or San Tomà. €€.
This smart little two-star place is well located, just ten minutes' walk from

Time Out
Travel Guides

Worldwide

All our guides are
written by a team of
local experts with a
unique and stylish
insider perspective.
We offer essential tips,
trusted advice and
honest reviews for
everything you need
to know in the city.

Over 50 destinations
available at all good
bookshops and at
timeout.com/shop

the station. The Venetian-style rooms are surprisingly upmarket considering the reasonable price; those on the second floor are newer. There is a comfy sitting area in the reception hall and a cosily beamed breakfast room.

La Villeggiatura

San Polo 1569, calle dei Botteri (338 853 1264/tel/fax 041 524 4673/www. lavilleggiatura.it). Vaporetto Rialto or San Silvestro.

A rather scruffy entrance and a steep climb will take you up to this guesthouse with its six spacious, beautifully decorated bedrooms. Thai silks, old parquet floors, electric kettles and interesting bathroom goodies all feature, while breakfast is served round a big table in the sunny dining area.

Locanda Sturion

San Polo 679, calle dello Sturion (041 523 6243/fax 041 522 8378/ www.locandasturion.com). Vaporetto Rialto. €€.

Although this thriving little hotel enjoys a prime Grand Canal location, only two of the rooms overlook the canal. Even if you decide you can't afford the view, you can enjoy it from the breakfast room. Be warned, however: it's a long haul up steep stairs to the hotel, and there's no lift.

Marconi

San Polo 729, riva del Vin (041 522 2068/fax 041 522 9700/www. hotelmarconi.it). Vaporetto Rialto. €€€.

The Marconi enjoys an enviable – though crowded – location right by the Rialto bridge. The sumptuous, olde-worlde reception hall has dark wood panelling and an impressive gold-embossed ceiling. Bedrooms are simpler but still old-fashioned; two of them look out on to the Grand Canal, but the others are much quieter.

Oltre il Giardino

San Polo 2542, fondamenta Contarini (041 275 0015/fax 041 795 452/www. oltreilgiardino-venezia.com). Vaporetto San Tomà. €€.

Accessed through a pretty garden, this attractive, brick-fronted villa has the atmosphere of a country retreat, yet it is just round the corner from the Frari church. Mother and son Alessandra Zambelli and Lorenzo Muner welcome guests to their stylishly eclectic yet homely hotel, where bedrooms and suites are equipped with LCD TVs, robes, slippers and Bulgari bath goodies.

San Cassiano – Ca' Favretto

Santa Croce 2232, calle de la Rosa (041 524 1768/fax 041 721 033/ www.sancassiano.it). Vaporetto San Stae. €€€.

The 14th-century Gothic building housing this traditional hotel faces the glorious Ca d'Oro across the Grand Canal. Bedrooms are quite elegant, while the airy breakfast room has huge windows overlooking the canal. There is a tiny but charming veranda right on the water, a great spot for an early evening *spritz*.

Sofitel

Santa Croce 245, Giardini Papadopoli (041 710 400/fax 041 710 394/www. sofitel-venezia.com). Vaporetto Piazzale Roma. €€€.

Convenient for both the station and piazzale Roma, the Sofitel somehow avoids the total anonymity of hotels of this international-chain type. Rooms at the front of the modern building overlook a canal and bustling campo Tolentini; those at the top have stunning views. Meals are served in a lofty, plant-lined winter garden.

Dorsoduro

Accademia – Villa Maravege

Dorsoduro 1058, fondamenta Bollani (041 521 0188/fax 041 523 9152/ www.pensioneaccademia.it). Vaporetto Accademia. €€.

Perennially popular, this secluded 17th-century villa offers comfortable, *pensione*-style accommodation. The stylish bedrooms are fairly traditional, with antiques and marble or wood floors. There is a wonderful waterside patio, as well as a grassy rear garden.

Agli Alboretti

Dorsoduro 884, rio terà Foscarini (041 523 0058/fax 041 521 0158/ www.aglialboretti.com). Vaporetto Accademia. €€.

A cosy, wood-panelled reception area leads to the simply decorated but comfortable bedrooms of this friendly hotel. Some are truly tiny, but they all have thoughtful touches, such as electric kettles and everything else you need for making hot drinks. A pretty, pergola-covered terrace makes a great spot for summer meals.

American

Dorsoduro 628, fondamenta Bragadin (041 520 4733/fax 041 520 4048/ www.hotelamerican.com). Vaporetto Accademia. €€.

Set on the delightful rio di San Vio, in a peaceful part of Dorsoduro, the pleasant American is a well-run and popular hotel. Bedrooms are generally spacious and decorated in antique Venetian style; the best are the corner rooms overlooking the canal.

Antica Locanda Montin

Dorsoduro 1147, fondamenta delle Eremite (041 522 7151/fax 041 520 0255/www.locandamontin.com). Vaporetto Accademia or Zattere. €.

Book well in advance for one of the simple yet cosy rooms at this charming canalside *locanda*. The hotel is also home to one of Venice's most famous – though very overrated – restaurants. Rooms are furnished with a rather eccentric mix of old and new; only half have private bathrooms.

Ca' Foscari

Dorsoduro 3887B, calle della Frescada (041 710 401/fax 041 710 817/ www.locandacafoscari.com). Vaporetto San Tomà. €.

The delightful Scarpas have been offering a genuinely friendly welcome to guests at this wonderful little

locanda since the 1960s. It's a bit of a climb up to the simple but homely rooms, which are done out in cheerful colours and spotlessly clean; not all the rooms have private bathrooms.

Ca' Maria Adele

Dorsoduro 111, rio terà dei Catecumeni (041 520 3078/fax 041 528 9013/ www.camariaadele.it). Vaporetto Salute. €€€.

Eighteenth-century Venice meets modern design at this luxurious guesthouse situated in the shadow of Santa Maria della Salute. Five of the 12 rooms are 'themed', including the ultra-sexy Sala Noire; others are more conventional. There's an intimate ground-floor sitting room (with chocolate-brown faux fur on the walls) and a Moroccan-style roof terrace for sultry evenings. Service is very professional and utterly charming.

Ca' Pisani

Dorsoduro 979A, rio terà Foscarini (041 277 1478/fax 041 277 1061/ www.capisanihotel.it). Vaporetto Accademia. €€€.

Ca' Pisani's luxurious, designer-chic rooms in 1930s and '40s style make a refreshing change from the usual fare of glitz, gilt and Murano glass; this was the first hotel to throw off the yawn-inducing pan-Venetian style, and though it's no longer the only one, it's still up there among the most effective. The striking pink-painted 16th-century palazzo is conveniently located behind the Accademia gallery. Bedrooms are all generously sized, and there's a restaurant with tables outside in the summer, a sauna, a roof terrace and a discount at the gym round the corner.

Ca' Zose

Dorsoduro 193B, calle del Bastion (041 522 6635/fax 041 522 6624/ www.hotelcazose.com). Vaporetto Salute. €€.

The enthusiastic Campanati sisters run this immaculate little guesthouse near the Guggenheim collection. There's a tiny, neat breakfast room off the cool white reception area; upstairs, the

Ca' Maria Adele p176

bedrooms are done out in a fairly restrained traditional Venetian style, with painted furniture.

DD 724

Dorsoduro 724, ramo da Mula (041 277 0262/fax 041 296 0633/www. dd724.com). Vaporetto Accademia or Salute. €€€.
Blink and you'll miss the sign for DD 724, a design hotel in miniature, where bedrooms are stylishly understated in pale shades and dark wood; several overlook the Guggenheim collection's garden, and one has a little terrace. Bathrooms are tiny but super-modern. Public spaces (and some of the bedrooms) are cramped, however, and the atmosphere is not exactly warm.

La Calcina

Dorsoduro 780, fondamenta delle Zattere (041 520 6466/fax 041 522 7045/www.lacalcina.com). Vaporetto Zattere. €€.
La Calcina is one of the best value and most pleasant hotels in the three-star category. Classical music plays in the white-painted reception area, while bedrooms have 19th-century furniture

and an uncluttered feel. The best rooms look over the sunny Giudecca canal, a view that is shared by the hotel terrace restaurant, which is built over the water.

Locanda San Barnaba

Dorsoduro 2785-2786, calle del Traghetto (041 241 1233/fax 041 241 3812/www.locanda-sanbarnaba.com). Vaporetto Ca' Rezzonico. €€.
Situated at the end of a quiet alleyway and with 13 comfortable, individually decorated rooms, the San Barnaba is one of the better hotels in this price range in the area. There's a small courtyard and a roof terrace.

Messner

Dorsoduro 216, fondamenta Ca' Balà (041 522 7443/fax 041 522 7266/www.hotelmessner.it). Vaporetto Salute. €€.
The Messner's modern bedrooms may not be very inspiring, but the location, the shady garden and the warm staff more than compensate. Between the main building and two annexes, there is a choice of rooms, from fairly basic standards to 'deluxe junior suites';

DD.724

V E N E Z I A

prices vary accordingly. The hotel also manages some apartments in the area.

Palazzo Dal Carlo

Dorsoduro 1163, fondamenta di Borgo (tel/fax 041 522 6863/www.palazzo dalcarlo.com). Vaporetto Ca' Rezzonico or Zattere. €€.

Roberta dal Carlo's elegant, yet laid-back and welcoming, palazzo-home on a quiet Dorsoduro backwater is filled with gorgeous heirlooms, antiques and pictures. She has three bedrooms available for guests, one of which has direct access to the roof terrace from where sunsets are pure magic.

La Giudecca

Cipriani

Giudecca 10, fondamenta San Giovanni (041 520 7744/fax 041 520 3930/ www.hotelcipriani.com). Vaporetto Zitelle or private launch from Vallaresso stop. €€€€.

Set in a verdant paradise on the eastern tip of the Giudecca island, the Cipriani has exquisitely decorated bedrooms and great facilities, which include a private harbour for your yacht; there's a higher-than-average chance of rubbing shoulders with a film star here. Alternatively, take an apartment in the neighbouring Palazzo Vendramin, complete with butler service and private garden.

Ostello di Venezia (Youth Hostel)

Giudecca 86, fondamenta delle Zitelle (041 523 8211/fax 041 523 5689/ www.hihostel.com). Vaporetto Zitelle. €.

This 260-bed youth hostel offers stunning and unique views across the lagoon towards San Marco. Book well in advance (through the website), in high season. Unadventurous, but very cheap, meals are served.

Lido & Lagoon

Des Bains

Lungomare Marconi 17, Lido (041 526 5921/fax 041 526 0113/www.
starwood.com/italy). Vaporetto Lido. €€€€.

Thomas Mann wrote, and Luchino Visconti filmed, *Death in Venice* in this glorious art deco hotel set in its own park. Des Bains has a private beach, plus access to tennis courts, a golf course and riding facilities. There's a courtesy boat to San Marco too.

Excelsior

Lungomare Marconi 41, Lido (041 526 0201/fax 041 526 7276/www.star wood.com/italy). Vaporetto Lido. €€€€.

The early 1900s pseudo-Moorish Excelsior hosts hordes of celebrities during the Venice Film Festival in September. A sea-facing room will provide you with a view of beach antics and the Adriatic beyond. There are luxurious beach huts, a swimming pool and private water taxis to take you the short ride to San Marco.

Locanda Cipriani

Torcello, piazza Santa Fosca (041 730 150/fax 041 735 433/www.locanda cipriani.com). Vaporetto Torcello. €€€.

This famous green-shuttered inn (Hemingway wrote *Across the River and Through the Trees* during his stay here) is still owned by a branch of the Cipriani family and is special enough to justify the remoteness of the setting, at least for a couple of nights. The six rooms are done out in understated, elegant country style. Don't miss lunch on the blissful, vine-clad terrace.

San Clemente Palace

Isola di San Clemente (041 244 5001/ fax 041 244 5800/www.sanclemente. thi.it). €€€€.

The restored buildings of a former mental hospital house this luxurious hotel set in extensive, landscaped grounds with 200-odd trad Venetian-style rooms, four restaurants, a business centre, a beauty farm and all the attendant facilities; there's even a three-hole practice golf course. A boat shuttle service takes guests to and from piazza San Marco.

ESSENTIALS

Getting Around

Arriving & leaving

Airports

Venice Marco Polo Airport – SAVE SpA

Viale G Galilei 30/1, Tessera (041 260 6111/flight & airport information 041 260 9260/www.veniceairport.it).
There are boat and bus services between the airport and Venice proper. Getting a boat may take longer and cost more, but the journey is infinitely more pleasant and may take you closer to your accommodation; clearly signposted, the dock for all boat and ferry services is located seven minutes' walk from the arrivals terminal. A porter will take your bags from the airport to the dock or vice versa for €4.50. A shuttle bus runs every ten minutes from the terminal to the dock (and vice versa) between 6am and 8pm; it costs €1. Bus services run from right outside the arrivals hall to piazzale Roma.

Treviso Sant'Angelo Airport – Aer Tre SpA

Via Noalese, Treviso (airport information 0422 315 111/www.trevisoairport.it).
ATVO's (0422 315 327, www.atvo.it) bus services run to Venice's piazzale Roma and back to coincide with flights. The journey takes 70 minutes, and costs €5 one way, €9 round trip (valid for seven days). Buses from piazzale Roma leave ridiculously far ahead of flights. Alternatively, take a train to Treviso (about 35 minutes) and then a bus or taxi (Cooperativa Radiotaxi Padova 049 651 333) to the airport.

ACTT's (0422 3271) bus 6 does the 20-minute journey from in front of Treviso train station to the airport at 10 and 40 minutes past every hour and costs €1.

Verona Valerio Catullo Airport

Verona Villafranca (045 809 5666/www.aeroportoverona.it).
A shuttle bus (0458 057 911) runs every 20 minutes between Verona's airport and train station from 6.35am to 11.35pm. The 20-minute journey to the station costs €4.20; buy tickets on the bus. There are regular train links between Verona and Venice (70-90mins).

By water

Società Alilaguna's (041 523 5775, www.alilaguna.com, no credit cards) Linea Rossa runs hourly in both directions; tickets (€12) for the 70-minute journey to/from San Marco can be purchased at Alilaguna's counter in the arrivals hall or on board. The service also stops at Murano, the Lido and Arsenale; after San Marco it proceeds to Zattere. This service can be included in the price of a VeniceCard multi-ticket (see box p55).

A water-taxi ride with Consorzio Motoscafi Venezia (041 541 5084, no credit cards) from the airport directly to your hotel in Venice will take 25-30 minutes and cost upwards of €90 depending on the number of people in your party and the stops you make.

The Bucintoro Agency (041 521 0632, www.bucintoroviaggi.com, no credit cards) runs the Airport Link shuttle service (€25) to fixed points in Venice. Book online at least 24 hours in advance.

By road

ATVO's (0421 383 672, www.atvo.it, no credit cards) number 35 bus runs between the airport and piazzale Roma in Venice. Tickets for the 20-minute trip cost €3.

ACTV's (0421 383 672, www.actv.it, no credit cards) bus 5 runs frequently between the airport and piazzale Roma in Venice. The 35- to 40-minute journey costs €2.

The Cooperativa Artigiana Radio Taxi (041 541 6363) charges around €30 for the 20-minute trip from the airport to piazzale Roma in Venice.

By rail

Most trains arrive at Santa Lucia station in Venice, though a few will take you only as far as Mestre on the mainland, where you will need to change to a local train (every ten minutes or less during the day) for the short hop across the lagoon.

By bus

Bus services to Venice all stop at piazzale Roma, which is connected by vaporetto (p181) to the rest of the city centre.

By road

Prohibitive parking fees in Venice's car parks make this one of the least practical modes of arrival, especially for stays of more than 24hrs. Note, though, that many hotels offer their guests discounts at car parks.

Most of the city's car parks are in piazzale Roma and on Tronchetto island, though a few are on the mainland. Expect to pay around €20 for 24 hours.

In town

Public transport

Public transport, including *vaporetti* (water buses) and buses, in Venice itself and in some mainland areas is run by **ACTV** (Azienda Comunale per il Trasporto di Venezia).

ACTV's marketing wing **VeLa** sells tickets for concerts and events as well as vaporetto tickets through its **HelloVenezia** outlets. The extremely helpful HelloVenezia call centre (041 24 24) provides information in English on ACTV vaporetto and bus schedules, and on events and tourist sights; the website www.hellovenezia.it has listings of upcoming events, and allows online booking.

Most services to and between destinations on the Venetian mainland are operated by **ATVO**.

ACTV-VeLa-HelloVenezia

Santa Croce 509, piazzale Roma (information 041 24 24/www.hello venezia.it). Vaporetto Piazzale Roma.
Public transport tickets **Open** 7am-8pm daily. No credit cards.
Event tickets **Open** 8am-6.30pm daily.

ATVO

Santa Croce 497, piazzale Roma (0421 383 671/www.atvo.it).
Vaporetto Piazzale Roma.
Open 6.30am-7.30pm daily.

Travelling with children

Vaporetto travel with children is far from cheap. Under-fives travel free; after that they pay full fare. It is perfectly acceptable to take your pram or pushchair on to *vaporetti* at no extra cost – although it is probably better to avoid doing this on the smaller boats at rush-hour.

Vaporetti

Venice's *vaporetti* (water buses) run to a tight schedule, with sailing times for each line that makes a pick-up there marked clearly at vaporetto stops. Regular services run from about 5am to around midnight, after which a frequent night service follows the route taken by Line 82 during the day.

Until you've grasped Venetian geography, it's remarkably easy

ESSENTIALS

to find yourself heading in the opposite direction to where you wanted to go. If you're standing with your back to the station and want to make your way down the Grand Canal, take Line 1 (slow) or Line 82 (faster) heading left. During peak season, ACTV runs express *vaporetti* 3 and 4 to San Marco from Tronchetto, piazzale Roma and the train station (Ferrovia).

Single trip (€6), 12-hour (€13), 24-hour (€15), 36-hour (€20), 48-hour (€25) and 72-hour (€30) vaporetto tickets can be purchased at most vaporetto stops, at *tabacchi* (p186) and at HelloVenezia offices. On board you can only buy a single ticket (€6, valid 60 minutes). There's also a 72-hour card (€15) for 14- to 29-year olds who must buy a €4 Rolling Venice card (on sale at HelloVenezia ticket offices) in order to be eligible. Tickets must be validated prior to boarding the vaporetto, by stamping them in the yellow machines at the entrance to the jetty.

Other boats

Gondole

Official gondola stops can be found in the following locations:

Fondamenta Bacino Orseolo
In front of the Hotel Danieli on the **riva degli Schiavoni**
By the **Vallaresso** vaporetto stop
By the **railway station**
By the **piazzale Roma** bus terminus
By the **Santa Maria del Giglio** vaporetto stop
At the jetty at the end of **piazzetta San Marco**
At **campo Santa Sofia** near the Ca' d'Oro vaporetto stop
By the **San Tomà** vaporetto stop
By the Hotel Bauer in **campo San Moisè**

On the **riva del Carbon** at the southern end of the Rialto bridge. Fares are set by the Istituzione per la Conservazione della Gondola e Tutela del Gondoliere (Gondola Board; 041 528 5075, www.gondola venezia.it); in the event that a gondolier tries to overcharge you, complain to the Gondola Board. Prices below are for the hire of the gondola, regardless of the number of passengers (up to six). Having your own personal crooner will push the fare up.

8am-7pm: €80 for 40mins; €40 for each additional 20mins.

7pm-8am: €100 for 50mins; €50 for each additional 20mins.

Vaporetti routes

Venice
The main lines follow the Grand Canal, or circle the island. Taking the wrong boat in the wrong direction is alarmingly easy. Pick up a timetable, (they frequently run out a month or two after the start of each season) from the central ACTV-VeLa office (see p181), tourist offices (see p187) or any large ACTV booth. A map is available at any ACTV ticket office.

Remember – if you're standing with your back to the station and are heading for the Grand Canal, take Line 1 (slow) or Line 82 (faster) heading left. During peak season, ACTV runs express *vaporetti* 3 and 4 to San Marco from Tronchetto, piazzale Roma and the train station (Ferrovia).

Southern islands
To get to the southern islands (San Servolo, San Lazzaro degli Armeni) take the 20 from San Zaccaria. Lines 1, 51, 52, 61 (and 82 in summer) all terminate at the Lido.

Northern islands
Murano: The DM line (Diretto Murano) departs every half hour

from Tronchetto, Piazzale Roma and Ferrovia for Murano. Between 10.15am and 4.55pm Line 5 departs from San Zaccaria every 20 minutes (with a break 12.15-1.15pm); the journey takes under half an hour. Lines 41 & 42 depart every ten minutes (4.20am-11.22pm) from Fondamenta Nove, and are replaced at night by the hourly Notturno murano service. En route to Murano, 41 & 42 also stop at Cimitero on San Michele.

All other services to islands in the northern lagoon depart from Fondamente Nove. The LN (Laguna Nord) Line leaves roughly every 30 minutes throughout the day from Fondamente Nove, stopping at Faro (Murano), Mazzorbo, Burano, Treporti and Punta Sabbioni. In the late evening (9.33pm, 10.28pm and 11.14pm) the LN also stops at Torcello. At other times take the half-hourly shuttle boat from Burano (journey time ten minutes); check the timetable or call 800 845 065 for information. Line 13 leaves hourly from Fondamente Nove to Faro (Murano), Vignole, Sant' Erasmo Capannone, Sant'Erasmo Chiesa and Sant'Erasmo Punta Vela. Some boats continue for Treporti.

Traghetti

The best way to cross the Grand Canal when you're far from a bridge is to hop on a *traghetto*. These unadorned *gondole* are rowed back and forth at fixed points along the canal. At 50¢, this is the cheapest gondola ride in the city, something to bear in mind when your children clamour for a gondola experience.

Water taxis

Venetian water taxis are jaw-droppingly expensive: expect to pay upwards of €90 from the airport directly to any single destination in Venice, and more for multiple stops. The absolute minimum possible cost for a 15 minute trip from hotel to restaurant, for a single person is €70, with most journeys averaging at a staggering €110 once number of passengers and baggage have been taken into account. To add insult to injury, between the hours of 10pm and 7am there is a surcharge of €10.

Avoid asking your hotel to book a taxi for you, as they frequently add a ten per cent mark up. Beware of unlicensed taxis, which charge even more than authorised ones. The latter have a black registration number on a yellow background.
Venezia Motoscafi *041 716 922/www.veneziamotoscafi.it*.
Open 24hrs daily. No credit cards.

Bus

Orange ACTV buses serve the mainland and the Lido. Services for the mainland depart from piazzale Roma.

Bus tickets, costing €1 (available in blocks of ten tickets for €9), are valid for 60 minutes. They can be purchased from HelloVenezia ticket booths or from *tabacchi* (p186). Buy tickets before boarding the bus and stamp them on board.

Driving

Central Venice has no road and consequently no cars. You can drive on the Lido. For car parks, p181.

Vehicle hire

The following companies all have offices in the Arrivals Hall of Venice airport.

Avis *Santa Croce 496G, piazzale Roma (041 523 7377/www.avisautonoleggio.it)*.
Europcar *Santa Croce 496H, piazzale Roma (041 523 8616/www.europcar.it)*.
Hertz *Santa Croce 496F, piazzale Roma (041 528 4091)*.
Maggiore *National Mestre railway station (041 935 300/ www.maggiore.it)*.

Resources A-Z

Accident & emergency

The hospitals listed below all have 24-hour *pronto soccorso* (casualty) facilities. For an ambulance boat, call 118. See also **Dental emergencies** and **Pharmacies**

Ospedale Civile *Castello 6777, campo Santi Giovanni e Paolo (041 529 4111/casualty 041 529 4517). Vaporetto Ospedale.*
Ospedale al Mare *Lungomare D'Annunzio 1, Lido (041 529 4111/ casualty 10am-8pm 041 529 5234). Vaporetto Lido.*
Ospedale Umberto I *Via Circonvallazione 50, Mestre (041 260 7111).*

Age restrictions

You must be 16 legally to buy cigarettes and alcohol. Alcohol can be consumed in bars from the age of 16. Anyone aged 18 or over can ride a 50cc moped or scooter; so can 14- to 18-year olds if they have a special licence. You must be over 18 to drive and over 21 to hire a car.

Credit card loss

American Express *800 864 046*
Diners' Club *800 864 064*
MasterCard *800 870 866*
Visa *800 819 014*

Customs

If you arrive from, or are travelling on to, a EU country, you are not required to declare goods imported into or exported from Italy if they are for personal use.

For people arriving from non-EU countries, however, limits apply.

For more information consult www.agenziadogane.it

Dental emergencies

Dental treatment in Italy is expensive; your insurance may not cover it. For urgent dental treatment, go to the **Ambulatorio Odontostomatologico** at the Ospedale Civile (above).

Disabled travellers

The very things that make Venice unique – narrow streets, bridges (almost 400), no barriers between pavements and canals – make the city an extra-difficult destination for travellers with impaired mobility or vision. Despite this, Venice should not be crossed off the holiday list altogether, as there has been an effort in recent years to make the city more negotiable for disabled travellers.

Super-helpful English-speaking staff at the city's council's **Informahandicap** service (*San Marco 4136, riva del Carbon (041 274 8144/www.comune.venezia.it/ handicap*) can answer queries over the phone and send information on accessible hotels, restaurants and museums in Venice.

APT offices (p187) provide a map (which can be downloaded at www.comune.venezia.it/informa handicap/files/va-carta-ita.jpg) showing bridges with wheelchair ramps, and accessible public toilets. APT offices also dispense the keys necessary for operating the bridge ramps.

Public transport is one area where Venice scores higher than many other destinations, as the large decks of standard *vaporetti* and *motonavi* enable easy travel along the Grand Canal, on lines 1 and 82.

Electricity

Italy's electricity system runs on 220/230v. To use British or US appliances, you will need two-pin adaptor plugs.

Embassies & consulates

For information, and in case of emergency, you will probably have to contact offices in Rome or Milan. **British Consulate** *piazzale Donatori di Sangue 2, Mestre (041 505 5990). Bus 7 from piazzale Roma.*

Embassies in Rome
Australian *06 852 721*
British *06 4220 0001*
Canadian *06 854 441*
Irish *06 697 9121*
New Zealand *06 441 7171*
South African *06 852 541*
US *06 46 741*

Consulates in Milan
Australian *02 777 041*
British *02 723 001*
Canadian *02 675 81*
Irish *02 5518 7569*
New Zealand *02 499 0201*
South African *02 885 8581*
US *02 290 351*

Internet

The techno-savvy will find unofficial hotspots (ie, open private networks) on the streets of Venice (try campo del Ghetto Nuovo and along fondamenta della Misericordia, both in Cannaregio).

Otherwise, there are any number of internet points around the city, where, to comply with infuriating anti-terrorism norms, you'll be asked to fill in a form giving all your personal details.

Internet Point Santo Stefano
San Marco 2958, campo Santo Stefano (041 894 6122/www.teleradiofuga. com). Vaporetto Accademia or San Samuele. **Open** 10.15am-11pm daily. No credit cards.

Pharmacies

Most chemists' are open 9am-12.30pm, 3.45-7.30pm Mon-Fri and 9am-12.45pm Sat. A small number remain open on Saturday afternoon, Sunday, at night and on public holidays on a duty rota system, details of which are posted outside every pharmacy and given in the local press.

Police

For emergencies, call one of the following helplines:
Carabinieri *112*
Polizia di Stato *113*
The Polizia di Stato's main station is at Castello 4693A, campo San Zaccaria; the Carabinieri's is at Santa Croce 500, piazzale Roma. Incidents can be reported to either.

Post

For information on postal services, call 803 160 (8am-8pm Mon-Sat) or visit www.poste.it.

There are local post offices around the city; opening hours are 8.30am-2.30pm Mon-Fri, 8.30am-1pm Sat. The two main post offices listed below open on alternate Saturdays in August and over the Christmas period.

Posta Centrale
San Marco 5554, salizada del Fontego dei Tedeschi (041 528 5813). Vaporetto Rialto. **Open** 8.30am-6.30pm Mon-Sat.

ESSENTIALS

Posta Piazzale Roma

Santa Croce 510, fondamenta Santa Chiara (041 522 1976). Vaporetto Piazzale Roma. **Open** 8.30am-6.30pm Mon-Fri; 8.30am-1pm Sat.

Smoking

In Italy it is prohibited to smoke anywhere with public access, including bars, restaurants, stations, offices, lobbies of apartment blocks and on all public transport except where a clearly designated, efficiently ventilated smoking room is provided. This is strictly enforced, and in general respected by local smokers. For where to buy cigarettes, see *Tabacchi*.

Tabacchi

Tabacchi or *tabaccherie* (identified by signs with a white T on a black or blue background) are the only places where you can legally buy tobacco products. You'll find them dotted all over the city.

They also sell stamps, telephone cards and tickets for public transport.

Telephones

Making a call

Venice landlines have the area code 041, which must be dialled whether you're calling from within or outside the city. To call Venice from abroad, dial your international access code followed by 041. Do **not** omit the 0.

Numbers beginning with 800 are toll-free. Numbers beginning 840 and 848 are charged at low set rates, no matter where you're calling from or how long the call lasts. These numbers can be called only from within Italy; some of them function only with a single phone district.

Directory enquiries

This is a jungle, and charges for information given over the phone are steep. The major services are: 1254 (Italian and international numbers) and 892 412 (international numbers, in English and Italian, from mobile phones). Italian directory information can be had for free on www.info412.it or www.paginebianche.it.

Dialling & codes

For international calls from Venice, dial 00, followed by the country code, area code (omit the initial zero of area codes in the UK) and number. Codes include: Australia 61; Canada 1; Irish Republic 353; New Zealand 64; United Kingdom 44; United States 1.

Mobile phones

Mobile-phone numbers begin with a 3. GSM phones can be used on both 900 and 1800 bands; British, Australian and New Zealand mobiles work fine; US mobiles will not work unless they are tri-band. Reception in central Venice is variable.

Vodafone Gestioni Spa

San Marco 5170, campo San Bartolmeo (041 523 9016/www.voda fone.it). Vaporetto Rialto. **Open** 10am-7.30pm Mon-Sat; 10am-1pm, 2-7pm Sun.

Public phones

There are public phones along the main tourist routes. Some bars also have payphones. Most public telephones operate only with phonecards (*schede telefoniche*), which cost €2.50, €5 and €7.50 and can be purchased at post offices, *tabacchi* and some newsstands. Some newer models take major credit cards.

Time

Venice is one hour ahead of London, six ahead of New York, eight behind Sydney and 12 behind Wellington.

Tipping

Venetians know that foreigners tip generously back home and therefore expect them to be liberal. Some upmarket restaurants (and a growing number of cheaper ones) have begun to add a service charge to bills. Italians rarely leave more than five to ten per cent, and nothing at all if they don't feel that the service has warranted it. In cafés and bars, leave 20¢-30¢ on the counter when ordering.

Toilets

Public toilets (*servizi igienici pubblici*) are numerous and relatively clean in Venice, but you have to pay (€1) to use them, unless you have invested in a Venice Card (see box p55). Follow blue and green signs marked WC. By law all cafés and bars should allow anyone to use their facilities; in practice, the majority of Venetian bar owners don't.

Tickets

Expect to pay *diritti di prevendita* (booking fee) on tickets bought anywhere except at the venue on the night. HelloVenezia offices (p181) are the best place to buy tickets for major and many minor events; some can also be booked by phone, though HelloVenezia adds a ten per cent surcharge for this service.

Tourist information

Several free publications provide comprehensive tourist information in Venice, available at APT and HelloVenezia offices, and some bars. Many events are advertised on posters plastered on walls all over the city.

There are 36 HelloVenezia offices at ports of entry and around the city centre.

Azienda di Promozione Turistica (APT)

San Marco 71F, piazza San Marco (041 529 8740/www.turismovenezia.it). Vaporetto Vallaresso. **Open** 9am-3.30pm daily.
Other locations: Palazzina Santi, San Marco 2, Giardinetti Reali (041 522 5150).
Venice-Santa Lucia railway station (041 529 8727). Open 8am-6.30pm daily.
Marco Polo Airport Arrivals Hall (tel/fax 041 541 5887).
Autorimessa Comunale, Santa Croce 465B, piazzale Roma (041 529 8711).
Viale Santa Maria Elisabetta 6A, Lido (041 526 5721).

Visas

EU nationals and citizens of the US, Canada, Australia and New Zealand do not need visas for stays of up to three months. For EU citizens, a passport or national ID card valid for travel abroad is sufficient; non-EU citizens must have full passports.

What's on

Il Venezia

www.ilvenezia.it
Local listings and a page of useful phone numbers and contacts.

2night magazine

www.2night.it
Pocket-sized monthly with art and nightlife listings for the whole Veneto region, in Italian.

Venezia News

A bilingual monthly with music, film, theatre, art and sports listings, plus interviews and features.

ESSENTIALS

Vocabulary

Pronunciation

a – like a in ask
e – like a in age or e in sell
i – like ea in east
o – like o in hotel or hot
u – like oo in boot
c – as in cat before a, o and u;
otherwise like ch in cheat
g – as in good before a, o and u;
otherwise like g in giraffe; **gl** – like
lli in million; **gn** – like ny in canyon
h – makes the consonant preceding
it hard (ch – cat; gh – good)
sc – like sh in shame, if followed by
e or i, if followed by a, o or u it's like
sc in scout; **sch** – like sc in scout

Useful phrases

hello/goodbye (informal) *ciao, salve*
good morning *buon giorno*; **good
evening** *buona sera*; **good night**
buona notte
please *per favore, per piacere*;
thank you *grazie*; **you're
welcome** *prego*
excuse me, sorry *pardon*,
(formal) *mi scusi*, (informal) *scusa*
I don't speak Italian (very well)
non parlo (molto bene) l'italiano
do you speak English? *parla
inglese?*
can I use/where's the toilet?
posso usare/dov'è il bagno?
open *aperto*; **closed** *chiuso*
entrance *entrata*; **exit** *uscita*
booking, reservation
prenotazione
I'd like to book… *vorrei
prenotare…*
… a table for four at eight *un
tavolo per quattro alle otto*
… a single/twin/double room
*una camera singola/doppia/
matrimoniale*
how much is it? *quanto costa?*

I take (shoe/dress) size *porto
il numero/la taglia…*
100 grammes of… *un'etto di…*
300 grammes of… *tre etti di…*
a kilo of… *un kilo di…*
five kilos of… *cinque chili di…*
do you take credit cards?
accettate le carte di credito?
where is? *dov'è?*; **(turn) left**
(giri a) sinistra; **(it's on the)
right** *(è a/sulla) destra*; **straight
on** *sempre dritto*; **is it near/far?**
è vicino/lontano?

Communications

dataport *attacco per il computer*;
broadband *ADSL (adiesselle)*;
mobile phone/cellphone
telefonino/cellulare; **courier** *corriere,
pony*; **fax** *fax*; **letter** *lettera*; **phone**
telefono; **postcard** *cartolina;*
stamp *francobollo*; **a stamp for
England/the US** *un francobollo
per l'Inghilterra/gli Stati Uniti*

Days

Monday *lunedì*; **Tuesday** *martedì*;
Wednesday *mercoledì*; **Thursday**
giovedì; **Friday** *venerdì*; **Saturday**
sabato; **Sunday** *domenica*
yesterday *ieri*; **today** *oggi*;
tomorrow *domani*; **weekend** *fine
settimana, weekend*

Numbers

0 *zero*; 1 *uno*; 2 *due*; 3 *tre*; 4
quattro; 5 *cinque*; 6 *sei*; 7 *sette*; 8
otto; 9 *nove*; 10 *dieci*; 11 *undici*; 12
dodici; 13 *tredici*; 14 *quattordici*; 15
quindici; 16 *sedici*; 17 *diciassette*; 18
diciotto; 19 *diciannove*; 20 *venti*; 30
trenta; 40 *quaranta*; 50 *cinquanta*;
60 *sessanta*; 70 *settanta*; 80 *ottanta*;
90 *novanta*; 100 *cento*; 200 *due-
cento*; 1,000 *mille*; 2,000 *duemila*

Menu Glossary

Antipasti (starters)

The dozens of *cicheti* – tapas-style snacks – served from the counters of the traditional *bacaro* (wine bar) are essentially *antipasti*; in more upmarket restaurants, these will be joined – or replaced – by an even larger and more refined selection, which will probably include: **baccalà mantecato** *stockfish beaten into a cream with oil and milk, often served on grilled polenta*; **bovoleti** *tiny snails cooked in olive oil, parsley and garlic*; **carciofi** *artichokes, even better if they are* **castrauri** – *baby artichokes*; **canoce** (or **cicale di mare***) mantis shrimps*; **folpi/folpeti** *baby octopus*; **garusoli** *sea snails*; **moleche** *soft-shelled crabs, usually deep-fried*; **museto** *a boiled brawn sausage, generally served on a slice of bread with mustard*; **nervetti** *boiled veal cartilage*; **polpetta** *deep-fried spicy meatball*; **polenta** *yellow or white cornmeal mush, served either runny or in firm, sliceable slabs*; **sarde in saor** *sardines marinated in onion, vinegar, pine nuts and raisins*; **schie** *tiny grey shrimps, usually served on a bed of soft white polenta*; **seppie in nero** *cuttlefish in its own ink*; **spienza** *veal spleen usually served on a skewer*; **trippa e rissa** *tripe cooked in broth*.

Primi (first courses)

Bigoli in salsa *fat spaghetti in an anchovy and onion sauce*; **gnocchi con granseola** *potato gnocchi in a spider-crab sauce*; **pasta... e ceci** *pasta and chickpea soup*; **...e fagioli** *pasta and borlotti bean soup*; **risotto... di zucca** *pumpkin risotto*; **...di radicchio**

made with radicchio from nearby Treviso; **spaghetti... alla busara** *in anchovy sauce*; **...al nero di seppia** *in squid-ink sauce*; **...con caparossoli/vongole veraci** *with clams*.

Secondi (main courses)

The choice of fish and seafood is almost endless – in addition to the *antipasti* mentioned above, you are likely to find the following: **anguilla** *eel*; **aragosta/astice** *spiny lobster/lobster*; **branzino** *sea bass*; **cape longhe** *razor clams*; **cape sante** *scallops*; **cernia** *grouper*; **coda di rospo** *anglerfish*; **cozze** *mussels*; **granchio** *crab*; **granseola** *spider crab*; **orata** *gilt-headed bream*; **pesce spada** *swordfish*; **rombo** *turbot*; **pesce San Pietro** *John Dory*; **sogliola** *sole*; **tonno** *tuna*; **vongole/ caparossoli** *clams*.
Meat eaters are less well catered for in Venice; the handful of local specialities include: **castradina** *a lamb and cabbage broth*; **fegato alla veneziana** *veal liver cooked in a slightly sweet sauce of onions*.

Dolci (desserts)

Venice's restaurants are not the best place to feed a sweet habit – with a few exceptions, there are far more tempting pastries to be found on the shelves of the city's *pasticcerie*. The classic end to a meal here is a plate of **buranei** – *sweet egg biscuits* – served with a dessert wine such as Fragolino. Then it's quickly on to the more important matter of which of the many varieties of grappa to order.

Index

ESSENTIALS

ESSENTIALS

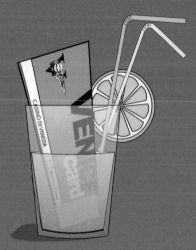